More Than Just a Friend

The Joys and Disappointments of Extramarital Affairs

Dr. Tom McGinnis

Prentice-Hall, Inc., Englewood Cliffs, New Jersey

More Than Just a Friend:
The Joys and Disappointments of Extramarital Affairs
by Dr. Tom McGinnis
Copyright © 1981 by Thomas C. McGinnis

Printed in the United States of America
Prentice-Hall International, Inc., London
Prentice-Hall of Australia, Pty. Ltd., Sydney
Prentice-Hall of Canada, Ltd., Toronto
Prentice-Hall of India Private Ltd., New Delhi
Prentice-Hall of Japan, Inc., Tokyo
Prentice-Hall of Southeast Asia Pt. Ltd., Singapore
Whitehall Books Limited, Wellington, New Zealand
10   9   8   7   6   5   4   3   2   1

Library of Congress Cataloging in Publication Data

McGinnis, Thomas C   date
   More than just a friend.

   Bibliography: p.
   Includes index.
   1.   Adultery—Psychological aspects—United States.
2.   Adultery—Social aspects—United States.   3.   Sexual
ethics—United States.   4.   Marriage—United States.
I.   Title.
HQ806.M3   306.7'3   80-25735
ISBN 0-13-600973-5
ISBN 0-13-600957-3 (pbk.)

Contents

Acknowledgments

Life was breathed into this book by all those who opened their hearts and shared the intimate details of their extramarital affairs with me. Although I cannot acknowledge them by name, I sincerely hope that the trust they placed in me to tell their stories will be validated by the benefits others like them will gain through the gift of their openness and honesty.

In addition to many hundreds of hours spent working with me on writing and editing, John Ayres brought to the book his particular knowledge, integrity, wise counsel, and sense of good taste. As close friends, John and his wife, Alice, helped me through the years of dreaming, agonizing, rewriting, and living with the manuscript as it took shape.

My associates on the staff of The Counseling and Psychotherapy Center in Fair Lawn, New Jersey, willingly accepted the sacrifices of my clinical time and personal involvement. For their cooperation and continual support, I am more than professionally indebted to Tom McGinnis, Jr., my son and colleague, and to Dr. Joel Becker, Marilyn Nusbaum, Irene Rapaport, Elaine Schiffman, Dr. Bert Schucker, Dr. Victor Solomon, and Dr. Stuart Weissman. Special thanks go to Barbara Kaufman for her suggestions and editorial assistance with the final draft and to Joan Gerhold and Virginia Aspden for their unflagging willingness to type and retype the many revisions.

I am especially grateful to the many people who read portions of the various drafts and helped me to refine them. Among these were Kay Bissantz, Marion Burden, Ingrid Cranfield, Carolyn DeBeer, Nancy DeVries, Harvey Dzodin, Bert Linder, Ruth Klot, Tony Mercantino, Gary Nunn, Bob Ryder, Joyce Sheinmel, Dian Schons, Barbara Steuert, and Janine Tremblay.

But all of our efforts might have been lost had it not been for Frances Collin, my literary agent, who believed strongly in my approach to this delicate subject and for Dennis Fawcett, my Prentice-Hall editor, whose patient guidance saw my work through the complex processes of production.

Words are simply inadequate to express my deep appreciation to my wife Mary Yorke; daughter, Karen Mercantino; and sons Tom, Jr., and Dick who offered suggestions and advice and encouraged me from the beginning of the project. No doubts, some families would have difficulty dealing with the reality of a husband/father writing on such a sensitive and controversial issue. "Yorkie," Karen, Tom, and Dick have met the challenge with dignity and respect.

How This Book Came To Be Written

It's adultery... cheating... being unfaithful.
A love triangle... playing around... a scandal!
It's cheap... dishonest... shocking... outrageous!
It's the shadow side of marriage... the destroyer
of lives... and marriages and families.

Sound familiar? These are traditional ways of referring to a forbidden—and frightening—subject. However, at this moment in history, when many of these strong moral judgments are being challenged and changed, we're also hearing bold, new, and sharply contrasting statements.

It's exciting... sharing... caring... loving!
A beautiful experience... I feel alive again...
A boost to my ego... A real growth experience...
I feel like a human being... My marriage has
definitely been helped... The best alternative
to divorce.

This books attempts to explore the true nature and significance of extramarital affairs. It deals with both the positive *and* negative aspects of affairs, their healthy *and* unhealthy characteristics, the joys *and* heartaches. The focus is on what *really* happens in affairs; who is involved, how, where, when, and why, as well as the possible consequences. It avoids taking a lopsided, harshly judgmental approach that holds affairs to be absolutely—and for everybody—wrong, shameful, and destructive. Nor does it promote affairs as always beneficial or desirable human encounters. Instead, this book came into being because I believe in the need for a balanced, honest, and realistic approach to this highly delicate and sensitive subject.

My twenty-five years as a psychotherapist specializing in marital and family therapy have proven to me that affairs are, in fact, complex relationships involving deep human emotions present in all of us. They simply cannot be dealt with in terms of black and white.

With approximately three out of every five married persons seen nowadays by staff members at our Counseling and Psychotherapy Center in Fair Lawn, New Jersey, reporting their own or their spouse's involvement in an extramarital affair, I am firmly convinced that affairs are neither right nor wrong in themselves. But they *are*. We have to deal with them.

Every married person—in fact, anyone involved in a couple relationship—has to make decisions at one time or another, consciously or unconsciously, about the nature and extent of relationships with others, both inside the marriage and outside. Helping people cope with and grow through the emotion-packed experience of an affair constitutes by far the most difficult and challenging part of my practice. Too often in the past, I found myself groping in the dark, for there are pitifully few established facts available about extramarital affairs. Probably less careful study has been given to understanding their sociological and psychological ramifications than to any other important human activity.

The reasons surrounding this lack of information are many. It's a fragile subject, tough to deal with, fraught with controversy, myth, and misinformation; one about which the people involved cannot talk without some risk. The very nature of their involvement implies that other people are included. Even in talking just about themselves, they may be betraying a trust which their extramarital partner has placed in them. And can they be certain that another person in whom they placed their confidence will keep the information secret and not use it against them at some future time?

Those in, or touched by, affairs make up a kind of subculture. Often only those involved know who they are. Sometimes they don't know whether to talk, when to talk, with whom, or even how. But many of these people thirst to share their feelings and experiences with someone—almost anyone who will understand and not judge their actions quickly and harshly. The sharing of such a confidence needs time and trust, and these cannot be developed easily. So, many feel isolated and alone. Because of their isolation, they are unaware of how many others like themselves are involved in similar experiences. If only it were safe for them to speak, they would find that they are really not alone after all.

I wrote this book to try to fill that void, to become a kind of spokesperson for them, as well as to contribute to a better public understanding of extramarital affairs. At the same time, I wanted to provide a vehicle to let many of these people speak for themselves in their own words and in their own ways.

As a psychotherapist who gets close to people, I feel and experience with them their isolation, their loneliness. Literally every human emotion can surface in an affair. One person may find an affair a joyous, growth-producing experience; for another, it may be a bitter, disappointing, life-wrecking ordeal. Having an affair is *always* risky. Its effects are unpredictable.

And in the closeness that develops between us, I share these people's pain and heartaches, along with their thrills and ecstasies. This has expanded my awareness of the destructiveness and dishonesty that affairs often bring with them, as well as the joys and the highs.

These people have also taught me a lot about marriage and family life. That's why this book is as much about marriage as it is about affairs. The two are very much interrelated—and the book shows how. From the experiences of hundreds of people, one can achieve perspective. And while no two affairs and no two marriages are alike, just as no two people are, there are lessons to be learned by all of us from all of them.

I've tried to provide a source of information—a resource, a guide— that I hope can be personally useful not only for people having affairs or thinking about them, but also for those trying to sort out their feelings about the affairs of their spouses or friends. I never recommend an affair as a solution to a marriage problem, any more than I would recommend marriage as a solution to a personal or family problem. Marriages and affairs are competitors in a game with no scores and sometimes no winners, but with high emotional stakes.

In writing this book, I soon found that in dealing with such a complex and personal subject, I could not be totally objective. To write with honesty, clarity, and conviction, it was necessary to examine some of my own pockets of privacy. My five years of work on this project have led me to appraise and reappraise my own values and behavior concerning sex, marriage, and extramarital affairs. As a result, I have gained a deeper understanding of affairs and a greater respect for people involved in them. It has enabled me to be more open and sensitive in working with troubled marriages, and has given me a clearer picture of the assets—as well as the liabilities—of traditional marriage.

I sincerely hope that you, the reader, will be able to appreciate and share my expanded awareness and that you will grow from your experience reading this book as I have grown by writing it. If we can draw a single conclusion from all the material presented, it is, simply, that options are available to all of us. No matter what the alternatives, the choices are ours to make.

Affairs are deeply human experiences flowing from people's minds and hearts. Whatever comes out of them begs for compassion and understanding, not condemnation and rejection.

Tom McGinnis

I am grateful to those who have shared with me their deepest joys and sorrows, and whose private lives have provided the basic material for this book. Of the cases cited in detail, some represent real people whose identities are masked, others are fictitious composites—making this book representative of hundreds of people in affairs. Personal recordings such as poems, letters, and written statements have been reproduced (anonymously) with permission.

Introduction

MORE THAN JUST FRIENDS

Whenever I see you my heart leaps.
I barely dare to look at you
Sure everyone can see how I care
Because we are more than "just friends."

Casually I speak
Wondering if they can hear how loudly my heart beats
Or if they can see through my expression to the joy
As I introduce you casually—as "my friend."

Images dancing in my mind
Passion soaring
Desire mounting
Wanting to feel your body pressed to mine
I hold my breath and try to seem unaffected.
Nonplussed—
Fighting the urge to add—No, we are more than "just friends."

In the beginning we're just friends. We like each other, we enjoy being together. There are no jealousies or fears of rejection. We don't wonder whom the other is with tonight.

Then something changes. We're no longer "just friends." We're absorbed in each other. We want to be together—we two and no one else. We're dating again—two persons seeking, needing, hoping, wanting.

Some moments seem as crisp and fresh as the day we were born. The currents between us are electric. We feel powerful and gentle, daring and dreamy, in touch with new feelings deep within us.

But we're committed to someone else (or at least one of us is). A spouse? Someone we're living with? Two spouses? There's our old life and our new experiences, our old pledges and our new longings, at war with each other. Problems! Uncertainties!

Our lives change in basic ways—how can our spouses not see? Symbols of the changed lives are the closed and bolted door, the pulled curtain, the car parked out of sight around the corner, the exchange of secret glances when in public. Now it's the fantasy come to life, the wonder and the hope, the fear and the guilt, the wish and the fulfillment. Now it's ecstasy, it's agony, it's honesty, it's lying, it's love, it's betrayal, it's beauty, it's ugliness and excuses. It's hours of talk and lovemaking. It's being wanted and appreciated. And it's the knowledge that there may be a price to pay: Somebody—perhaps a number of people, including ourselves—may get hurt.

We meet in out-of-the-way places. Risky! We dare not telephone. We dare not write. We dare not be seen together. We dare not even give gifts that can be traced. Life gets excessively complicated. Silence and deception hang over us like a thundercloud. Practical matters intrude: Why were you late? Whose turn is it to bring the wine, cheese, and crackers? There is pain, anxiety, shame, fear. Am I still loved? Why doesn't he/she call? I haven't heard in more than a week. Is there someone else? Have we been found out? Have I destroyed my marriage? Or my lover's marriage? Suddenly I know what it is like to be the "other woman" or "other man."

This is an extramarital affair*: one of life's blockbusters... exhilarating ... mysterious ... rewarding ... frightening ... dangerous. Value systems are upended. Heartaches juxtaposed with thrills, like the whirl and rush of a roller coaster. To be loved, admired, made to feel important to someone else; to respond; to share: Such are among life's thirsts. Dreams trickling to the surface from deep inside, spawning fantasies, stimulating feelings, desires, and laughter.

An affair—it's the shadow side of marriage; the hidden, disreputable side. Great numbers of people in every walk of life experience it in a thousand variations. Through it we see our marriages as we may never have seen them before: the hurts, scars, misunderstandings, resentments, careless habits, boredom, feelings of neglect and faded love. But also the loyalty, steadfastness, dependability, caring, sharing, hard work, and the moments of joy.

Underneath the extramarital affair and propelling it are a person's unmet needs, dreams, unfulfilled wishes, deprivations, and hurts, often not successfully dealt with in the early years. Yesterday's child is the architect of today's affair. For an affair doesn't just happen; it boils up out of the past. You don't suddenly become unhappy with yourself or your marriage. And in a society where people unashamedly seek greater satisfactions, want to "do their own thing," and feel an urge to live independently and creatively, much of the old resistance is ebbing.

Affairs are increasing to an extent that is historically unprecedented. According to available studies,† every socioeconomic group, every age group, every occupation is affected. Few marital partners today are so well adjusted or so happy in their relationship that an affair is unthinkable or impossible. Affairs have become everybody's concern.

How can we regard the extramarital affair? Can we dismiss it as simply cheating on a spouse? Sinful? Against the law of God? Injuring our children? Running out on our marriage instead of staying with it and trying

---

*For the purpose of this book, I define an extramarital affair as any adulterous relationship between a married person and someone other than the spouse. I include also any relationship of a similar kind that affects an unmarried couple living together.
†See discussion of the statistical evidence in Chapter 1.

to work through our problems? Are we participating in the final disintegration of the moral basis of our society—a new fall of Rome? Is sociologist Amitai Etzioni correct when he warns that sexual license is weakening the family and that "no political society has ever survived without its nuclear family intact"?[1] Or Tony Lake and Ann Hills when they warn that the loosening of sexual attitudes can go only so far before it threatens the fundamental structure of society?[2]

Or is there a more positive, hopeful side of the extramarital affair? Can an affair be a learning experience, a stimulus to personal growth? Can affairs help revitalize some marriages or preserve marriages that otherwise would fall apart? Is conventional marriage, as we've known it, too restrictive, too stifling, too lacking in stimulus for people who've tasted the freedom to live a rich and varied life? Are we in trouble because so many of us have married unwisely and for unhealthy reasons, expect too much of marriage and have had no adequate training for a stable, satisfying marital relationship? Is the extramarital affair a means of breaking out of the straitjacket some marriages impose? Is it a viable alternative to divorce?

We may ask even more searching questions. Can the growth of extramarital affairs be viewed as part of the vast movement of emergence by which great numbers of people, who had felt themselves restricted (e.g., blacks, the poor, the young) are throwing off shackles of every kind and demanding personal recognition and an opportunity for fulfillment? Will the affair come out of the shadow of marriage and insist on social acceptance in its own right? Can it be seen as a challenge to marriage to put its house in order? Might the extramarital affair be seen as a cry for a gentler, freer, more kindly social order in which human feelings and human relationships are more honored and in which there is less restriction, repression, and cruelty?

Dare we ask such questions? Yet dare we not ask them? For affairs can no longer be hidden behind locked doors. They've already become a social avalanche threatening to bury traditional beliefs and values. Yet we still shrink from looking squarely at what's happening because, as Lake and Hills point out, a threat to the general concept of marriage puts our own legitimacy in question. And even our identity![3]

Marriage is changing, becoming looser, less structured, and less restrictive. It offers more options, more variety of life-styles than in the past; the roles of the partners are more flexible and interchangeable (or, as some would put it, more confused!). Wives are freer and more independent; but so, in a different way, are husbands. Because many people do not know how to handle a situation so unstructured and so vulnerable to pressures, and perhaps have entered marriage with unreasonable expectations, marriages are crumbling on every hand. Yet for people who have developed skills in human relationships, today's marriage offers a better opportunity for long-term rewards and personal growth than marriage ever did in the past. Today's young marrieds have a unique opportunity. But the assumptions on which marriage has traditionally been based will have to change.

An affair versus marriage: How do the two kinds of relationships compare? What has each to offer? Where do children fit in? Can marriage be as interesting, stimulating, and satisfying as an exciting affair? Some married couples, we know, are able to keep the zip in a marriage. Help is available through marriage enrichment programs and in other ways. But how many of us are trained for marriage? How many pick the right partner at age twenty? How many of us know what we want out of marriage, let alone how to build a rewarding life together? Or how to give freely of ourselves? On the other hand, how well are most of us prepared to deal with the strains, uncertainties, complications, and consequences of an affair?

Affairs present everybody involved, including the therapist, with a dilemma. As a marital and family therapist, one of my objectives is to help people strengthen and enrich their marriages and family lives. An equally important objective, however, is to help them grow as individuals; develop their capacities; get in touch with their feelings; learn to recognize what is going on within them; acquire healthier attitudes and values; improve their communication; interact more constructively with each other, with their families, and with other people; explore new alternatives in marriage and family living; and thus learn to live their lives with more awareness, sensitivity, humor, and joy. These two objectives sometimes collide. I am committed to working wherever possible for a blend of both. But if that doesn't work, the decision as to which to put first—personal fulfillment or marriage and family needs—has to be made by the individual. The therapist cannot and should not make it.

More Than Just a Friend starts with the obvious fact that affairs *are.* They not only are, they are going to continue because people want satisfying qualitative couple relationships, and if they don't find them in their marriages, they'll look for them elsewhere. Some people prize their affair as the only meaningful human relationship they have ever had. People who have been in affairs have things to tell us—not only about themselves, but about marriage, human relationships, love and sex, and the changing nature of society as they've experienced it. We needn't agree with their views, but theirs are voices not often heard.

It will be evident as soon as we look closely at extramarital affairs that there is far more to these experiences than the gratification of sexual appetites. The urges underlying affairs are deeply human and active in us all. We'll see that there are many different kinds of affairs with different motivations and different effects. (For a person hurt by the affair of a spouse, this can be valuable knowledge.) We'll compare affairs with marriages and look at the ways in which affairs can evolve out of dull, poor marriages or even good marriages. We'll experience through the confidential stories of people in affairs their hunger for love, their itch for excitement, their longing for fulfillment, their fear, miseries, and guilt. We'll consider what qualities in people most often lead to affairs, and why.

We'll learn how some people have made their marriages better by bene-fiting from experiences in affairs, and how others have destroyed their marriages. We'll find out who are *not* involved in affairs, and why not.

Learning about affairs is a way of learning about marriage from a new viewpoint. We begin to see what makes both affairs and marriages healthy and what causes both to go downhill. To our surprise, certain personal qualities that make a marriage satisfying—such as the capacity for affection—can also make an affair satisfying, and many of the qualities or attitudes that hurt a marriage can equally hurt an affair. I hope this knowledge will help people avoid blunders and misery. Stumbling upre-pared into an affair (as into a marriage) can be disastrous. Yet how often, because the issue had never been faced, do people find themselves in an affair they'd never imagined. "Someone else, yes. But *me*? I thought never!" I hope this book will provide a service to men and women everywhere by taking the wraps off a difficult issue, examining it, and drawing up some constructive guidelines for handling personal relationships—within the marriage and outside.

In this book we'll take a detailed look at what happened in the cases of twenty-five couples involved in extramarital affairs, all but two selected from our files of case histories to illustrate the variety and scope of affairs. The people involved could well represent your neighbors, your friends, your coworkers—possibly your children, your parents, your spouse . . . or yourself.

It will be noted that more than half the affairs described herein are portrayed from the viewpoint of the woman in the affair rather than from that of the man. There are two reasons for this. One is that when an affair occurs, it is the woman who is more likely to experience emotional turmoil, pain, and rejection because cultural tradition and religious teach-ings about fidelity have borne down much more heavily on her. Hence it is women who more often seek therapy in these situations. A second reason is that affairs by wives seem to be increasing proportionally faster today than are those by husbands (though wives have not yet caught up).

The revolutionary changes taking place in traditional values, attitudes, and practices challenge us to reflect on our personal lives and to look at fidelity, commitment, and trust in new ways. Can we relate con-structively to what's happening? Can we find grounds for hope rather than despair?

1. *Extramarital Affairs: Past and Present*

Thou shalt not commit adultery.
—Seventh Commandment

Thou shalt not covet thy neighbor's house,
Thou shalt not covet thy neighbor's wife . . .
Nor anything that is thy neighbor's.
—Tenth Commandment

THE CRIME OF INFIDELITY

Extramarital sexual activity must have been a problem in ancient times, for the Ten Commandments struck at it twice—directly in the seventh, indirectly in the tenth. The tenth commandment had to do with respecting other people's property—wives included.

So the attempt was made, backed by the authority of God, to clamp iron chains on extramarital sexual relations—chains that have begun to be loosened only in recent times. Not that these taboos were ever fully effective. People are adept at slipping through chains. But the prohibition kept extramarital activity underground, invisible in the daylight, recognizable only as ghostly forms, pressed hands, and moist lips under cover of darkness.

For centuries, among our forebears, adultery by a wife was a crime—long punishable by death. In certain parts of the world it still is. Infidelity of a husband was often viewed less seriously; his act was a crime if he "stole" another man's wife or seduced someone's cherished daughter, but otherwise little attention was paid. Thus the double standard of sexual conduct has a very long history, and its imprint on our psyches is deep.

To warn against infidelity of wives, the most bloodcurdling tales were told. The fairy tale of Bluebeard, for example, is the story of a husband who, when he leaves on a journey, tests his wife's faithfulness by forbidding her to enter a certain room in the house, but leaves the key with her. When he returns, the key has blood on it; he knows she has been in the forbidden room (unfaithful) and he kills her (as he had killed all his previous wives).

In *The Thousand and One Nights* a sultan, disillusioned by the infidelity of one of his wives, vows never again to let a woman betray him. His solution is to sleep each night with a fresh virgin and kill her in the morning before she has a chance to be unfaithful. The brave and beautiful Scheherazade undertakes at the risk of her life to cure the sultan of his blood lust. She succeeds by telling him the stories of *The Thousand and One Nights*.

The killing of a wife for infidelity was accepted practice in Old Testament times. It was frequently backed up by social custom and law. And a man who committed adultery with another man's wife was also liable to severe penalties; a wronged husband could, and sometimes did, kill a man who tampered with his wife. Or, if the husband didn't do it, the law did it for him, as stated in Leviticus 20:10:

> *And the man that committeth adultery with another man's wife, even he that committeth adultery with his neighbor's wife, the adulterer and the adulteress shall surely be put to death.*

It is interesting that in this code adultery is defined by implication as a connection involving someone's wife. It says nothing about a husband who has intercourse with an unmarried woman. In fact, there seems to have been no law in those times that forbade a husband to have coitus with a woman not under some man's protection.[1]

Long before the Judeo-Christian tradition, the Babylonians and Assyrians also punished a wife's adultery with death.

Moving forward in history, penalties for adultery gradually softened. Thus, Jesus was able to prevent the stoning of an adulteress by the words, "He that is without sin among you, let him first cast a stone at her" (John 8:7). He also said, "Neither do I condemn thee; go, and sin no more" (John 8:11). But, most significant of all, he clearly implied that the woman was not the only sinner; the *man* shared the blame.

Yet even up to comparatively modern times, the penalties for adultery by women remained harsh. In Hawthorne's novel *The Scarlet Letter,* a woman found to have committed adultery was required to display a large letter *A* on her clothing, bringing upon her sneers and contempt. In Greek culture, even today the killing of a wife and her paramour by her husband is not unheard of and is tolerantly regarded among some Greeks as an "honor crime."

Our language clearly reflects the traditional attitudes toward adulterous women with terms like *whore, slut, tart, tramp, harlot, floozy, home wrecker,* etc. The terms applied to an adulterous man are much less damning: *wolf, womanizer, Don Juan, libertine, rake, lecher, old goat,* etc. The latter terms can be used with a laugh and a wink—"Come on, you old goat!" Shakespeare's Falstaff, a notorious rake, is portrayed as an entertaining buffoon. But an adulterous woman was no joke. She was a threat to the social order, the family, the community, and the church.

Clearly, adultery has existed for thousands of years—almost always condemned. George Murdock's research shows taboos against adultery in 120 of 148 societies studied.[2] It seems that monogamy, even though buttressed by powerful legal, social, and religious sanctions, has been a difficult life-style to maintain. It proved difficult even when villages were small and everyone knew the comings and goings of neighbors.

With this long history, it's understandable that even in our society of relaxed sexual attitudes, a woman's adultery sometimes carries with it an almost unbearable burden of guilt. The taboo remains powerful. But a social trend modifying its effects is the movement toward equality of women. The historical condemnation of adultery by a wife was based squarely on the subordinate position of women. Men, not women, wrote all the rules of conduct and shaped religious doctrines. A man's wife in ancient times was totally subject to his direction and control.

An echo of this idea of possession in present-day practices is the question asked in certain wedding ceremonies: "Who gives this woman . . .?" Gives! The assumption is that the father could have "given" the daughter to anyone he pleased. In an earlier age he did so.

There were, of course, very practical reasons for condemning a woman's adultery. A man wanted to be certain his children were his own. Bloodlines and kinship were enormously important, and any uncertainty about parentage had serious legal, economic, and social consequences. To be conceived by unwed parents could put a stigma on a person for life ("bastard!").

All these conditions and attitudes are now changing with incredible speed. Cultural intermix has reduced the emphasis on bloodlines and kinship. Birth out of wedlock no longer carries the stigma it formerly did. The position of women has been altered enormously and irrevocably. Wives no longer feel constrained to obey their husbands. They have power to control childbirth and the even more crucial capability of self-support. They feel much less obliged to become household drudges. Husbands, in turn, feel less obligation to protect and support their wives. The result is a change in the entire atmosphere of man-woman relationships. To the extent that the traditional code was based on women's subjection, the foundation of it is crumbling. This does not mean that the coast is clear for everyone to commit adultery, for adultery still threatens the integrity and stability of marriage and the family. But it needs to be recognized that the issue has shifted its base. And no one knows what the ultimate effects of this shift may be.

CHANGING MORAL PERSPECTIVES

Moral guidance in our society has traditionally been a function of churches and the family. Both are losing effectiveness. Still, it is important to look at the religious aspect of extramarital affairs, for the feelings of sin and wrongdoing arising from the violation of deeply held religious beliefs can arouse inner conflict. Church teachings say, unequivocally, "Don't do it. It's wrong."

But the churches' positions on divorce, remarriage, and premarital sex have been almost as uncompromising. It is only within the lifetimes of some of us now living that divorce has emerged from being an act of disgrace and shame. And it is only within the last two decades that premarital sex has dared come out of dark corners and reveal itself. Many

churches still regard divorce and premarital sex as wrong; but their condemnation has lost a great deal of its sharpness. After all, it is often their
own members, their children and even, in some cases, their clergy who are
violating the ancient codes.

Traditional church teachings, in effect, leave single people with
only two choices consistent with their religious beliefs: marriage or celibacy.
This puts enormous pressure on young people to marry. Yet if, as a result of
this pressure, they make an unfortunate choice of partner, they are expected
to live with the consequences for the rest of their lives. It doesn't work any
more. People have become too used to freedom.

A basic difficulty for the church is simply that marriage is not the
same institution it was when the biblical injunctions were written, and
neither is the society around it. When Moses, Jesus, and Saint Paul spoke of
marriage, each had in mind something so different from modern marriage
that, if he returned today, he probably wouldn't regard the unstable form
we now have as marriage at all. Marriage in Old Testament times was part of
a closely knit patriarchal structure tied in with a nomadic way of life. A
family's survival depended on having many sons. The wife's responsibilities were to serve her husband, to do whatever work was required of her
and to bear and raise children. Her subordination to her husband, later
buttressed by the teachings of Saint Paul, became entrenched in custom,
church doctrines, and law that, to some extent, continue even to the
present, although women now are increasingly challenging this inequity.

Of course, there is no way that marriage can be restored to
anything resembling what it was when the teachings of the church were
shaped. Yet altering any of the teachings to adapt them to modern marriage
is strongly resisted because the ancient concepts are embedded in doctrines
that many people feel are God given and cannot be touched. Unfortunately, the teachings are based in part on assumptions about human beings
that do not accord with modern knowledge and everyday observation. One
basic assumption, for example, has to do with the nature of love. Church
teachings have often treated love less as an emotion flowing from the heart
than as a moral duty following a commandment. You love your spouse (if
you do) because you are instructed to do so; human feelings to the contrary
are minimized. You are expected to love that person for a lifetime ("eternal
love"). Any other love that intrudes tends to be viewed as false and a
betrayal. Thus, we are instructed to suppress and smother feelings that run
contrary to these injunctions.

We know from many studies and observations of human beings
that the consequences of such suppression of feelings can be dire. They put
a person at war within himself. With such inner conflict, he or she cannot be
true, cannot be whole.

In real life, love seems to be neither exclusive ("one only") nor
eternal. On the contrary, it can be very fragile. But we cling strongly to the
"one only" idea. To abandon that would be to undermine the very basis of
marriage as we know it. Yet the "one only" rule of love is applied solely to

the marital relationship. There are many kinds of love, none of which—except marital love—do we limit to one person. For example, we don't limit parental love to one child, nor altruistic love to a single favored individual. Why is marital love thought to be different? Social custom and centuries of tradition would seem to be the answer. But, looking at the way people actually live, we frequently encounter multiple loves. This is what many extramarital affairs are. And even when there is no affair as we have defined it, there are multiple friendships with strong emotional content—loves, in fact. They do not necessarily diminish each other or cancel each other out. Often they enhance each other.

Church statements often reflect other beliefs about human beings that conflict with observed facts about how people think, feel, and act. For example, in a 1940 statement by the Federal Council of the Churches of Christ in America, the ideal Christian marriage is described as "a union dissolved only by death and unspoiled by the memory of pre-marital indulgence or by degrading episodes after marriage."[3] The statement takes for granted that the recollection of premarital sex would be a cloud on a marriage. Perhaps this may have been true of many individuals forty years ago, but I know very few people today who feel this way. Premarital sex is extremely common, and many married people recall it with respect and appreciation. As for "degrading episodes after marriage," individuals who have actually had extramarital affairs do not, as a rule, feel these experiences to have been degrading. Many feel the opposite—they are glad they had the experience. The statement by the Federal Council of Churches reflects a deep fear of sex that has pervaded much of Christian thought from its beginning and typifies a basic assumption made by the church that the preservation of a marriage is far more important than whether people are happy in it. The clear directive is "Stay together at all costs," based on Jesus' injunction (Mark 10:9, 11, and 12):

> *What therefore God has joined together, let no man put asunder. Whoever divorces his wife and marries another commits adultery against her; and if she divorces her husband and marries another, she commits adultery.*

In Jesus' time, the divorce of a woman by her husband often left her nowhere to go. There were few or no jobs for women, and so she was likely to become an outcast. Such a divorce was a cruel, unfeeling act, and Jesus was understandably against it. Today, the situation is quite different. Many women can now make independent lives for themselves. As for the effects on children, staying together at all costs when a marriage is failing can sometimes hurt the children much more severely than divorce and separation.

Because of these immense social changes and changes in attitudes, some religious leaders are attempting to rethink and reinterpret their positions on marriage and sex. An influential churchman who did such rethinking was John A. T. Robinson, Bishop of Woolrich, England, who in 1963 came out with a controversial book, *Honest to God.*[4] This book stirred an uproar in the religious world. He wrote that Jesus was not teaching a set of rules or a fixed code of conduct, such as the old Jewish law, but was trying to open people's minds to a more spiritual understanding of God and man. As the Bishop viewed it, Jesus was *not* telling us never to divorce under any circumstances, thus making a rule out of an admonition, or even never to have sex before marriage. Jesus made one simple commandment: to "love one another." And certainly forcing a badly mated couple to stay together in a loveless marriage where everyone is hurting could scarcely be considered to accord with the principle of love. Rules have their place; but the commandment to love takes precedence, and circumstances and human feelings always have to be taken into account.

Although Bishop Robinson was furiously attacked for these and other views believed by some to undermine faith and morals, no one could accuse him of not knowing his Bible or of not being familiar with the background of Christian faith.

Few religious writers have dared go so far as to come out with an open admission that an extramarital affair might, in certain circumstances, be an act of genuine love and therefore right for the persons involved. Among the few taking this position is the husband and wife team of Rustum and Della Roy in their book *Honest Sex,*[5] published some ten years ago. They state quite bluntly that sexual relations with a person other than the spouse, if a genuinely loving act, may not necessarily destroy or damage a marriage and may, in certain circumstances, be understood and accepted by the partner not involved. They feel that extramarital relationships are bound to increase and that it is "the church's urgent business to provide guidelines for the most creative conduct within them."

There has not been much response as yet to this appeal by the Roys; and, as Kenneth and Betty Woodward have pointed out, "every religious group that has mushroomed so far in the 1970's—from fundamentalist Jesus freaks to Hare Krishna—stresses sexual continence."[6] Clearly, older attitudes have strong supporters too, and unquestionably, placing sexual conduct under strict control resolves a lot of doubt and confusion.

THE EMERGENCE OF WOMEN . . . AND OPPORTUNITY

The biggest social earthquake of our time, now altering moral perceptions on a vast scale, is the change in women's relationship to the outside world. The opportunities for women to engage in all kinds of activities have expanded beyond anything formerly conceivable. Doors are open wide. The sheltered environment has vanished. Chaperones are gone. Trained and educated women are claiming rights, positions, and privileges previously reserved for men. Along with men, they enjoy more freedom and leisure than their ancestors ever imagined. The telephone puts them in private communication with anyone they wish to talk to. Automobiles, trains, planes, taxicabs, and buses are at their disposal. Hotels, motels, and restaurants are everywhere. Contraceptives remove or reduce the pregnancy threat. Sex can be freely enjoyed without undue fear of consequences. Privacy can be secured. It is easy for a woman to meet a variety of men—at school, at work, at restaurants, at resorts, at clubs, at church, in public conveyances, at political and professional meetings. And, of course, it is equally easy for men to meet a variety of women.

Can we grasp how historically unique this condition is? It's revolutionary! In a rural area before the age of the automobile a married woman during her entire lifetime might meet—how many men? A dozen, perhaps? Twenty? Thirty? And how many of these might she meet with her husband not present? Very few, I daresay. Yet the married woman in our society today probably meets hundreds of men in her lifetime, the great majority of them without her husband present. She is approaching the position men have long enjoyed. Merely on the basis of numbers, the opportunity for participation in extramarital affairs by both men and women has increased beyond measure over that of all previous societies.

These changes are, without question, challenging, modifying, or eliminating many of the old protections and restraints that once kept extramarital affairs within bounds. Qualified observers are in wide agreement that *opportunity* is the most powerful single factor in precipitating affairs. This was clearly evident, for example, in a survey of *Psychology Today* readers, summarized in 1970,[7] in which 80 percent of respondents stated that they would probably find an affair acceptable under certain circumstances. This suggests that conscience and morality may not, today, be the most powerful deterrents. Conscience is largely a product of early moral training and many people in adult life move away from the teachings of their childhood. Furthermore, as Gerhard Neubeck[8] has pointed out, "Our culture, while explicitly puritanical, promotes social affairs which are, in fact, institutionalizing men-women opportunities." Office parties, the cocktail hour, the discotheque, and girls for entertainment at business conferences are all examples.

Opportunity for an affair can develop in any of three different ways:

1. By accident or by institutional arrangement, as at a party or conference where two people are thrown together under circumstances or plans not of their own making. (Example: finding each other alone together, with both spouses away, in a place where privacy is easily available.)

2. By deliberate plan, as when one or both participants arrange matters to facilitate their coming together.

3. By unconscious intent, as when the meeting occurs as a result of unconscious manipulation of events by one or both participants. (They want it, but don't admit it to themselves).

Yet despite its importance, opportunity is far from being the only factor. Many men and women, regardless of opportunity, have no interest in having affairs. For some, the universal exposure may even have reduced the desire. When married women were secluded, hard to meet, and their bodies were concealed under multiple layers of clothing, they may have been more enticing to men. Hidden gold can be a greater challenge; inaccessibility enhances value.

EROTIC LOVE VERSUS PREVAILING MORAL RULES

The'conflict between erotic love and prevailing moral rules has been the theme of innumerable legends, sagas, songs, poems, plays, novels, paintings, and sculpture. We meet it in the Old Testament in the story of Potiphar's wife, who tried unsuccessfully to seduce Joseph (Genesis 39:7 ff.). In Greek mythology there was Helen of Troy, whose affair with Paris, a Trojan prince, precipitated a war of revenge that ended in the destruction of ancient Troy. There was King Arthur of the Round Table, who was conceived (say the legends) in an extramarital tryst in a castle with the husband away. The Arthurian legends are rich in illicit romances, including the affair between Sir Lancelot and King Arthur's wife, Queen Guinevere, and the love of Sir Tristan for Isolde, wife (or intended wife) of King Mark.

These were fateful love affairs: Each led to tragedy and death. All through literature the motives of love and death have been intertwined, just as Shakespeare intertwined them in *Romeo and Juliet.* This can be explained in part by the enchantment of drama: A great love affair is high adventure; the lover is a hero overcoming all opposition to win his loved one, but in the process he often sets in motion forces that destroy them both. We are moved by the passion of the lovers, their bravery in the face of implacable enemies, and the tragedy of their deaths.

Stories like these reach into the depths of the psyche, where dreams originate. They give rise to fantasies; they stimulate feelings and desires. Who can resist the vision of a knight in armor carrying off a beautiful queen? People pretend in this cynical age that romance is old-fashioned, that love is mere sentimentality, that heroism is ridiculous; but at a deeper level they don't believe it and never have believed it. Who knows how many extramarital affairs have grown out of fantasies nourished by these archetypal visions?

Because extramarital affairs generally involve a conflict of loyalties and strike at the basic relationship and obligation between husband and wife, they can let loose hurricanes of emotion. They can upset people's beliefs about who they are and who their marital partners are. They can throw their value systems into confusion. I have seen individuals, honest in most matters, become expert in lies and deception; gentle people turn violent; humane and kindly people become cruel, harsh, and vindictive. I have seen shocked or enraged partners submerge their feelings in drink or drugs or act them out in suicide or murder. A secret extramarital affair can be a hazard to any marriage, undermining trust and threatening to blow to bits what had been thought safe and secure.

But there's another side. An affair can also be a joyous—indeed, a transforming—experience. It can help some people to grow emotionally, to come alive, to cast off old limitations that had bound them as though in chains, to discover strengths and capacities they never knew they had, to become warmer, more lovable and loving, more understanding and compassionate. And sometimes the marriage, too, is rejuvenated. I've encountered that side of affairs also, and have had many an occasion to reflect upon it.

In conversation with people about extramarital affairs, certain patterns begin to emerge. People who have never had an affair tend to condemn. Often they have little sympathy with participants in affairs, regarding their troubles as "their own fault" or as "deserved punishment." It's often different with most people who have had one or more affairs. They tend to see an affair as a human relationship rather than as a moral lapse, and feel concern and understanding for the individuals involved.

The incredible change in the attitudes of some people toward extramarital affairs is illustrated by this excerpt from a letter I received from Lynn, an intelligent and sensitive woman with whom I have worked:

> *The people I know are really smack in the* middle—*they aren't tied by old-fashioned morality, but they don't want to abandon their marriages, either—and they find the idea of an affair very exciting. They are on the brink, and the temptation is overwhelming. A new viewpoint on marriage is creeping in—they expect much less from marriage itself but much more from life as a whole. The spouse is not expected to provide* all *the solace,* all *the sex,* all *the stimulation. My friends look more to themselves than to others—the new "I am I" and "you are you." That's exciting because it places less stress on marriage. . . . If we are open, experiencing people, we are bound to find many people we can relate to—and some will be very attractive. So it becomes easier and easier to find potential extramarital partners. . . . As for me, I've only really had* positive *reactions to my extramarital affairs. They have been* growing *experiences—and I have learned that nothing hurts too much when the alternative is being emotionally "dead"—not feeling, not doing and not experiencing.*

Here is a radical reappraisal of the whole meaning of marriage and sex. How seriously can we take such thoughts? Very seriously, I believe. Lynn isn't alone; there are many who feel as she does. Note that she's not giving up on marriage. She recognizes that marriage has its value. But she has ceased to expect that her marriage will ever give her *all* the satisfaction she seeks. She expects to fill the gaps outside.

Another significant comment was made to me by a man having an extramarital affair (his first). Said he:

> *I've told several of my friends about my affair. In each case, to my utter surprise, my friend confessed an extramarital relationship of his own. Each one said I was the* only *person he had ever spoken to about it; and*

each poured out his feelings as if I had opened a valve that had been stuck shut. This has happened in five instances (totally unsuspected by me). In each case my acquaintance implored me to say nothing to anyone—a pledge of secrecy. It has almost become a memory game for me, for I try to remember that Bill has a "friend" in Houston, Jim has one in Washington, Ted one in New York, etc. . . . It's a struggle to recall whose girl is where and not to get them confused.

It would be easy to jump to the conclusion that practically everybody is having affairs. Not true. A woman having difficulties with her marriage writes:

Until last year the thought of an affair never crossed my mind. . . . I was not ready to admit that I was very unhappy in my marriage. Even now it seems wrong, somehow, not to keep trying to make the marriage work. The first time I found myself attracted to another man, I was shocked at myself and felt scared and guilty. Of course, I didn't give him the slightest encouragement. Since then, I've come to realize I have emotional needs my husband will never fill because of his basic personality. The thought of finding happiness through someone else doesn't frighten me so much any more. But I have trouble imagining it in the context of my marriage, and it still seems wrong to me. I'm not the kind of person who would find casual sex rewarding. I have two small children who are with me most of the time and I would need a baby sitter if I were to go out. And the only man who has shown interest in me (and whom I find attractive) is the husband of my very best friend. I couldn't do that to her. Catch 22! I suppose if the right man came along, I might surmount the logistical problems. But I would feel more ethically comfortable if I were divorced.

Here we've heard the voices of the enthusiastic adulterer; the naive, somewhat inexperienced adulterer; and the wistful "might-be" adulterer. But also there are nonadulterers with happy marriages who should be heard. One of these, now in his seventies, writes of his marriage of fifty years:

I can't express how wonderful it is to live with a woman like Anna May. She's extraordinary, and you have to live with her for fifty years to realize how true that is. Ours is not a perfect match. I don't think there is any such thing as a perfect match and I'm not sure I'd want one. We've certainly had our differences. We still do. We irritate each other at times, and we've had to work through problems of getting along. Many a time, while pouring out our feelings, we have talked in bed until three o'clock in the morning trying to achieve understanding, and then have celebrated our final success with passionate love-making. A lot of crises can occur over fifty years. But the fact that we were and are different stimulated growth in both of us. This is the way we want it. In fact, I wouldn't care for a marriage where the partners are in such harmony that they don't stimulate each other's growth (if such a one exists).

But even when our relationship was under strain, we never contemplated separation. We allowed no outside entanglements to threaten what we had. And do you know, I'm proud of that! I'm happy about it. I don't know where I'd be if it were not so.

GATHERING STORMS OF CHANGE

All four of the people just quoted are living amidst wrenching social changes that are fast unraveling traditional marriage. They *feel* these changes. They react to them daily. Even the man with the fifty-year marriage has to deal with them—he perhaps more than most because the span of his marriage bridges two utterly different worlds. All four individuals are aware that their own marriages are not like those of their parents and grand-parents. People today are dealing with new strains, new problems, new uncertainties. Their goals are less clear than those of earlier generations. Often they feel lonely and alienated. They may not always be aware of how nearly universal these feelings are. They might feel less isolated if they had a clearer understanding of what has been happening to marriage and other human relationships during the last several decades.

Here is a summary of social changes that have profoundly affected marriage and laid the groundwork for the current growth of extramarital affairs. Individually, these developments are familiar and have been widely written about and discussed; but they are not often brought together to form a total picture, nor looked at in the light of their bearing on affairs.

1. *Decline of the extended family and weakness of the nuclear family.* It is hardly news that the extended family—in which several generations lived together and various uncles, aunts, cousins, and other relatives were within easy reach—has fallen a victim to urbanization and industrialization. When the extended family was at its best, it offered a stable, growth-enhancing interaction between the generations and a rich variety of interpersonal experiences. Family members came to each other's aid in crises, took some of the burdens off each other, advised, counseled, helped with the children. The extended family was replaced by the nuclear family (parents and children only), which offers far less scope for interpersonal relationships and puts all the burden on two people. This form seems to be inherently unstable. Now the nuclear family, too, is declining; and between 1970 and 1978 there has been a fifty-four percent increase in *one-person* households (compared with a twenty percent increase in all households).[9] The two-parent family with father at work and mother at home with the children (which many people still think of as the standard American family) has declined to less than one-fourth of all households.[10] Today, mainly as a result of separations and divorce, eighteen percent of American children are growing up in single-parent households.[11] Such households have doubled between 1965 and 1975 from two and a half million to over five

million.[12] It has been estimated that nearly one-half of all children born today will spend a meaningful portion of their lives in a single-parent situation before they reach age eighteen.[13]

Some of the consequences of the strains on family life have been a rapidly rising number of divorces (for every two marriages which took place in 1979, there was one divorce),[14] an alarming increase in teenage drug abuse and alcoholism, a flood of children who run away from or are forced out of their homes (two million every year),[15] increasing rates of juvenile delinquency (one child in nine can be expected to appear in juvenile court before the age of 18), a serious public-health problem of child abuse, and a rise in suicides among young Americans to make this the second leading cause of death for persons between the ages of fifteen and twenty-four.[16] The nuclear family obviously is in critical need of help. It faces strains often beyond its capacity to handle; and it should surprise no one if its problems and confusion are reflected in extramarital affairs.

2. *Changes in the nature and purpose of marriage.* People do not marry for the same reasons they once did, and this is affecting the nature of marriage itself. Such motivations as settling down, having children; establishing a permanent home; perpetuating the family name; legitimizing sexual relations; providing economic security for the wife; and forming an economic and social unit are dwindling in importance in the United States. Modern middle-class marriage stresses companionship and a high-quality rewarding relationship between the partners, who often regard each other (at the beginning) as best friends and lovers. This is a very recent concept, not contemplated in the older teachings about marriage and certainly not known in the marriages of biblical times. Children are not always the primary object of modern marriage. Partly, this is economic; whereas children were once regarded as an economic asset, they are now close to an economic disaster. The out-of-pocket cost to an average middle income family of raising and educating a child from birth to age eighteen and then sending him to a public university is estimated to be $85,000, according to the Population Reference Bureau,[17] and this does not include the income the mother may forego during the child-raising period. Many people, of course, want children regardless of cost, but others are not prepared for the sacrifice or do not feel they can afford to have them. The proportion of marriages that are childless increased from 42.8 percent in 1968 to 48.6 percent in 1979.[18]

A number of the purposes for which people once married (sexual relations, for example) now are being accomplished without marriage. And there has also been a steady decline in the concept of marriage as a religious sacrament and a lifetime contract. The median duration of marriages is less than seven years.[19] Yet many people still want to marry; they yearn for some degree of commitment, some feeling of stability and dependability, some assurance that their union has meaning and purpose. When couples break up, remarriage is common; some eighty percent of the formerly married remarry.[20] Such a succession of marriages is called serial monogamy—formerly the prerogative of movie stars and rich heiresses, but now expanding to the population at large. And I suspect that in many cases the bridge from one marriage to the next will be the extramarital affair.

3. *Change in attitudes toward sex.* The change from concealing sex behind drawn curtains to emblazoning it on the front page has probably been one of the fastest social changes in all history. The fact that a change this basic could have occurred so rapidly suggests that the emotional groundwork had already been laid in the minds of older generations long before it became overt in practice. Now that the genie is out of the bottle and resists being put back, it is becoming more and more difficult to restrict sex to marriage. Already, couples living together without marriage have more than doubled in number since 1970.[21] And, as we shall see shortly, extramarital activity is rising steadily.

Much slower to change, on the other hand, is the double standard. Many men (but not all) still feel free to find sex wherever it is available, while naively expecting their women to remain faithful. Some women are in rebellion against such a one-sided viewpoint, which may account in part for Morton Hunt's startling finding[22] that the percentage of married women ages eighteen to twenty-four who have been unfaithful seems to have tripled since Kinsey's 1953 study, going from eight percent at that time to twenty-four percent in 1972–73. Hunt believes this reflects not so much a break with the ideal of sexual fidelity as an assault on the double standard. Another aspect of the matter was brought out in *The Hite Report*,[23] which indicated a wide dissatisfaction among women with the sexual responses they were getting from either husbands or lovers.

The sexual picture today is one of incredible confusion—people do not know clearly where they stand with each other. As psychotherapist Lillian Rubin has pointed out,[24] there is not even a generally acceptable term in the language to describe a man with whom an unmarried woman lives, or the woman with whom an unmarried man lives. Friend? Lover? Paramour? Apartment mate? Existing words are either imprecise or disparaging. It is as if the person in such a position has no acknowledged identity or status.

4. *Depersonalization of modern life.* With the rise in big corporations, big government, big labor, big cities, big schools, etc., friendships and other human relationships are becoming more temporary and superficial. Alvin Toffler calls these "throw-away friendships." Your boss is probably not someone you grew up with; he was sent from a company headquarters in another city and will soon be replaced by someone else. Classes are huge, teachers remote. Ethnic neighborhoods where people once felt a common bond are declining. Most of the people in an urban or suburban area are strangers or mere nodding acquaintances. People become lonely and long for someone to be close to, with whom to share their thoughts, fears, hopes, wishes, joys, and sadness. When marriage doesn't provide this, and friends and relatives are remote, many people turn to affairs.

5. *Intermingling of cultures.* A middle-aged Jewish couple came to me in deepest distress. "Our only son is living with a Gentile girl," said the father, "and we think they are in love. We don't so much mind their living together, but we're terribly afraid they may get married. That would be a tragedy for us. Look: Our people have suffered through countless centuries to keep our beliefs and customs intact, and I personally lost my parents and a sister in the Nazi holocaust. Are we now to lose our only son in marriage to a pretty Gentile girl after carefully raising him in our faith?" He broke down and cried. The intermingling of cultures through travel and urban life is accomplishing what no amount of persecution ever did: the cross-fertilization and dilution of racial, religious, and ethnic groups. Catholics marry Protestants, blacks marry whites, persons brought up with a strong religious faith marry agnostics. Belief systems carefully cultivated and defended in the past when people of similar convictions lived in one community and married only each other are now crumbling under the impact of conflicting beliefs. There are few accepted values and convictions on which an entire community is in agreement. This is a recipe for marital disharmony, for everyone who marries brings into the relationship the values he or she grew up with, and may discover eventually that the marital partner holds different—perhaps incompatible—values. Such conflicts can lead to extramarital affairs. The anonymity of urban life, of course, makes secret arrangements easy.

6. *Rise in expectations of the quality of life.* Earlier in our nation's history, people worked hard for long hours at low pay because they had to. Self-denial was a virtue. People were much too occupied with surviving and building their future to worry much about the quality of life. They had neither inclination nor leisure to wonder whether they were happy or to brood on whether they were getting enough out of life. But now that we have achieved mass production and technological marvels, our hours of work are shortened, our vacations are lengthened, we have social legislation to protect us from want, our expectations about life are much higher, and we have time for self-development, education, travel, and cultivation of personal relationships. Also for entertainment, sports, self-indulgence, and worrying about ourselves. Searching for something new and better has become a way of life in America. It is expressed in the struggle for upward economic mobility—for better jobs, higher incomes, better homes, better environments. And sometimes the search is for new and "better" sex partners and companions.

7. *Social movements of the sixties and seventies.* We have just had two decades of unprecedented social ferment marked by the emergence of the counterculture, the antiwar movement, the civil rights and black power movements, the women's movement, the agitation for gay rights, the senior citizens' movement, and more recently the American Indian movement. All are saying, "Look, we're here. Recognize us. Give us the same rights and opportunities everyone else has." This trend is worldwide. And in some respects the rise of extramarital affairs grows out of a similar urge to

challenge old restrictions and break out of the status quo. In many cases the participant in an affair is saying by his or her actions, "Look, I'm here. I'm a person. Pay attention to me."

8. *The human-potential movement.* Parallel with the social movements (and, like them, arising from the desire for self-realization and equal opportunity) is the human-potential movement and its many offshoots: e.g., sensitivity training, encounter groups, consciousness raising, marathon encounters, the experiential activities at Esalen, California, the development of therapies focused on personal and interpersonal growth, and a variety of related movements, some of them fads and some adopting the trappings of religion. Through these movements, many people have come to be more aware of themselves as feeling, thinking, self-actualizing individuals. They've grown accustomed to experimenting with new life-styles, and their experiments sometimes include extramarital affairs.

9. *Conflict between career and family demands.* Forty-two percent of the labor force in the United States is now made up of women. Nearly half of these working women are married.[25] Many are strongly committed to careers. Business or professional demands often separate husbands and wives, and sometimes parents and children, for extended periods. Or the partners get so absorbed in their work that they neglect each other and the children. Sometimes spouses work different hours (such as one at night and one in the daytime), or in different cities where they can come together only on weekends. All these situations have the potential of leading to affairs.

10. *The tensions of the middle years.* A powerful impulse to engage in affairs is felt by some individuals in midlife. A man at this stage may begin to doubt his masculinity and a woman her continued attractiveness. They may have more money and freedom than in earlier years. Their children need less day-to-day care. The wife, in many cases, has gone back to work. The partners are beginning to reassess their relationship. They are probably no longer struggling quite so hard to build a life jointly or to make ends meet. That's a challenge that in the earlier years may have helped hold them together. Husband and wife are beginning to think in terms of individual fulfillment. ("What am I doing with my life?") They may begin to see their lives slipping by and suddenly realize that they are bored with each other. Sexual relations in the marriage may have become perfunctory; the husband may have developed signs of impotence and the wife of frigidity. This worries them both. The husband may be tempted to test his masculinity with another woman and the wife her capacity to attract another man.

Gail Sheehy in her book *Passages*[26] fixes age thirty-five for women, as the "beginning of the dangerous age of infidelity." This agrees with Kinsey's findings and coincides fairly closely with women's sexual peak (about thirty-eight). Many women, Sheehy says, and men, too, in mid-life are not prepared to give up the comforts of their marriage and don't want to risk being left alone. But they are becoming aware of bodily decline and may be tempted to seek a narcissistic experience to assuage their panic at the approach of older age. These women may have tired husbands, high sexual ardor, time on their hands, and lack of direction.

11. *Lengthening life span of women.* Many commentators have noted the greatly extended life span of women and the new strains this puts on long-term marriage. James Ramey, in *Intimate Friendships*,[27] writes:

> *The female lifespan in 1900 was 48 years, and 18 of those years—from age 22–40—were devoted to maternity. In 1970 the female lifespan was 74 years, and 10 years—from ages 20–30—were devoted to maternity (see Sullerot, 1971). The average American woman today completes the family size she desires by age 26 (Udry, 1974). . . . the vast increase in nonmaternity years for women will have a marked effect on their world-view and on their life-styles.*

Gail Sheehy points out[28] that the average American married woman who has been out of the labor market to raise children reenters the working world at about age thirty-five and can expect to be part of the work force for the next twenty-four years or more. This is an enormous change from a generation or two ago. What does it mean for the future of marriage? Clearly it adds to the pressures for divorce and for engaging in extramarital affairs.

HOW PREVALENT ARE EXTRAMARITAL AFFAIRS?

Extramarital affairs are spreading to an extent that is historically unprecedented. They occur in poor marriages and relatively good ones; among people you might suspect of unconventional behavior, but also among "pillar-of-the-community" types. Affairs happen at the bottom of society and at the top; among the poor and disadvantaged and among the educated, the rich, and the powerful. Presidents, senators, social workers, corporation executives, stewardesses, physicians, clergymen, secretaries, housewives, truck drivers, garbage collectors, farmers—extramarital affairs have occurred in every corner of society, every occupation, every locality.

Yet strangely enough, fewer careful studies have been made on this topic than on any other important social trend of our time. The only surveys of any real statistical depth (and even these were criticized for sampling deficiencies) were made in the 1940s and early 1950s by the late Dr. Alfred Kinsey and his associates, who analyzed data furnished by more than five thousand men and nearly six thousand women.[29] He concluded that by age forty, twenty-six percent of married women and fifty percent of married men in his samples had, at some time during their marriages, experienced extramarital sexual intercourse. He believed these figures were probably underestimates because respondents are likely to cover up this experience more than any other.[30]

Kinsey's figures were not only criticized but also widely mis-interpreted. On their face, they left the impression that a shocking amount of promiscuity was taking place. This is an incorrect reading of the data. A person who had only one extramarital sexual contact in his or her entire married life was counted as having had extramarital experience. Obviously, not all the people who reported having engaged in extramarital sex had been habitually involved in the practice or were necessarily engaging in it at the time the survey was made.

What Kinsey's figures do show is that a great many married people do not succeed in maintaining absolute faithfulness for a lifetime. They may have been faithful most of the time and perhaps meant to be faithful for life, but as years go by unanticipated events occur. What the figures show, really, is the astonishing variety of human behavior and experience.

Kinsey's figures by age groups reveal highly significant differences between men and women. For men, extramarital sexual activity reached its peak in their late teens. (Keep in mind that this survey was done during the Korean War when many newly married young men were being drafted into military service. Trailing close behind, the next highest incidence of extramarital affairs occurred in the early thirties. The latter probably would have been the higher had the survey been conducted in peacetime.) For women it peaked in the thirty-six to forty age group. Of the women who reported extramarital experience, forty-one percent had confined their relations to a single partner, and another forty percent to two to five persons—mostly other married men. The remaining nineteen percent had relations with more than five partners. Women who engaged in premarital sexual relations had a somewhat greater propensity to extramarital intercourse than those who had not.

Kinsey's findings are now some thirty years old. The percentages today would certainly be higher. In personal correspondence to me in 1980, Dr. Paul Gebhard, successor to Dr. Kinsey at the Institute for Sex Research at Indiana University, "guesstimated" them to be about sixty percent for males and thirty-five to forty percent for females—the same figures he suggested twelve years earlier to Morton Hunt.[31] Dr. Wardell Pomeroy, another Kinsey successor and personal friend, recently shared with me both his current estimate—sixty to sixty-five percent for males and forty to forty-five percent for females—and his end of decade (1990) estimate—an additional five percent for each of the sexes.

No in-depth survey as comprehensive as the Kinsey study has been made since his work, but there have been a number of limited studies that are provocative and interesting. For example, in a recent nationwide survey of 4,000 men by Anthony Pietropinto and Jacqueline Simenauer[32] forty-three percent of married men admitted extramarital sexual activity, and four percent engaged with their spouses' consent and knowledge. Nearly two thirds (sixty-two percent) said they would have an affair under certain circumstances (i.e., opportunity).

Several surveys have been made of the extramarital affairs of women. *Redbook* magazine's poll of its readers in 1975[33] reported that nearly *half* the women who work had experienced extramarital sex and had met their partners on the job or in related situations. Robert Bell, in his 1974 Australian study, found that forty-three percent of Australian women between ages twenty-six and fifty had had extramarital sex experience.[34] The quasi-replication of the Kinsey study by Hunt[35], referred to earlier, revealed that the most significant increase in the frequency of extramarital sex since Kinsey has occurred among the younger women, ages 18–24. Larry and Joan Constantine express the opinion that "the age 20–25 married group today has already experienced more transmarital sexual intimacy than all other age groups have experienced in their entire lives."[36]

A whopping 106,000 women responded to a survey on sexual attitudes and behavior taken by *Cosmopolitan* in 1980. Among those which the magazine designates as "Cosmo Girls" (employed women between the ages of 18 and 34, who live in cities with populations of more than one million) fifty percent indicated that they have had at least one extramarital experience. For those over age 35, however, the proportion jumped to 69.2 percent. (The geographical distribution and employment status of this group was not included in the survey report.)[37]

Nobody knows if the nationwide survey of men or of *Redbook* and *Cosmopolitan* readers or of Bell's and Hunt's respondents are typical of the populations from which they were drawn. There is obvious need for a new, more comprehensive, and more reliable study.

THE OUTLOOK

Considering the vast increase in the opportunities for affairs in the contemporary world, it is surprising that the growth of affairs has not been even greater than these studies indicate. Its moderate growth suggests more restraint on the part of more people than would appear at first glance from the raw data. Unquestionably, many individuals—regardless of both opportunity and desire—are reluctant to let go of the "one only" convictions with which they were raised. These convictions are important to their own sense of right living and stability. But what appears to be happening among the youngest age group may be a warning that in the next generation the population may exercise less restraint. Traditional marriage may be closer to breaking down than even these statistics show.

We are in a dilemma. While society offers increasing opportunities to engage in extramarital affairs, people are also encountering great difficulty in creating and maintaining the healthy human relationships necessary for marriage to be satisfying, stable, and permanent. The problem, it seems to me, lies in the conflict between what we were brought up to expect of marriage and our newly awakened desire for freedom and personal fulfillment. The two are not always compatible. If we insist that marriage is for life, that our spouse belongs to us exclusively, and that it's impossible to love more than one person at a time, we are more and more going to find these embedded beliefs colliding with the urge toward openness, broadened experience, and freedom. Historic and religious teachings and values regarding marriage need to be respected, understood, and responded to with perspective as we, at the same time, continue our learning about human relationships. Ultimately, I'm convinced, if we are to preserve marriage, we will need to rethink some of the values we have taken for granted in the past . . . and expand our options.

2. *Myths About Affairs*

I've had two extramarital affairs. They've helped me grow up. . . . I've come to understand my spouse much better. I realize that a lot of the complaints I had about him were my fault, too. Too much of the past had crept into our relationship—unknown to us both. Through my affairs I became far more aware (and helped him become more aware) of what was missing in our marital relationship, whereas before the affairs I knew something was amiss but couldn't zero in. Yes, we're trying harder now and things are better between us—still lots of room for improvement, but I have no intention of terminating my marriage. What's "out there" isn't so great, either!

Andrea

HOW MYTHS GROW

No topic is more beclouded by myths than the extramarital affair. Activities that are private and hidden are particularly susceptible to myths because they are so poorly understood and seemingly irrational. Some myths help produce affairs. Other myths are partly responsible for the suffering and damage resulting from affairs.

The growth of a mythology around extramarital affairs has not been accidental. Myths have always been powerful agents for encouraging approved and discouraging unapproved behavior. They can be much more powerful than flat prohibitions—for prohibitions can be seen, thought about, argued over, and sometimes defined. But myths work themselves subtly into the psyche, stirring up fear and shame by use of words like *whore, adultery, immorality,* and *lust,* and thus exert powerful restraints at both conscious and unconscious levels. This makes them exceedingly effective in social control. They become an integral part of a person's system of dos and don'ts.

What I call myths are of course merely beliefs, not well founded in fact, that have become ingrained and stereotyped. Most contain some truth; if they did not, they would probably not have survived or had such influence. Many are true for certain people, in certain circumstances, part of the time. What makes them myths is that we assume them to be *always* true for *all* people in *all* circumstances, and they are not.

As long as there is general social agreement on dos and don'ts, the prevailing myths are rarely questioned. It is only when moral beliefs are in doubt or under attack that we are impelled to examine our myths. That is the situation today, and the steadily widening gap between precepts and practice makes such an examination urgent business. Otherwise, the strains on marriage and the family produced by conflicting values and unexamined beliefs could have disastrous social consequences. I believe this will become clearer as we contrast the myths with present knowledge.

Sorting out myths about extramarital affairs exposes an astonishing network of interlocking assumptions about such matters as the function of sex in human relationships, the meanings of marriage, commitment, fidelity, and love. A few such assumptions were examined in Chapter 1. We'll discover others.

COMMON MYTHS

The myths I encounter most frequently are these:

Myth 1. Extramarital affairs are nothing new—there always have been affairs. True, but misleading. The present widespread participation in extramarital activity detailed in the previous chapter does not resemble anything in the past. We have a new world here. It's scary, and we don't know what to do with it.

Myth 2. An affair offers a carefree relationship with no strings attached. This is pure fantasy. Whatever affairs may be, few turn out to be only lighthearted amusement. By their very nature they can scarcely remain carefree, especially if long continued. An affair can become as loaded with problems and anxieties as a marriage. The notion that you can enjoy sexual relations with somebody for a time and then simply break it off, like snapping a twig, leaves out the emotional element. What if either or both partners develop strong emotional ties and become close companions? Or fall in love? Emotional attachments can be as difficult to break as legal ones. And conflicts, rivalries, jealousy, and suspicion can undermine affairs as they can marriages.

When strong emotional attachments are formed in an affair, the knowledge that the relationship is impermanent can throw a shadow over it almost from the start. Carefree? Hardly! There is a heightened sense that life is fleeting. Enjoy it now—there may not be a tomorrow! Wrote a woman who was engaged in an extramarital affair:

NOW IS FOREVER

What is Forever,
What meaning does it have?
Beyond tomorrow . . .
I have no plans for us.
Nothing is forever.

Enjoy today.
Love me hard; love me now.
Savor every moment.
Love me more day by day—
Just as I love you.
But do not plan on tomorrow.
Nothing is forever.

Let us be the most we can.
As I give you my all, give me yours.
Do not look forward, do not look back.
Here and now is what we have.
It is shining seconds, breathless passion,
Awe at the "us" we have become.
We have it now, and now is forever.

Myth 3. Extramarital affairs arise solely from sexual lust. This notion arises from a belief that men and women are subject to insatiable sexual lusts that must, at all costs, be curbed. Judaic, Christian, and Moslem teachings all assume this. While sex is certainly a factor, the physical desires behind extramarital affairs are often subordinate to emotional wants or needs such as a longing for affection, love, attention, excitement, comfort, solace, companionship, and other qualities of a genuine human relationship. Sex, in many cases, is only a shortcut to satisfying these deeper desires.

Myth 4. An affair is always the product of a poor or unsatisfying marriage. It often is, but not always. Although unsatisfying marriages do frequently breed affairs, it is possible for affairs to occur in good marriages, too. An affair may happen on impulse for reasons of adventure or excitement, or to satisfy curiosity about what an affair is like. Or it may happen when the partners are separated for extended periods. An attractive third person may, under certain circumstances, catch the fancy even of a happily married man or woman. If an unusual opportunity presents itself, such as the pair finding themselves together while away from home and the mood is right, an affair can happen.

It is not often recognized that good marriages have their own patterns of vulnerability. One reason is that people in good marriages are apt to have very high expectations, which may or may not be fully satisfied in the marital relationship. Success is a notorious creator of discontent. How many people, after achieving success, give a sigh of relief and say, "Now I have enough for my needs—I don't want any more?" I remember a three-year-old child on Christmas morning sitting down happily to play with his first Christmas present. But along came another, and he laid aside the first to play with the second. Still more gifts were unwrapped, and soon he was crying confusedly, "Is there another? Is there another?" And when the stream of presents came to an end, he asked in a disappointed voice. "Is that all?" Like the child, a person in a happy marriage may not be ready to say, "I'm happy enough now. This is all the happiness I need." He or she, if inclined to discontent, may look for even higher levels of satisfaction, possibly through experiments with new partners. Richard Farson[1] wrote a few years ago that "good marriages probably fail more often than bad ones." They fail, he says (referring to divorce), "precisely *because* they are good." The trouble is that expectations may get too high to be reasonably met. John F. Cuber, in a study of the adulterous behavior of 437 distinguished white Americans who were not psychiatric patients,[2] found that successful extramarital affairs can accompany successful marital relationships.

None of this, however, means that good marriages have *more* extramarital affairs than bad ones. They probably have fewer. The point is that a good marriage cannot be assumed to be a guarantee against an affair.

Myth 5. Having an extramarital affair shows character weakness. This is widely asserted or tacitly assumed, even by some professionals in my field. It is sometimes true; there are people who cannot resist temporary attraction or sexual desire. But in other cases, having an affair might be regarded as a sign of character *strength.* Sometimes it takes a long period of personal growth for an individual who feels victimized by a sterile or loveless marriage to summon the courage and imagination to claim a better life for himself or herself. Engaging in an affair might, for such a person, actually be a triumph of overcoming inner obstacles, prohibitions, and fears. It could be a sign, too, that low self-esteem is being overcome; the person may for the first time have reached the point of being willing to go out and chance a new kind of relationship with a new person. Said one very shy man: "All my life I've been afraid of rejection, and this has blocked me from making new women friends. I was always afraid they wouldn't like me or accept me. It's wonderful to be freed from this terror and to discover that women do like me. I may never have an affair, but if I don't, at least it will not be fear of rejection that holds me back."

Myth 6. Having an extramarital affair signifies emotional instability or an unhealthy psychological state. Not necessarily. An affair is a *human relationship,* often a very qualitative one—in some cases more qualitative and growth enhancing than the interaction in the marriage. Engaging in a meaningful human relationship is one of the signs of emotional health; it is usually disturbed people who are unable to develop such relationships. Sexual desire is a normal reaction of human beings and is not unhealthy in itself. Nor is it unhealthy to desire sexual variety or to experience the reawakening of romantic urges, or to long for excitement and adventure. On the other hand, it is true that many affairs are unhealthy. There are individuals who engage in compulsive, manipulative or ego-bolstering affairs lacking meaningful emotional involvement. There are affairs pursued in retaliation against a spouse or to gain a power advantage of some kind. There are escapist affairs in which people use an affair to run away from responsibilities or problems. And sometimes affairs are psychological replays of childhood relationships with parents, siblings, or others in ways that are not healthy. Each situation has to be looked at individually.

Myth 7. The "other woman" is bad and immoral. (The "other man," too, although he's not quite so criticized.) Writers of advice columns in newspapers often accurately reflect the prevailing moral views. They do not, in fact, dare stray far from them. One of these writers recently castigated women who "play around" with married men, using terms like dishonest, stupid, cheap, shortsighted, and cruel. This diatribe was merely a restatement of myths. The "other woman" is called dishonest; yet it is the roaming husband, not the "other woman" (unless she's married), who is violating marriage vows. The unspoken assumptions are that the husband is only doing what (for a man) comes naturally, that he is susceptible to a woman's wiles, and that *she* is to blame for not putting a stop to his advances. This is the old *double standard* with an extra twist. The myth is that this standard is immutable, embedded in human nature. Another myth is illustrated by the writer's use of the words stupid and shortsighted. There is an unspoken assumption here that the "other woman" is seeking a permanent relationship—in other words, that she's trying to displace the wife—and she's stupid because she is unlikely to succeed. But, in fact, capturing a husband may not be her objective at all. She may simply like the man and enjoy being with him whenever it is possible. She may be seeking attention and affection, or perhaps some fun and excitement. Or maybe she likes sex. Many "other women" (and "other men," too), far from being cheap, are loving, understanding, sympathetic, helpful human beings capable of enriching another person's life. The affair may not necessarily be a cruel act directed against the partner's spouse. This assumption, too, is a myth. Not every affair damages a marriage. What if the marriage is helped because the affair contributes to the well-being and happiness of one or both marital partners?

Myth 8. Men want sex more than women do (that's why they have more affairs). Not necessarily true. Some men do. Some women want it more. One of the more interesting revelations of modern sex research recently highlighted by *The Hite Report*[3] is the number of women whose husbands do not satisfy them sexually. The research by Masters and Johnson[4] has shown that a woman's sexual capacity is biologically much greater than a man's. She can have more sex and more orgasms than a man, she can continue intercourse longer without being exhausted. As women further emerge from the cultural restraints that have inhibited them in the past, it will become increasingly evident that this myth is contrary to fact.

Myth 9. Practically all husbands have extramarital sex. Not true. Some men use this myth to justify their own affairs ("All husbands do it. Why not me?"). But if Gebhard's estimate that sixty percent of married men have engaged in affairs by age forty is reasonably accurate, obviously forty percent have not done so—which is a far cry from "all."

Myth 10. An affair by a wife is much more reprehensible than an affair by a husband. The old double standard, again. Husbands have traditionally kept for themselves the right to have extramarital sex contacts (mistresses, concubines, etc.) while denying a similar right to their wives. Marriage has never in all history been regarded as a contract between *equals*, nor is it commonly viewed as such even today. But the concept of a wife subordinate to the husband is losing ground. Women are increasingly inclined to reject it, and men will find it more and more difficult to sustain it in their own minds. The trend is clearly toward equal moral responsibility of both marital partners.

   Myth 11. An affair is a repudiation and rejection of the spouse. Some affairs are. Some are not. *Repudiation* and *rejection* probably do not accurately describe the typical attitude of a person in an affair toward his or her spouse. An affair might reflect some decline in interest in the spouse, perhaps some degree of fading of the love that had burned more brightly earlier in the marriage. But this does not necessarily mean repudiation and rejection. By assuming the latter, the spouse may kill chances for repairing the marriage.

   My impression from working with people in affairs is that most affairs *do* reflect some degree of dissatisfaction with the marriage, although people in the early stages of an affair are sometimes reluctant to admit it. A lot of covert signals are apt to take place between spouses. In some marriages there seems to be an unspoken agreement that affairs will be tolerated as long as they are discreet and kept under cover. For this reason, as Ramey[5] points out, it may be hard to draw a clear line between consensual adultery (agreed on by both spouses) and nonconsensual (usually secret) adultery. We may not be quite sure which it is.* In a study by John Cuber and Peggy Harroff,[6] it was found that a majority of the upper-middle-class sample "ignored the monogamous prescriptions about sex. While holding the marriage bond to be inviolable, they condoned extramarital sexual relationships. Some did so quite openly, but most practiced more or less effective concealment and observed various conventional pretenses." Clearly, the spouse in many cases knew what was going on but chose not to make an issue of it, and the marriage continued as before. This does not suggest that either spouse saw the affair in terms of repudiation and rejection. But neither does it indicate a strong vital relationship between the marital partners.

   Myth 12. The "betrayed" spouse suffers most from an affair. Not necessarily. I've known cases where the spouse is relieved. Trying to satisfy all the needs and demands of the partner is, for some, too great a burden. But even if the spouse knows about or suspects an affair, he or she may not be the only— or even the chief—sufferer. I'm not minimizing the distress a spouse may feel when a partner's affair is discovered; it can be agonizing. But there are a number of ways in which the person in the affair may be suffering, too. In the first place, the affair may have come about because of suffering arising from a poor marital relationship. Many affairs are the result of silent (or not so silent) anguish in reaction to a hostile, preoccupied, indifferent, or unloving spouse. Then, also, there may be intense suffering by the person in the affair from

---

Ramey's third type of extramarital relationship common to many so-called monogamous marriages is swinging, or co-marital sex. This may involve two or more pair-bonded couples who mutually decide to switch sexual partners or engage in group sex. Swinging may also involve couples and singles in either triadic or larger group sexual encounters.

feelings of guilt and shame. And the relationship between the extramarital partners themselves can be painful. There are few experiences causing more heartache than unrequited love (which can easily happen in an affair) or that can produce more anxiety than wondering from day to day whether one is still loved. When one extramarital partner is more deeply in love than the other, the more ardent one may begin making demands (such as urging divorce) that may scare off the other person, abruptly ending the affair. Or a person may discover that his or her extramarital partner is having an affair simultaneously with someone else. Situations like these have been known to lead to depression, drink, or suicide.

Myth 13. *Extramarital affairs are destructive for everyone involved and invariably cause suffering.* Sometimes yes. Sometimes no. Unless an affair is undertaken as an act of hostility toward the spouse, it is not usually a destructive act in itself. An affair may, however, be handled cruelly, as when the participant, feeling guilty, throws the blame on the spouse ("You are such a lousy sex partner that I . . ." etc.) The degree of destructiveness and suffering resulting from an affair depends very much on the personal qualities of the individuals affected: on how considerate the spouses are of each other, how well they communicate, how tolerant they are of their differences, how much self-esteem and sense of security each has, their capacity for forgiveness, and so on. If the marital partners can interact constructively, suffering is minimized.

There are many affairs, like Andrea's (see quotation at the head of this chapter), that leave a marriage stronger than before. In Andrea's case the improvement came about through her increased self-esteem and knowledge of herself. Her affairs were valuable learning experiences. They helped her achieve insights as to what was wrong between her and her husband. She put her new insights to use in developing a better marital relationship.

Myth 14. *An extramarital affair is an intolerable disruption of the marital relationship and the spouses can never trust each other again.* This is a deeply embedded belief that goes with possessiveness ("*my* wife," "*my* husband"). The marital relationship is assumed to be sexually and emotionally exclusive and inviolable. There can be no allowance for a love interest or even a temporary sexual attraction outside the marriage. Either is considered a betrayal. This reaction comes in part from insecurity and fear, and from the belief referred to earlier that you cannot love more than one person at a time and that a new love necessarily drives out the old. Consider Andrea again. Recently she wrote: "My marriage is pretty stable now. I'm contented for the most part. I love my husband and we're still trying to make our marriage better. I wouldn't want to leave him, but obviously I got something out of my affairs that was missing in our marriage." Andrea kept her affairs secret. Would her husband have felt betrayed if he knew? Very likely he would. He might have walked out of the marriage—he is a product of traditional teachings, including the double standard. Yet not all spouses would react this way. Attitudes of marital partners toward affairs range all the way from physical violence or murder to complete forgiveness for a spouse's affair. Some people regard an extramarital relationship as so different from a marital one that it hasn't much to do with the marriage. As they see it, the two kinds of relationships can go on side by side, just as wives and mistresses have coexisted in European upper-class life for centuries.

Kinsey[7] discovered a fair number of cases in his sample where the husbands had encouraged their wives to have affairs. Some forty percent of the wives who reported having had extramarital coitus believed that their husbands knew it, and another nine percent believed that their husbands suspected it. Yet a substantial proportion (forty-two percent) of the women who believed their husbands knew it or suspected it felt that their marriages had not been seriously damaged because of it. These findings put in question the common view that extramarital relationships inevitably do damage to a marriage.

Myth 15. Extramarital affairs threaten the stability of marriage as an institution and undermine the family and society. There's no doubt about the instability of marriage and the family, as divorce rates show. But to attribute it to extramarital affairs is questionable. The assumption is that affairs destroy marriages. Sometimes, of course, they do. Sometimes they do not. And sometimes, as we've indicated, they help preserve or even revitalize marriages that were on the verge of disintegrating. Moreover, affairs are more usually symptoms or outcomes of marital instability than its cause. By the time an affair occurs, the marriage may already be in shaky condition for a variety of reasons: e.g., neglect, lack of love or affection, poor communication, inability to negotiate, closed personality styles, mismatched temperaments, conflicting values, divergent careers, etc. But a more basic factor in the weakness of modern marriage is the isolation of the nuclear family, which we referred to earlier, and which has been rather thoroughly studied. The modern nuclear self-contained household is a very recent development, confined mostly to the United States, and inherently unstable. Ray Birdwhistell[8], noted anthropologist, calls it the "closed dyad" and regards it as a diseased form that cannot possibly survive as presently constituted. Isolation is an untenable condition for any organism. Marriage and the family have to get back into the world somehow, multiplying rather than restricting their contacts with the outside. Looked at in this way, extramarital affairs might be seen as the struggle of marriage to escape from its disconnected, closed-in state. A crude, painful way of breaking the isolation, no doubt, but possibly necessary for its own survival.

MORAL JUDGMENTS THAT UNDERLIE THE MYTHS

Many of the myths are based essentially on moral judgments. But it is not always clear whether the moral judgment produced the myth or the myth produced the moral judgment. The seventh commandment, for many people, settles the matter: extramarital affairs are intrinsically wrong and never can be justified under any circumstances. Yet this pronouncement leaves many unanswered questions. Adultery is conventionally defined in terms of coitus. What is *coitus*? I've known people who strictly avoid intercourse in order not to be guilty of adultery, but go to the very edge of it with an extramarital partner, including heavy petting, mutual masturbation, and oral sex. Is this adultery as the seventh commandment defines it? Jesus, in the Sermon on the Mount, gives a very clear answer (Matthew 5:27–28):

> *Ye have heard that it was said by them of old time, thou shalt not commit adultery. But I say unto you, that whosoever looketh on a woman to lust after her hath committed adultery with her already in his heart.*

What mattered to Jesus was not so much what people's bodies were doing as what their hearts and minds were doing.

But this leaves unanswered questions, too. Must a loveless marriage take precedence over a truly loving extramarital relationship? Must a vow made in one state of a person's development block, for the rest of his or her life, any opportunity for personal happiness or growth? Jesus condemned divorce, too, but many people do not feel bound by a teaching that envisaged an entirely different social order and concept of marriage than prevails today.

Are morals deteriorating? It is true that some thoughts and actions believed immoral in one age are perceived as moral in a subsequent one, and vice versa. Until a few generations ago, sexual intercourse even *within* marriage was believed to have only one proper function—procreation. If not performed to produce a baby, it was a grave sin. This was the teaching of both Saint Augustine and Saint Thomas Aquinas,[9] who shaped many church doctrines, and its echoes still reverberate in the condemnation of contraception by the Roman Catholic Church. The sex act, unless cleansed by the word of God through the sacrament of marriage, was considered evil. Some religious writers called it "damnable."

These dictates didn't stop sexual activity, but they did take much of the pleasure out of it and tended to make it furtive and guilt-ridden. For centuries sexual intercourse was disallowed as a legitimate expression of love, and was totally unthinkable as an aspect of warm companionship.

Contemporary moral judgments appear to be moving toward evaluation of the quality of human relationships rather than what people do with their bodies. Contraception has been a powerful agent in bringing that about. What counts more today is whether the relationships—either within or outside of marriage—are characterized by affection, kindness, generosity, consideration, sensitivity to feelings, openness, nonpossessiveness, and honesty. If human relationships have these qualities, there is less concern about their sexual morality.

Nevertheless, extramarital sex, to a large extent, is still in the furtive, guilt-ridden stage. This is because two moral issues still remain unresolved: fidelity and honesty. Breaking a vow that has been made in good faith is undeniably a moral issue. So is the lying and deception that accompanies many affairs. Resolving these issues is a painful struggle in many people's minds.

The essential difficulty, as in many real-life situations, is that two or more moral principles are in collision. The issue of fidelity may conflict with the responsibility for one's own personal growth and fulfillment. The principle of honesty may conflict with the responsibility to be kind and considerate of another's feelings. How do we resolve such antitheses? The solution offered by most moralists is to set one imperative above the other—to put fidelity, for example, above personal growth and fulfillment, or to put honesty above kindness and consideration for another's feelings. This is an answer if one can live by it. But whether it serves the greater good is less clear. Is it good that fidelity to a partner for whom one no longer feels an emotional closeness should permanently block personal growth and fulfillment? Is it good that certain people should suffer agonies to serve the moral cause of total honesty? And where does responsibility for one's children fit in? The answers can only be worked out by each individual in the depths of his soul.

Our society's attitudes, inherited from the past, do not make this resolution easy. In their book *Affairs: The Anatomy of Extramarital Relationships,* based on the English experience, Lake and Hills[10] show how deeply our society is split on the question of sexual behavior. Officially, they say, we are a monogamous society; but the behavior of millions of us is polygamous. In theory our marriages are supposed to be "havens of peace." But in reality many marriages are economic arrangements "wherein we spin a web of deceit to hide our deepest joys and protect our moments of true peace."

Cuber, whose study was referred to earlier,[11] finds "adultery" a misleading "moralistic-legalistic-theological" term that lumps together many different kinds of behavior as if they were morally equivalent; hence, its use, he says, "can lead only to error." Thus, it equates the impulsive action of someone who had one too many at a party with the licentious behavior of a habitual lecher. It lumps this, in turn, with the affairs of unhappily married people who feel trapped in their marriage and look for warmth and comfort outside, and the affairs of those whose marital situation is so miserable that they depend on an outside relationship for emotional sustenance. Dumping all these different kinds of situations into one moral bag produces only confusion.

The attitude of society as a whole seems to be overwhelmingly against extramarital sex. A sampling survey of 1,044 registered voters throughout the United States in 1977, made by Yankelovich, Skelly, and White,[12] asked whether it is morally wrong for a married man to be unfaithful to his wife. Yes, said seventy-six percent of the respondents. Is it morally wrong for a married woman to be unfaithful to her husband? Yes, said seventy-nine percent. Yet what seems to be happening is that a great many people who are against infidelity in their public statements (and their replies to questionnaires) are privately practicing it. A common attitude is, "It's generally a bad thing and I don't believe in it, but my own case is special." What we find, however, when we look closely at what is happening in people's lives is that *every case is special*. In every case there is a unique combination of thoughts, values, needs, hopes, longings, past experiences and present problems, and stresses. No moral generalization or rigid rule of conduct can take these infinite variances into account. This will become more and more evident as we proceed.

3. *Hunger for Love*

WHY?

I cried last night
For you—for me
For us
For what we had
For what we never had.

Sad and lonely without you.
Constant on my mind
The need for you
The ache
The desire
The helpless feeling.

I cried last night
Filled with desire
Needing you to penetrate
My mind
My body
Wanting you to fill me too full
I ache
And I wonder—why?

For lack of an answer, I cried.

THE LOVE URGE

When we look at real people and learn of their struggles, hopes, joys, and sadness, the unique quality of every extramarital affair emerges. There is no "typical affair"—for there is no "typical" man or woman.

But there are universal longings. One is the hunger for love and for someone to love. Who has enough love? In many ways we inhabit a loveless world (of our own creation), and we suffer for it. Even those who have been hurt by love and draw back from it still hunger for it at a deeper level. What they are really trying to avoid is being possessed.

The affairs I'm about to describe—all of real people—are unsung and hidden from public view. Yet the emotions that precipitate them and swirl around them are as intense as anything the romances portray. The kingdom that totters may be someone's marriage or someone's life. But the extramarital affairs of today are not quite like those of old. Our affairs have the flavor of the motel, the automobile, the cocktail lounge, the contraceptive device or pill, and the "new freedom." Still, they remain the outpouring of urges as old as mankind and human to the core.

I begin with an affair that superficially comes closer than most to matching the stereotypes people have about affairs. The characters in the drama seem to leap right out of soap opera: the straying wife who wants to be loved, the outraged husband, the unscrupulous seducer, and the scandalized parents. Naturally, the affair disrupts the marriage and everybody is upset, as the myths say will happen. But as we look more closely, the focus changes. We wonder: Is it the *affair* that upsets everybody and causes all the anguish? Or is it the way people's minds are set and how they react to it?

"She's become a tramp!"
Charlotte and Bill—and the rock singer

Charlotte was sent to me by her husband and her parents, shocked by discovery of her affair. She's in her twenties, pretty, soft-spoken, appearing delicate and fragile. She said, "I know I've done wrong and I feel miserable about it. But how could I have known marriage would be such a bore? Bill and I don't *do* anything together any more—we hardly ever go out—we just look at TV night after night and fall asleep in front of the set. I like to go places and *do* things. I recently started going to dances and rock concerts with a friend of Bill's, and at one of these concerts I met the rock singer I had the affair with. But when I go out with someone else, Bill grinds his teeth. In our engagement days Bill was fun to be with. But now he's gotten so stodgy that it takes a crowbar to pry him loose. How could a man change so much in less than three years?" Then, with a rising tone of sarcasm, she added: "Wouldn't you think it would occur to him—and to my mother, too—to wonder *why* I've been unfaithful? But no, they don't ask. Mom just calls me a slut! Bill is giving me the silent treatment, and I'd rather he'd scream at me. I'm in a mood to walk out on him. Yet I don't really want to. And it would kill my mother." She burst into tears.

As I talked with Charlotte's parents and later with Bill, it became evident that each of these three people perceived Charlotte's involvement narrowly, in terms of a very restricted value system. To Charlotte's mother, the supreme virtues for a girl are obedience and respectability, and she summed up both in one sentence: "Charlotte has repeatedly disobeyed me since she was a child, particularly in her behavior with boys, and now she has disgraced us all." To the father, chastity and fidelity are most important for a girl: "I'm shocked beyond belief that Charlotte has lowered herself to adultery in the face of everything we've tried to teach her." Bill reacted to Charlotte's behavior as a wronged husband. Outraged by her infidelity, he saw it as a personal slap at him and as proof of innate character weakness in his wife: "I thought I had married a girl who would make a fine wife and mother, and now it turns out she's a tramp." Charlotte felt herself wretchedly abandoned and unloved—ashamed, but also furious at being called a tramp. "Tramp is one thing I'm not!" she stormed.

Said Charlotte, "For twenty-three years I've been criticized from my hair to my toenails—nothing about me seems to have pleased my parents or my teachers—or my husband."

"Nonsense!" the mother interrupted. "How dare you say that? You were our favorite child. We gave up everything for you."

I searched for evidences of love or sympathy in the voice tones, facial expressions, and gestures of the three accusers. I could find none. Charlotte withdrew gradually into a despairing silence.

Later, during individual therapy, Charlotte said, "I had no intention of committing adultery. I knew perfectly well adultery is a terrible sin. I don't have to be preached to about it. What happened was that I met this famous singer at a rock concert. He gave me a look that just melted me. I know how adolescent this sounds, but after that concert all I could think of was being in his arms. It's as if I'd become a teenager again. A lot of teenage feelings came back that I thought I had outgrown.

"There was his tanned, hairy chest peeking out of an open-front shirt—a come-on if there ever was one. But I fell for it. I wanted to stroke it. Next time we met, he whispered in my ear, 'You're so lovely! I've never seen anyone lovelier.' These words brought back more teenage feelings. In one part of my mind I knew he was handing me a line. But in another I wanted to believe he meant it. I had had a similar feeling when I was fourteen years old and joined the Jesus movement in my church. We girls swooned at the thought that Jesus loved us. Now I was swooning at the thought that a famous rock singer loved me. Only I was swooning alone—there was nobody to swoon with me.

"When the guy invited me to his apartment, I had all kinds of mixed-up feelings. I admit I shouldn't have gone. Once there, though, it was like a dream. He undressed me and kept the most divine music playing all the while. He sang to me—he, a big star, sang to *me*! I felt completely loved for the first time in my life. When I left his studio in the afternoon the sensations of electric shock were still going through me like needle pricks. But I was ashamed. I thought everyone I passed in the street was staring at me. I returned to that dullard, my husband, who had *never* said to me 'You're lovely.'

"Of course, I couldn't stay away from my new lover. He taught me things about lovemaking that I wouldn't dare let Bill suspect I know— things I suppose a prostitute does. While I was doing it I knew I was degrading myself, yet I didn't want to stop because it was so terribly exciting. But one day a neighborhood loudmouth spotted me emerging from his studio, and I guess one look at my flushed face told her all she needed to know. She spread the word around. My mother heard and told my husband—and the whole thing exploded."

Charlotte fell into adultery partly because of her innocence. She was friendly, trusting, romantic, and far too willing to believe that loving words must come from a loving heart. Love and sex were mixed up in her mind like a stew. She didn't disentangle them until one day a few weeks later when she made an unannounced visit to her lover's studio. He answered the door casually pulling on a bathrobe while behind him stood another woman trying to cover herself up. "My God!" said the woman. "Who's that?" "Just a kid I know," replied the singer, and then to Charlotte: "I can't see you now, Sis. Come another time." And bang went the door.

An extramarital affair like Charlotte's confronts everyone involved with a choice between growth and disintegration. The outcome depends on who learns what.

What has Charlotte learned? Certainly not to be so naive. She's had a personal demonstration of how sex can masquerade as love. She may have learned not to be so carried away by glamour, public acclaim, or honeyed words. But will she sour on love itself? Will she smother the yearnings that rise so naturally in a young heart? Will she become disillusioned by the harshness with which her parents, her husband, and finally her lover have treated her? Will she become emotionally numb, dull and cloddish along with her husband, suppressing what is most precious in her: her capacity to feel and to express and share her feelings? I think, in Charlotte's case, this will not happen. But with some people it does.

Has Charlotte learned anything about her marriage? She's been too upset recently to reflect on it, but she has an opportunity to do some basic thinking. She's discovered for herself one of the disadvantages of casual sex: Somebody else comes along, and you're out. Just now she can't imagine coming home and finding Bill in bed with another woman. But that is possible if Bill gets as bored with the marriage as she is. He might even do it in retaliation against her affair. Charlotte is wondering now whether part of the boredom is her own fault. Should *she* be doing more to keep her husband's interest and love alive?

And what has husband Bill learned? Has he learned to give more of himself to his wife, to nurture their relationship, to spend time with her, to laugh with her, to show her affection, to let her know he loves her, to take her out on dates, to *dance* with her, physically or figuratively? Has he learned to forgive and forget her affair? Or has he convinced himself (because other people keep saying so) that she's a tramp?

And Charlotte's parents—what have they learned? To be forgiving? To forgive themselves for any mistakes they've made? To stop assuming they have failed in bringing up Charlotte? To extend love to her instead of condemnation? To help her recover her faith in people? To comfort her in her torment? Or will they continue to berate and disapprove until Charlotte either severs her ties with them or breaks down?

With constructive attitudes, Charlotte and Bill could build a better marriage than they've had. An extramarital affair can be a catalyst to revitalize a marriage. This is their chance. But if they don't take it, the marriage will almost surely disintegrate.

These are questions and dilemmas that develop in many extramarital affairs.

As we examine these affairs, we encounter very basic questions: What are the motivations that drive people? Why do so many people react differently today than they would have, say, fifty years ago? (Charlotte's grandmother would almost certainly not have reacted to a dull marriage as Charlotte did.) Are the taboos against adultery crumbling? Why are some marriages dull? Why do people let them get that way? What's happening to marriage today? What's the outlook for marriage in this changing society? And many others.

Hunger for love takes different forms—as illustrated by the following persons who share their experiences.

"My marriage is sheer hell, and without my affairs I'd have gone mad!"
Becky and Reggie—and the night worker

Becky's two affairs are ones I often think of when I run across the argument that *no* extramarital affair can be justified. Becky's affairs literally saved her from emotional collapse.

When Becky first came to me, she was a tired-looking woman in her forties who wore thick glasses and kept her hair clipped short with a mannish look. She was twenty pounds or so overweight and had a neglected appearance.

"I know what it's like," she said, "to be in the grip of an octopus that's sucking the life out of you. That's how I feel about my husband, Reggie. He's been sucking my life away for twenty years." She took a long breath and pulled herself together. "Twenty years of nonliving!" she sighed. "All those years when I might have done something with my life.

"I'm trapped now. He's a sick man totally dependent on me. I hate him, yet I can't leave him. He was disabled by polio when quite young and has had to walk on crutches ever since. But his condition has deteriorated and now he seems to be affected mentally as well. Sometimes his memory slips, he gets confused about business details or his tax records, and then blames *me*. The sicker he gets, the meaner he is. I can't tell you what it's like to live with the guy. It isn't that I mind doing for him—changing his bedding, mending his clothes, giving him his meals and all. I'd do that gladly. But all I get in return is abuse. And the worst of it is our sex life."

She paused and didn't know how to go on. There was a look of despair in her eyes. "He rapes me–every day. Yes, I mean *rape*. Isn't it rape when you have sex forced on you against your will by physical compulsion or threats? It's even easier for a husband than for someone else because he's got more opportunity. I try as best I can to keep out of Reggie's way, but our apartment is small and I have no separate bedroom. When our son was at home, his presence kept Reggie from being too brutal. But now I have no one to protect me. And he . . ." She shut her eyes in pain and couldn't continue.

There's something very appealing about Becky. She's at the same time helpless, yet wondrously strong. Although very insecure and unsure of herself, she's also tough and resilient.

"Twice I've almost walked out on him," she went on. "Once I

even had my clothes packed. Then I stopped to think. To leave him suddenly like that wouldn't be right. And I'd be a fool. I suppose he could hire a practical nurse to take care of his physical needs and a housekeeper to run his home. But what would I do then? Where would *I* go? He keeps tight control of all the money. Maybe I could get my old teaching job back. But I've been away from teaching so long I'm afraid they wouldn't hire me now. I fear I couldn't make it on my own.

"But I've found one answer that helps keep me going." She searched for words, and her expression was a mixture of distress and hope for understanding. "About twice a week I leave the house in midafternoon to do a little shopping and get some fresh air. Reggie fusses and fumes; he never wants me to go anywhere. But I tell him we need supplies and I say, 'Look, I've got to get out of here just to breathe.' He says, 'You go out too goddamn much!' After shopping I drop in to see a neighbor I'm fond of—a man who works at night for the power company and is usually at home in the afternoon. His wife works downtown during the day and doesn't get home until after five. So he and I usually have maybe an hour and a half we can be together in his apartment. I don't quite remember how I started doing this. I guess I was lonely, and so was he. It's not exactly the love match I used to dream of. The guy is untidy and fat. He's no great conversationalist. But even if he's not a dreamboat, he's warm and he has a heart. We both have unhappy marriages. We can unburden ourselves with each other. He listens—he even lets me cry in his arms when I can't talk any more. I look up, and he has tears in his own eyes. We make love—it's soothing and comforting, like putting an ointment on a burn. Or sometimes we come together gleefully and it's very exciting. We got to prancing all over the apartment in the nude. We both looked so ridiculous we had to laugh. I don't think I had laughed in years. What a relief!"

"So you've been feeling mistreated by your husband for twenty years," I remarked. "What are your thoughts and feelings about why you and your husband didn't work on your relationship years ago?"

"I didn't want to face the truth," Becky replied. "I know I'm partly to blame for Reggie being the way he is. His mother had spoiled him as a child by waiting on him and babying him, and when we married they both expected me to do the same. They were a kind of joint committee on the education of the bride. Like a fool, I fell right into his mother's pattern. Then the baby came. It's hard to undo something like this after it's been going on so long. And I'd have felt much more guilty if I had walked out on my husband and son than I do in having an affair. My affair isn't harming anyone. Neither of them know about it. But walking out on Reggie really would hurt him.

"So you still feel trapped?" I asked.

"I'm still trapped," admitted Becky. "But I'm not quite so helpless. I think one of these days I'll break out of the trap."

Becky today is almost unrecognizable from the defeated-looking woman of a year ago. She has trimmed off her excess weight. She's taking better care of her appearance. She wears her hair more becomingly, dresses better, and is more attractive in every way. Her extramarital affair, combined with therapy, has bolstered her belief that she's a worthwhile person—she's proved to herself that someone can love her. She's always been bright and capable, but now her whole life is opening up—she's becoming more interesting and alive, keeping up with what's happening in the world, achieving a victory over an extremely repressive childhood. Her parents had been supercritical—as much so as Charlotte's but in a different way. They had criticized everything about her and left her with an "I'm-no-good" feeling that has taken years to overcome.

Reggie observes these changes in his wife and is deeply suspicious. But he's also afraid to bring the issue to a head. He knows he can no longer hold Becky under his thumb. He sees her growing stronger while he grows weaker, and probably realizes that if he pushes her too hard, she may very well leave him. And he needs her more than she now needs him.

Becky's affair with the night worker came to a sudden end when the man's wife came home unexpectedly, caught them together in the nude, and had hysterics. "I was so embarrassed I wanted to die!" Becky said. "The woman rushed at me as if she'd tear me apart and screamed, 'You bitch! You bitch!' Before I knew what was happening she'd kicked me out into the public corridor without a stitch on and slammed the door. I was about to knock and ask for my clothes when the door suddenly opened and my clothes came sailing out—all except my panties, which were under her pillow. One shoe just missed my nose and an earring almost hit me in the eye. I was scrambling to gather everything up when the door of the adjoining apartment opened and a bearded man put his head out and stared in astonishment. Recovering quickly, he said, 'Don't dress up, come just as you are,' and gestured with a sweep of the arms for me to enter. I fled down the stairwell and pulled on my blouse and skirt on a landing two floors below. I then discovered I had left my wristwatch and bracelet behind.

"I didn't go back. But when I got home Reggie, who misses nothing, said, 'What have you been doing? A dog chase you?' 'I've taken up jogging,' I replied.

"He looked closer. 'Where's your wristwatch?' 'Oh,' I said, 'I think I left it at the jeweler's to be fixed.' He said, 'You had a bracelet, too. Did you leave that to be fixed also?' 'No,' I said, 'it rolled into a sewer grating.' 'You're a liar,' he said. But he didn't pursue it further. Afraid to, I think.

"I was sure the news of my escapade would spread all over the neighborhood. It did, but nobody knew it was me. The wife didn't know me and I felt certain her husband wouldn't inform on me. I felt sorry for him, stuck with a wife like that. I never went back, of course. I thought I'd done enough damage to his marriage."

Later we learned that the affair didn't damage his marriage at all, but instead made his wife realize she'd be smart to treat him better. She was nicer to him after that.

Becky's hunger for affection was so great that she sought (and eventually found) another lover, more nearly her social and intellectual equal, and she's prancing in the nude again. But now she has a more attractive figure to show off.

Becky and Charlotte, though far apart in age and personality (Becky is nearly twenty years older) are alike in one respect: Each is a woman who would almost certainly have remained faithful if she had been given sufficient love and affection by her husband. Each was reluctant, in the beginning, to violate her marriage vows. Becky, however, had put up with a terrible marriage for twenty years before it even crossed her mind to seek a lover. The idea crossed Charlotte's mind a lot sooner (her third year of marriage, in fact). Does this mean that Charlotte is less moral than Becky? Or is the explanation that Charlotte had more self-respect and was less willing to accept a husband's insensitivity and lack of consideration? Whichever way you look at it, the difference in responses of the two generations suggests a profound change that has taken place in people's views of themselves and of marriage. Younger women today are inclined to put up with much less neglect and unpleasantness. And this probably applies to today's younger men as well.

"I nearly killed my wife and myself!"
Richmond and Diane—and Andy

Here we meet another woman in midlife hungering for love, but very different from Becky. My first encounter was with the husband.

Richmond is a member of a prominent law firm. He's short, stout, quiet-voiced with a pleasant manner, talks easily, and is invariably courteous, with professional smoothness. He gives the impression of being in control of his life and seems to look down with some disdain on people who are not. He was not one of my patients at the time he called me, and I knew little about his personal life.

Late one afternoon my phone rang and the smooth conventional mask was torn to shreds. Over the wire came a hoarse scream: "I've got a gun and I'm going to kill my wife and myself!"

"Come to my office," I pleaded. I rescheduled the rest of the afternoon appointments.

Into my office strode a tormented man, barely able to hold himself together. "My wife's been having an affair and I'm going to kill her."

We sat late into the evening while he poured out his feelings. Bit by bit the story unfolded.

"My wife, Diane, was downtown shopping this afternoon getting some things for a trip she was planning for tomorrow," Richmond said.

"She told me she needed to visit her father, who is ill. I didn't suspect anything—she likes to visit her family from time to time. But I was looking for our joint-account checkbook and I thought she might have put it in her handbag, which she had set out with her suitcase ready for tomorrow's trip. I looked in her handbag. And in the handbag—" He broke down, shuddered and for several minutes couldn't go on. "In the handbag," he finally resumed, "I found her diaphragm, a book of erotic poems, and a packet of love letters, some dated as long as three years ago, written to her and addressed to a post-office box downtown. I phoned her family and found they weren't expecting her. I glanced at one or two of the love letters, and— God!

"This is *Diane* I'm talking about!" He slammed his fist on the table. "This is *Diane*, who's been my wife for twenty-three years and the mother of my two children! *Diane*, whom I trusted as I'd trust my own right hand! *Diane*, for whom I've worked and devoted my entire life! And today, within the hour, I discovered that she's been for years a deceiver and a whore!" He got up and stamped around the room in agony. "What would you do, Tom McGinnis? What would you do?"

I suggested he'd do well to put his gun away and work with me a while. But it took a number of sessions to bring out what had really happened.

I got part of the story later from Diane herself, a charming, beautifully groomed woman in her early forties with black hair and luminous dark eyes. "Yes, I'm in an affair," she said. "It hasn't been much of a secret, really. Several of our friends have known about it for more than a year because I'm really crazy about this man and I see him every chance I get. If Rich ever really paid *attention* to me, he'd have found out about it long ago. The fact is, he didn't want to know. The idea of my having an affair is terribly threatening to him—he can't face it. You know, the big thing with Rich is *appearances*. He doesn't really care whether our marriage is any good or not, but it has to *look* good. He has to appear to the world like a man in charge! That's why he worked himself up into such fury. He has to be the big he-man. Some he-man! He can hardly get it up in bed!" Her voice grew scornful.

"Believe me," she went on, "my husband's anger has nothing to do with love for me. He's never loved me. He married me because I was a pretty little flirt and because he was a poor boy while my family had money and social position. Sure, I admit I set bait for him. He was good looking and smart and I figured he'd be successful someday.

"It took me some years to realize what an empty shell Rich is emotionally. If he has any feelings at all, he pours them into the interpretation of corporate contracts. If love could be expressed in legal language, he'd be an expert at it.

"But now I've found someone who knows how to love." Diane's face softened. Her eyes grew warm and moist. "Andy loves me. Love is what we all really live for, isn't it? What else is there? If Rich thinks I'm going to trade real love for a mostly absent husband with a big career and no feelings, he's never known me at all.

"Andy is everything Rich is not. Every time we meet I learn something new about him. We play music together, talk, read poetry, dance, take long walks, go to plays, make love by the hour with our bodies and minds and souls. We're alive! Our love is full of color and flowers and whispers and touches. My husband couldn't possibly understand any of this. He spends his waking hours in endless conferences with other lawyers and corporation executives. What a deprived life! In a way, I feel sorry for him."

Where did all this hostility come from—Richmond in a mood to murder his wife (probably not a new idea to him in spite of what he said) and she holding him in such withering scorn? And how could they have been so ignorant of each other, especially the lawyer who seems to have totally misappraised his wife?

Richmond is somewhat emotionally stunted, to be sure, as a result of his childhood upbringing. But he's not nearly as complete a dud as his wife portrays. Diane is hostile and angry partly because of past frustrations with him and partly because of accumulated anger at her own parents, some of which she takes out on Richmond. Though she doesn't perceive her husband fully, much of what she says is true. Her insight as to why he was infuriated by her affair is deadly accurate. Appearances *are* very important to him, and his manhood was profoundly threatened.

Richmond can pour out words effortlessly in telling what he thinks (and he has no end of thoughts), but has trouble putting half a dozen words together to tell how he feels. He's particularly afraid of expressing tender feelings like affection. Words like "I love you" he can't get out—they stick in his throat; they sound absurd to him. His personality is characterized by a tendency to concentrate on a narrow range of interests at the expense of spontaneity and awareness of feelings. Personality types like this tend to appear and reappear from generation to generation in a family. Thus, Richmond describes his father as "quite a lot like me—he couldn't express feelings, either." Nor could his mother. So Richmond grew up emotionally isolated, handicapped in his ability to supply emotional nurture and affection to the people close to him. Yet he too has a hunger for love that Diane doesn't recognize. The problem is that although he wants love desperately, he can't accept it in the excessively demonstrative form Diane had offered it.

Diane did offer it for a number of years, and her husband might long ago have had her love. Diane is a woman of intense but not very controlled emotions. She overdoes her expression of them. When she feels loving she gets very physical, smothers the object of her affection with hugs, kisses, caresses, and words of endearment. This is too much for Richmond—he pulls away. Diane feels his withdrawal as rejection and her affection turns to rage. Richmond is accustomed to his wife's rages. He's much more comfortable with anger than with overblown affection. His way of dealing with her anger is to ignore it, as one might the tantrums of a child. While she rages, he calmly lights his pipe and turns to reading the *Law Review*. To him, as to his father, this is the adult way of handling a hysterical woman: Be controlled, be superior, laugh at her a little.

Diane eventually ceased looking to her husband for affection and began flirting with other men. She had several brief extramarital affairs that nobody knew about. Partly she was driven by sexual hunger, for the couple had nearly stopped having sex. Richmond was devoting more and more of his energy to building his career. And Diane didn't enjoy having sex with him anyway; the act was too mechanical, it was over too quickly, and left her feeling used and frustrated.

About five years ago, Diane met Andy at a party. Without a word being spoken, and before either knew who the other was, their eyes met across the room and locked. Though neither could have explained it, each was instantly aware that the other was ripe for an affair. They maneuvered as if by prearrangement to be alone together and left the party early. Their affair blossomed within a week.

Diane was probably right in saying that Richmond didn't consciously want to know of her affair. For a bright lawyer, he certainly ignored plenty of evidence. Is it not strange that he never noticed the sparkle in his wife's eyes as she anticipated spending an evening with her lover, never sensed her increased vivacity as the "weekends with her family" approached, never observed the fetching way she was dressed or her obvious eagerness to be off? Of course, at any time during those several years a simple phone call to her family would have blown her cover, yet Richmond never made that call until proof of her infidelity stared him in the face. Was this really the complete trust in his wife that he insisted it was? Trust, like other human feelings, is made up of a number of components. One of them, in Richmond's case, probably was the *need* to believe.

After uncovering Diane's infidelity, Richmond immediately moved out. Diane was delighted to be free of him. She was set on marrying Andy, who at that time was obtaining a divorce from his wife. They married within the year.

More recently, Richmond has begun to circulate again and is contemplating remarriage himself. He's found a less demonstrative but very loving woman who admires him and gives him the appreciation he longs for. In therapy, he's getting in touch with his feelings and learning to be more alive and responsive. Although his reaction to Diane's affair put an end to his marriage (which was headed toward dissolution anyway), it seems to have paved the way for enhanced personal growth and the promise of happier relationships in the future for four people, including Richmond himself. (The two children, away at school, seem not to have been hurt too much. Actually, both voiced relief that a poor marital relationship had ended and were pleased their parents were embarking on new lives.)

Some affairs pose moral and emotional dilemmas that are extremely difficult and confusing. Such was that of Sydney, which we'll look at next.

"My affair brought a dazzling vision."
Sydney and Francine—and Barbie

Sydney is a cultured man in his thirties whose profession is the highly competitive one of screenplay director. He's quiet, rather retiring, and looks like a person who would be more at home in the reflective life—maybe as a professor of philosophy—than in the storm and stress of filmmaking. But he's many-sided. He has a storm-and-stress side, too. His work is strikingly original and provocative. His problem is that his films tend to be a bit too intellectual and so fail to draw the big audiences he wants. He feels he is approaching a crisis where he will either have to produce a big hit or retire from the film business.

While Sydney is capable of strong feelings, his emotions had gone mostly into his screenplays. His wife and two small children have received rather little from him. A feeling of emotional inadequacy was one of the concerns that brought him to me.

"I confess I haven't given my wife and family much of myself," he said in one of our early sessions. "My work is extremely demanding and that's where my energies go." But this initial statement was not quite truthful. A considerable part of Sydney's energies and time (and some of his money) went into an extramarital affair with a young, unmarried script-writer he calls Barbie.

Sydney's affair was not (like those we've previously looked at) a response to a consciously unhappy marriage. His marriage had been comfortable but unexciting. He found it pleasant to have a well-ordered home and family to come back to after weeks of feverish activity. To him, home was a place of refuge, a retreat to which he could return for spiritual renewal after battling in the rough world. He loathed hotel rooms (unless Barbie was in them); their impersonality and standardization repelled him. When at home he could read his books, play his stereo, romp with his children, and watch the birds on the feeder outside his window. In its quietness he could gather inspiration and renewal for his next creative venture.

This kind of home life left his wife, Francine, rather on the sidelines. But she hadn't particularly minded, she said. She's an extremely reserved person, didn't feel herself strongly involved in the marriage relationship nor even very much with the children. "I'm a loner," Francine said. "I've always been a loner—I like to go on walks alone and even take vacations alone. For a long time I thought I was an ideal wife for a man like Sydney because it didn't bother me when he was away for weeks. In fact, it was kind of restful when he wasn't around. I knew he loved his home and would come back, so I didn't worry."

Sydney told me of his affair, which at the time was unknown to his wife. "It started very simply," he said. "Barbie's a captivating person.

She's tiny and doll-like, which is how I got to call her Barbie. But her appearance fools you. She has a sharp mind, she's been around, and she's one of the best scriptwriters in the business. Her scripts have rare qualities of humor and charm. From the first day I met her, I've not been able to get her out of my mind. She's not only enchanting to be with, but she makes penetrating judgments. I guess I tend to downgrade somebody who looks like a doll, and it seems as if she can't have an idea in her head. Then, over and over, she puts me in my place by making some acute observation I wonder why I hadn't thought of myself. But she does it without making me feel she's trying to outsmart me.

"When we were working together in Mexico last year I slept with Barbie a few times. What an experience! Up to then I had coasted along on the assumption that Francine and I did pretty well together—we're adjusted to each other, although we don't have sex often. Francine is quiet and self-contained, and sex with her has always been quiet and self-contained. But Barbie! Comparing Barbie with Francine is like comparing fireworks with a heating pad.

"Barbie has helped me realize how unfeeling I've been in my relationships with people. I suppose I'm not a very emotional person in some ways, although I can get very excited about films and scripts. Barbie's feelings flow all through her and burst out all over, which simply staggers me. When she's happy, she just bubbles, and she has an infectious laugh that I hear in my dreams. When she's sad, tears come to her eyes and every bit of her is sorrowful—I have to take her in my arms. Never do I get the impression—as I often do with Francine—that what she is saying has little to do with what she's feeling. With Barbie, what she's saying and feeling are one and the same. So when she says, 'I love you, Sid'—God! I know she does. It's not just a line. And it thrills me.

"Barbie and I often talk by the hour and sometimes make love in and out of bed for an entire afternoon. I've never done that with anyone else, and least of all with my wife, who has considerable reticence when it comes to sex. But Barbie is as wholehearted in lovemaking as she is in other ways. We're both wildly in love. Now what do I do? I'm married!"

Francine came to me some weeks later, greatly distressed because she saw signs that Sydney was withdrawing from her. "I'm scared," she said. "I've never been really scared before. I'm an easygoing person. Life has been good to me. And Sydney has been good to me too. I've never had grounds for complaint against him—except that he annoys me sometimes by being perfectionistic. But it suddenly hit me—is he turning to someone else? We've had a comfortable and happy marriage. We haven't been close—each of us goes our own way—and that's been one of the nice things about our relationship. We never quarrel. I don't think we've ever even raised our voices at each other. It's been the smoothest marriage I've ever heard of. We're seen by everybody as an ideal couple. How can a marriage like ours go suddenly sour?

"Sex? I admit we don't have much sex any more. Once or twice a month, maybe. We don't need it. I can do without sex entirely, myself. And Sydney hasn't seemed to want it much. But, my God! Suppose he does like sex but is getting it with someone else? Maybe I should have *given* him more sex all along. Maybe I haven't been as good a wife as I might have been. What's the answer? I'm bewildered."

Francine has covered up and suppressed feelings all her life, and the practice is now reaping bitter fruit. The best chance she has to save her marriage is to get in closer touch with the emotional side of her own nature. She needs this to help her with her children, too, who often feel little emotional connection with her. She has begun, belatedly, to do so in therapy. It's a rough path for her, yet it opens new possibilities. She realizes this is the only way she'll ever be able to compete with her unknown rival. She's feeling more and more rage as her emotions rise to the surface. Anger had piled up in her for a lifetime—first, hostility at her undemonstrative parents for not expressing more love to her as a child, and now anger at her husband for turning his affections elsewhere. She's kept all this locked up. But now she has to meet and acknowledge it within herself, otherwise it could erupt and destroy her and those around her (as Richmond's fury so nearly did). The bland, artificial smoothness of her marriage is suddenly revealed to her as a mirage—an escape from reality. Her relationship with Sydney is moving, as it were, from a placid lake into rock-strewn rapids. No one can predict how it will turn out. For Sydney is growing in all his capacities. He may be outgrowing her.

His affair has ended now as divergent career ambitions have separated the extramarital partners. Barbie has taken a job in a distant city. Sydney recently poured out his feelings in blank verse:

THE DAWN OF 35

One day I forgot how old I was;
    where I'd been, and why.

That same day I began to think:
    How many days have I left?
    Where am I going? Who am I?
I'm 35. It is dawn.

The memories of my love affair linger, all but blotting out the negative feelings, the problems and complications.

I think of myself as having been blind for 35 years. Then suddenly I was SEEING things I'd only felt before. I began to grow at 35. With my affair dawned a dazzling vision . . . etched in gold. In the dawn of 35, I forgot how to frown.

I see two pairs of thirsty eyes (Barbie's and mine), anxious, gentle. The eyes would speak feelings . . . the hearts would listen. One thought . . .

one mind . . . a special kind of mental momentum . . . a force, a vibrance that lasted throughout the affair.

Every gesture, every movement still lives in memory: her perfume, hair, softness of skin, clothing, demeanor, facial expression. But most of all . . . the eyes.

I like to think of my eyes as windows of my heart . . . Before the affair: shuttered . . . During the affair: glistening . . . After it: receptive and wide open.

At 35 I began at last to feel, to see, and be.

> *Dawn has faded. So has 35.*
> *The days are brighter.*
> *My love affair left a legacy*
> *of hope . . . a vision of*
> *where I'm going, how to get*
> *there and WHO I am.*

In a reflective mood Sydney said to me, "If you've once experienced something supreme, how can you settle for the mediocre? I realize now that my marriage has been mediocre—ho hum. To be merely 'OK' and 'nice' leaves a lot to be desired. Once I thought 'OK' was plenty and 'nice' was fine. But not any longer. I know Francine is growing tremendously as a person, and I'm happy about that. But I've been close to the mountaintop in a relationship with a woman. I don't want to hurt Francine. We've had a good relationship in many respects—like a brother and sister. But that doesn't satisfy me now. Yet if I leave Francine, I'm afraid she'll take it very hard. I dread what might happen."

Barbie is gone. Sydney at times feels lost. "Where am I?" he writes. "I never dreamed I'd find myself so alone. . . . Frustration— throbbing frustration! . . . And I want desperately to change that—to squash 'so-so,' mangle mediocrity, drop 'ho hum' into the past."

In the deep emotions of a flesh-and-blood affair like Sydney's, questions of moral justification seem less and less relevant. Who could say whether Sydney's affair was justified? The affair *was*. It *is*. And through it two human beings reached a more qualitative level of living. Whether the marriage will survive is still in doubt.

"A knight in shining armor!"
Renee and husband—and Eric

Often, the hunger for love stems from fantasies about love derived from myths. Such love, not based securely on reality, can crumble. Rather than describing Renee, I will quote verbatim from her writing about her experiences:

I'd always had a fantasy of a lover. A knight in shining armor who would adore me, pursue me, tell me how beautiful and sexy I am— though deep down I really didn't believe it. During the early years of my marriage, I imagined lovers, friends, men I flirted with, who would fulfill these desires.

When I was thirty-two, I was attracted to a new neighbor, Eric, eventually discovering that he felt the same way about me. I wasn't able to make any advances, due to an old fear of rejection, but kidded around a lot (safe!). Finally, Eric let it be known he was interested in having an affair, even though he said he loved his wife. We played games—he pursued me constantly. I saw him almost every day. . . . I felt very much in love and could think of nothing else. He seemed to be everything I wanted in a man—much that my husband lacked. In the beginning we just kissed and petted—teased each other. I eagerly responded because he kept desiring me as a woman, something I'd never felt before. I dieted and lost twenty pounds, changed my way of dress; my whole outward appearance changed. I felt then like a sexy, sensuous, and a very desirable woman, but I also felt terribly guilty, for this playing around went against my strict moral upbringing. . . .

I decided to take the final step, and meet Eric at a motel. With great trepidation, fear, and shyness, I did it. But I felt so miserable I couldn't enjoy it. I know I made him uncomfortable, too. . . .

After that, things changed—he cooled off. . . . He became more distant and defensive. Of course, all I could see was rejection and being made a fool of. He wouldn't go to a motel anymore . . . so I guess I figured it was better than nothing to let him come sporadically to my house for a "quickie." I was never satisfied, and all the tender love and intimacies I had been looking for were nil. As I tried to get closer, he became more distant. I understand now he couldn't handle intimacy, either. Why I let this go on so long (four years, on and off) was, I guess, because I felt this was all I deserved, not liking myself very much. Gradually the tables were turned—I was pressuring him, wanting assurance, love, etc. that he couldn't and wouldn't give. He started to criticize me, my children, and my husband—and tear down my self-respect—yet I still let him drop by occasionally on his bicycle, awaiting him for a "quickie," felt awful when he left, as there was no follow-through with love.

During this time, I was so emotionally screwed up I could neither recognize nor cope with the damage my affair was doing to my self-respect and my marriage. Nor could I understand myself—what drove me. I was badly hurt, and so was my husband, although he never understood why, either. It brought a lot of painful things to a head in our marriage, as I kept comparing my lover with my spouse, and was dreaming for a while of how great it would be if I were only married to my lover. I paid a heavy price in depression, guilt, and terrible anxiety. I finally sought professional help from you because I had to get my head screwed on right. It was some *time before I came to realize that I was a worthwhile person and that I had a better husband than I had thought. Now we are trying to improve our marriage, and things are going better between us. But still I'm not sure I will ever be fully satisfied with only one man's attention and affections.*

There is a great variation in the emotional intensity with which the hunger for love in these five case manifests itself. Diane's love for Andy involved her whole being. So to a large extend did Sydney's for Barbie. Charlotte's and Renee's, on the other hand, were fantasy loves, ultimately extinguished like dying embers. Although Becky hungered for love in her struggle for survival, she never reached the deepest emotional levels; part of her always remained outside, observing and wondering.

4. *Itch for Excitement*

You say you do not love me,
        But you come to me with feeling.
I say I do not love you,
        But I come to you with pride.
I give with love, and so do you.
And so, if you do not love me, nor I you, what matter?

Every time we meet with tenderness and passion
        My being grows.
I watch you watching me, and
I see joy and affection in your eyes.
Then I feel boundless, timeless delight.
Why then does love matter?

For the moment we are raindrops suspended
        Between sky and earth.
We come to give and to share.
With you I soar beyond feelings grown familiar,
Carrying with me the destiny of life's cycle.
Such is life: a moment suspended like a raindrop.

THE ADVENTURE SEEKERS

Hunger for love can be also an itch for excitement. For what is more exciting than being in love? It's not always possible to separate the two. In all five affairs we have described, the hunger for love and the itch for excitement were virtually identical.

But there's also a desire for excitement that isn't love. It pursues excitement for its own sake. Children feel it, and adults too. It's the urge to drive cars fast, take big risks, get into fights or scrapes, and sometimes do all manner of unwise things. But it's also a part of the urge to explore, to experiment, to seek new worlds, to cross unknown seas, to invent new hypotheses, to question old teachings, to engage in new activities, to feel new feelings, to reach emotional highs, to sustain peak experiences. The urge is profoundly human. And it's a major motivation for extramarital affairs.

Modern life seems especially to awaken this urge, though the urge itself is ancient. Perhaps this is because so much of day-to-day life is dull. We're separated from the storms and upheavals of the natural world as no people ever were before. We're sheltered, insulated, heated, protected.

Many of us have dull jobs, dull marriages, and dull family lives. Even our recreations often are unrewarding, unimaginative, and repetitive, like playing slot machines or lying for hours on a beach. Our friendships tend to be superficial. The vicarious excitement we derive from the entertainment media is short-lived and leaves a void. There's not much for our adrenaline glands to do. We have, sometimes deep down, a yearning for *real* excitement.

A great number of extramarital affairs, in fact, start because of this urge, including many that later becme true love relationships. Lake and Hills[1] suggest that the emotional tensions, narrow escapes, and risks of disaster accompanying these escapades have much in common with the experiences of mountain climbers and single-handed yachtsmen. As these authors put it, the lies and deceit (for certain people) "become a means to feeling alive... to doing something with a part of the self which the marriage no longer uses and perhaps never did."

For many people, having sex with a new partner, seeing and feeling a different body with a different quality of skin and hair and different smells, experiencing a different personality with as yet unknown responses, reactions, new rhythms and emotional patterns, can be enormously exciting. Some find it the most exciting thing they have ever known.

Here are several affairs that arose out of this itch for excitement.

"We set each other aflame!"
Monica and Jimmy—and Slim

Monica had been strictly brought up in a fundamentalist church community and had attended a school run by a religious order. Sex was never talked about in her family. When anything remotely connected with it crept into the conversation (such as a remark that so-and-so was going to have a baby), Monica's mother would give a horrified "sh-h-h" and not another word would be said. Monica didn't know where babies came from until she was in sixth grade. "Imagine my amazement," she once told me, "when I first learned that babies came out of the place where no man should ever go. I began right then to suspect that men sometimes go there." She was nevertheless a virgin when married, and neither she nor her husband, Jimmy, had much knowledge of what marriage is all about.

Monica today is an attractive woman of about twenty-eight, with clear complexion and dimpled cheeks that break easily into laughter. In her school days and the early years of her marriage she was perfectionistic and fastidious. She had no preparation for sex in marriage and at first found its physical aspects repulsive. And Jimmy was no help. He was silent, moody, unaffectionate, and uncommunicative. He didn't care much for sex himself—which in some ways was a relief to Monica, yet left her feeling that there was an unfilled gap in her life.

Jimmy got more and more involved in his business as a salesman of industrial goods, and began to be away for extended periods. Even when at home, he made no attempt to be a companion to his wife. He preferred the friendship of his old cronies from school days. He was a "man's man," and left his wife often lonely and at loose ends.

There was a neighbor in the next block—a bachelor known by his friends as Slim—who drank a great deal and gambled on horse races (nearly always losing). He was physically attractive, when not drunk, and had a mocking, teasing manner that intrigued Monica. She was too inexperienced then to see the hollowness behind it. For Slim was unemployed much of the time; he had a reputation for unreliability—sometimes he'd show up for work and sometimes not.

Slim was a bundle of conflicts and confusion. For a short time he came to me in the hope I could help him. I think Moncia may have persuaded him to seek therapy. She came with him a few times. But Slim had little staying power and broke off therapy before he had made appreciable progress. Monica stayed with it until she had resolved her mixed feelings about Slim.

Slim described his first meeting with Monica: "I met her one day at the city park when she was wheeling her baby in a stroller. She was damn attractive. There was a kind of sad, forlorn look about her. Yet she was exciting, too. I found out pretty quickly that she was lonely and felt neglected by her husband, and she seemed eager for somebody to talk to. She was like a ripe fruit ready to pluck. Then I discovered she lived only a block from my apartment. There were a number of repairs needed in her house, and I offered to do them for her. Soon I was going to her house almost every day. And we got acquainted.

"She resisted having sex for quite a long while. I guess it was the strict way she was brought up. But we drank together a good deal and laughed and smooched a lot, and one day she had a few more drinks than usual and we went to bed, and she just exploded like a firecracker. She'd been holding it in for years, it seems. I don't think she ever had a notion what it was like to really let herself go. Well, she found out! And after that she couldn't get enough!"

"It's true," Monica said with some embarrassment. "I'd been brought up to think of sex as something horrid that no nice girl does. But I knew that when a girl gets married she has to do it for her husband's sake. With Jimmy, sex was awkward, fumbling, and always left me disgusted. I'd never been aroused sexually in my life until Slim came along, and one day when we were fooling around he took my clothes off. And what happened then was like Fourth of July fireworks. God, it was exciting! I'd never dreamed sex could be like that. I can't wait to do it again. With Slim, that is. Not with my husband."

Monica has a rare capacity for enjoyment of new experiences. She loves to try new foods, loves travel and nature study, loves music—and, once her inhibitions were broken, she came to love sex. Slim had sensed this robust quality in her when they first met, and it had been one of her attributes that had charmed him. But she has a sharp mind, also. She questions.

"I can't understand my parents," Monica admitted one day. "What could have been their motive for hiding sex from me and my sister the way they did? Did they think we'd never find out? Mom and Dad seem to have hated their own sexuality and been embarrassed by it. I think they looked on sex as one of God's puzzling mistakes. Maybe the Devil winked at Him the day He made sex." And she laughed merrily.

Monica's clear-eyed comprehension of her parents' hang-ups enabled her to throw off the chains they had tried to weave around her. She had long felt rebellious at the restrictive teachings of her childhood; when she saw how absurd some of them were, she was able to discard many of them with a minimum of guilt feelings. "I'm a child of the new age," she'd say. "Sex is for enjoyment."

For eighteen months, Monica and Slim carried on a flaming sexual affair, sometimes in his bachelor's quarters but also often in Monica's home when her husband was away. She took rash chances, such as inviting Slim over when her husband had merely gone downtown on an errand, risking Jimmy's unexpected return. This added to the zest. It excited her to imagine the horrified look that would come over Jimmy's face if he should come back suddenly and catch her with Slim, especially in the middle of one of their more erotic postures. She almost wished it would happen just to enjoy the effect.

What really happened was that Slim began to feel contemptuous toward Jimmy and to ridicule him in Monica's presence. This stung Monica. No matter how neglectful Jimmy was as a husband, he *was* the man she had married and she was outraged by Slim's smug attitude of superiority.

"I began thinking about this," Monica related afterward, "and I realized that Slim was a conceited ass who had nothing to be conceited about except his prowess in bed. He couldn't control his drinking, he couldn't hold a job, and he never had any money. The few dollars he picked up from odd jobs he blew on the races. He couldn't, to save his soul, manage his own life. At no time would I have considered marrying the crazy guy or running off with him—he would have been a total disaster as a husband. It's a funny thing about Slim. I don't really understand him at all. He's interesting, he has intriguing ideas—he kind of twists everything around backward. He's a dreamer. He can spout poetry by the hour from memory. And he had been very attentive to me at first, which I loved. But I can't respect him! How can you love someone you don't respect? He's a sponger, a freeloader, always getting free rides from somebody—generally me. I'm ashamed to think of all the money I've lent him that I knew he'd never pay back. . . . And all the free meals I've cooked for him. And the free sex." She made a face.

"And there's something else that bothers me. The sex has been wonderful and it's released a part of me that had been totally blocked. But there's no love in it. To Slim, sex never had anything to do with love. It's just conquest. He thinks he's quite a man to have seduced a married lady! I guess I sensed this from the start. But now I want to get rid of him."

Monica came to realize that her affair with Slim had been dominated by ego drives on both their parts. Slim was using sex to prove his manhood (which he otherwise had reason to doubt) and Monica was using sex in part to prove that she could rise to a man's sexual expectations which she had previously had reason to doubt). No matter how exciting thier sex was, it was wearing a false face. And Monica was hungering for real love. Once she found that, she was quite capable of fidelity and responsibility.

Getting rid of Slim was not easy. Beneath his mocking, teasing exterior was a paranoid streak, and he revealed an insane jealousy of Monica's husband and even her young child. When Monica told him their affair was ended, he went into a rage and threatened violence and suicide. She knew him too well by that time to be moved by his protest. She saw him as a talker but not a doer and refused to see him any more. Eventually Slim drifted out of her life and moved to a different locality.

No sooner had Monica's affair ended than she discovered that her husband, Jimmy, also had been having an affair. She was furious. The fact that she'd been having one didn't mollify her. Notions of justice or fair play were irrelevant to her. Jimmy's affair tightened Monica's resolve to seek a divorce. Later Monica met a gentle, kindly school administrator several years older than she, fell in love with him, and married him.

"I had a great fling," Monica told me recently, "and it was an important learning experience for me. It's no good going into marriage as ignorant about basic human experiences and feelings as both Jimmy and I were. But it's over. I don't think I'll ever have another affair. I have a *real* husband now—he's beautiful, I love him, and I'll never turn my back on him." She flashed me an enchanting smile. "And he even loves my little boy, which Slim never did. I'm happy!"

Was Monica's affair with Slim essentially different from Charlotte's affair with the rock singer (previous chapter)? In certain respects, yes. Charlotte was basically a woman of conventional morals who had, for a short time, been carried off her feet by a glamorous figure in the entertainment world. Though Charlotte enjoyed her fling for a time, she never had any doubt that what she was doing was wrong by the only standards she knew. (Her parents hadn't failed as badly as they thought.) Monica, on the other hand, once she tasted sexual adventure, became avid for it, fanned the flames of her desire, had no compunction about enjoying physical sex to the utmost, and didn't mind (at first) that the man she was having it with was one she couldn't respect. She was a woman in full rebellion against convention. Yet ultimately both Charlotte and Monica arrived at the same place: Both wanted love and affection.

We come now to a very different type of case in which both spouses had affairs, broke their marriage, but maintained an amicable relationship.

"When I finally accepted my husband's affair, I began to live my own life for the first time."

Harry and Henrietta—and their extramarital partners

The family of Harry and Henrietta was oriented almost entirely to having a good time. They entertained a lot; their life was a round of tennis, golf, swimming, boating, cocktails, and weekend trips. They took nothing very seriously. If a problem came up, it was treated as a joke and made the occasion for amusing repartee. As a result, no one in the family really confided in anyone else. Harry brushed off all attempts by his wife or their three teenage children to deal with any substantive issues. Parental discipline was lax or nonexistent, and the children frequently got out of hand.

Clever repartee is an effective form of blocking communication; so practiced was Harry at this game that nothing of significance could be talked out. It made for a poor marriage, since feelings were invariably locked up. Henrietta had no way of knowing how her husband really felt about anything, and as the years went by she ceased to care much.

There seems to have been no interest in extramarital affairs until this couple reached their midforties and some of the bloom had worn off their frenetic way of life. One day at dinner Harry let drop the casual remark that he was having an affair with a girl in town and presented the information as if it were an amusing incident—just another fun adventure. Henrietta was deeply hurt. Obviously, Harry hadn't even thought about her possible feelings in the matter. She abruptly left the dinner table and went to her room to sort out her emotions. "He's done it at last," she said to herself. "I was afraid he would some time. But at least he hasn't done it behind my back." She was wrong. He'd been in the affair for several months before he revealed it, and his admission of it was a hint that it was about to get serious.

Henrietta, thoroughly upset, came to me. As she described the situation: "I went to Harry after I'd had time to get a grip on myself. I said, 'Harry, what does this mean? Are we finished?' He laughed as if it were a big joke. 'Come on, little one,' he said, 'wipe those tears away. It's nothing. Only a little affair with a girl young enough to be our daughter. Forget it, Hetty.' 'You'll have to give that girl up if we're to stay married,' I told him. 'Aw, you're taking it too seriously' he said. 'It's nothing. Have a drink. Let's play a game of gin rummy.'

"That's the way it always went," Henrietta continued. "I never could pin him down. But instead of giving up the girl, I discovered he was taking her with him on business trips and weekend jaunts. He was spending more and more time with her and less and less with me. I caught a glimpse of the girl once and understood why. She was a real stunner—young and vivacious. I knew I couldn't compete with her for Harry's interest. I'm no longer young and at that moment I felt terribly over the hill."

But Henrietta is no woman to whine or retire in defeat. "I said to my husband, 'If you're going to have an affair, I intend to have one, too.'

'Excellent idea,' he said. 'You have my blessing. It's better if we're both free to do as we like.'

"Well, I have lots of friends," Henrietta went on. "All I had to do was direct an interested look at the right man and the dates fell into my lap. I saw that Harry was becoming more and more infatuated with his girl friend—he was taking her everywhere. But do you know, painful as this was, I began to feel actually *relieved*! I felt free for the first time in my life. I didn't have to go to all those stupid fun places my husband likes. I could decide for myself where I wanted to go and with whom. I began to enjoy doing the things *I* like, and it was easy to find people to do them with. I prefer a quieter life than Harry. I like to stay in one place for a while and absorb its atmosphere, which bores Harry to death. I'm beginning to think that all our married life I've been doing the things *he* liked and never the ones I liked."

Harry eventually moved from his big suburban home to a city apartment with his girl friend, while Henrietta reveled in her newfound freedom. She wasn't particularly interested in sexual affairs. But she met an older man whose tastes matched hers and soon developed a close relationship with him. Harry and Henrietta divorced. Harry married his girl friend, and Henrietta is living with her older companion. She's enjoying the freedom of the unmarried state and doesn't want marriage just now. Both former marital partners are happier in their new attachments.

Henrietta grew substantially as a result of being thrown on her own resources. With the help of therapy, she became a stronger, more self-reliant individual, much less dependent on others. This helped steady the children, who had been suffering from the unsatisfactory personal relationships in the family and the lack of discipline. As Henrietta grew stronger, the children responded with improved behavior. Harry kept a friendly relationship with his ex-wife and children, continuing his financial support after the divorce. But according to Henrietta, he's still preoccupied with seeking fun and seems likely to continue so.

In three of the affairs we've looked at (Diane's, Monica's and Harry's) the marriages broke up. Yet it would not be accurate to say that the affairs *caused* the fracture of the marriages. Those marriages were already headed for breakup.

The Harry and Henrietta case suggests a possible way of looking at certain kinds of extramarital affairs. Such affairs might be seen as a reshuffling process by which people who had been poorly matched are able to find partners better suited to their personality patterns and ways of living. We saw how Richmond's wife, Diane, whom he wanted to kill, found Andy, who came far closer than Richmond ever could to satisfying her emotional and sexual hungers. We saw how Sydney's love for Barbie raised his whole perception of what a qualitative human relationship could be. And in some of these cases, even the so-called injured spouse ultimately benefited. Richmond and Henrietta, for example, found happier lives with new partners. Perhaps such a reshuffling of partners is necessary for many people under the conditions of modern life, given the poor marital choices so many people make.

"We have a sexually open marriage, and it works."
Kevin and Deborah and extramarital partners

The ability to enjoy a succession of affairs without serious disruption of a person's marriage or personal life is rare in our culture. It's an accomplishment as difficult for most of us as riding a floating log down a river. But I know a couple who make it work by being open with each other and taking care that their own relationship comes first, while granting each other full freedom to have outside relationships (sexual or otherwise) without keeping them secret. The couple I'm about to describe approached me after participating in a workshop I had conducted on Understanding and Coping with Extramarital Affairs.

"We feel we have a constructive alternative to offer," they said. "We have a sexually open marriage. You might be surprised to hear that it works—for us." They consented to a series of personal interviews, on which the following account is based.

"Early in our marriage each of us had a few affairs." Kevin was speaking. He is a deeply tanned, athletic man, an expert tennis player who talks rapidly, waving his arms with vigorous gestures. But behind his physical vigor, kindness and gentleness are apparent. "The affairs gave our marriage a jolt. When Deborah found out about mine, she was terribly hurt."

"It was like skating along and suddenly, without warning, falling through the ice," Deborah said. She flashed a smile at Kevin, and it was clear they understood each other. She's a warm, vital woman of about forty whose attractiveness lies not only in her physical beauty but in her sparkle and responsiveness.

"I was astonished at how hard she took it," Kevin continued. "I hadn't thought of my affairs as big deals. They were casual—the sort of thing any man might have done in similar circumstances. She found out by accident when a motel receipt fell out of my pocket. And she let out a shriek you could have heard in the next county."

"It was the deception that upset me," Deborah put in. "I had trusted my husband, and I had thought we were one couple who were up front with each other. It was disillusioning."

"I love my wife," Kevin went on, "and I decided that if she was so bothered by my having an affair, I'd promise not to have any more. I didn't really need an affair—it was only a bit of adventure. Debbie is a marvelous companion and sex partner so I tried to stay away from other women. But it was tough! I have a roving eye for pretty girls." Deborah gave him an amused look and nodded. "He does."

"Then Debbie hit *me* between the eyes. *She* had a secret affair. Two of them, it turned out. And *I* was upset."

"Let me tell how it happened," Deborah broke in. "Kevin was building his own business at the time—he's a machine-parts jobber—and he had to work long hours and travel a lot. When he came home, he was usually bone tired. This wasn't good for our marriage. I'd always hoped Kevin would get more involved with our two children; they hardly knew him, he was away so much. He wanted to, also. We made all sorts of plans to do it. Then some crisis would come up in his business and he would have to back out. It happened over and over again. Almost like a gremlin that didn't want us to succeed with each other.

"I finally made up my mind that I'd go ahead with our vacation plans even if Kevin couldn't join me," she went on. "I got tired of cancelling holiday arrangements and trips we'd planned to take together. One day, about seven years ago, it happened again for the umpteenth time. Kevin's key assistant got sick and Kevin had to spend our intended vacation doing two men's work. Well, I went to the shore by myself (the children were at their grandmother's), and on the boardwalk I unexpectedly ran into an old flame—his name was Vern—whom I'd been very fond of years ago, before I'd met Kevin. My old friend, hearing of my predicament over a cocktail, moved in with me for a week and we had a ball. I guess it was partly resentment at Kevin that led me to this silly thing. I'd reached the limit of my patience. But there was something else, too. Sex with Kevin had gotten a little dull." She gave him a coy glance. "I loved him, you understand, but even with someone you love you can fall into repetitive patterns without quite realizing it. You stop using your imagination. And with Vern—who's quite a guy!—sex got back a lot of its old thrill for me. I returned home refreshed and very aroused sexually, and the next time Kevin and I had sex, I surprised him. He remarked on how exciting I was and I was delighted. 'You've learned some new tricks, too,' he observed. This scared me. I didn't want him to know what I'd done. 'Oh,' I said, 'I just realized we weren't using our imaginations enough. Let's be more inventive!' He loved the idea. And sex with Kevin became more interesting again. At the same time, our relationship grew closer.

"On a weekend later that summer, Kevin again had to cancel out, and I had a second affair—not with Vern, with another friend. Just one night that time. But it was a sizzler, and again I returned to Kevin sexually aroused and again he was surprised. But this time he was suspicious. 'Debbie, you've been up to something,' he said to me. I tried to deny it but I felt guilty and he saw right through me. We've always had an open relationship, and these two affairs were the only goings-on I had ever tried to hide from him. I thought, 'God, our marriage is finished!'

"Well, I broke down and admitted both affairs and I cried in his arms. I kind of threw myself on his mercy, which a woman shouldn't have to do nowadays. But I wanted to stay married to him—he's a wonderful husband. And then he proved to me how wonderful he really is. He said, 'Debbie, this shakes the hell out of me because I love you so much, but who am I to complain? I can't say I blame you. I let you down. I know I did.' I held him tighter and we made passionate love. He said, 'I won't make an issue of your affairs. I know you love me and I love you and we're going to stay together.' "

"Up to this point," Kevin broke in, "we both were in the traditional marriage bind. We believed we had an obligation to be sexually faithful; each of us felt hurt and resentful if the other slipped, and the one who slipped felt guilty and ashamed and afraid to tell the other. We talked about this dilemma, and the more we thought about it, the less we could make sense out of it. It seemed to us we had two options: one was to remain sexually faithful by sheer effort of will, and hope we could succeed. The other was to agree to be sexually free and open and to keep no secrets from each other. We gave serious consideration to the first option. It is the most socially acceptable and certainly the simplest. If either of us had insisted on taking that course, the other would have tried very hard to live up to it—for the last thing either of us wanted was to disrupt our marriage.

"But it turned out, after a lot of soul-searching, that neither of us thought the first option would work for us over a long period of time. Some people do make it work. But for us it seemed too rigid. It left no freedom for impulses or for the stirrings of the heart."

Deborah eagerly took up the story. "I was pretty sure Kevin would have trouble with a strict undertaking to be sexually faithful. He's an experimenter. He's too fond of adventure. I've mentioned that roving eye of his." She again directed at him a look of tolerant understanding. "And if he failed after making such a pledge, he'd be tempted into secrecy. That could really undermine our marriage. But, on reflection, I doubted whether I wanted to be bound this way either. Up to that week with Vern, I had resisted friendships that tended to get sexual. This resistance had undoubtedly put an end to some friendships I would have liked to continue. There are different kinds of friendships. I have several close men friends with whom I *never* have sex. One, for example, is a well-known drama critic. I love the guy, and I adore spending an evening alone with him in his apartment (his wife is away a great deal), drinking his Spanish Fino sherry and discussing every subject under the sun. But sex just isn't part of that friendship. It's a strange thing how one person, for some unknown reason, will draw out, say, your wit, and everything you say draws a laugh until by evening's end you're so witty you don't recognize youself. But someone else will draw out your serious side and you couldn't make a joke if you tried. My drama critic draws out my wit, and he responds in kind; so we laugh until the tears roll down our cheeks. We're affectionate and we embrace and kiss a little sometimes, but nothing more.

"On the other hand, there are men who draw out my sexiness. I seem to have a lot of it, and if the man has a lot of it too, I may be mentally in bed with him before we're together an hour. Of course I can mentally walk right out of bed also, and that is what I used to do before my caper with Vern. But putting up the bars often terminated a friendship; the man felt rejected. With some types of men, as I've since discovered, a friendship doesn't begin to take on depth until we've gone to bed a few times. It's as if this kind of man has to test himself with a woman sexually before he can open himself up intellectually and emotionally. I sensed this a long time ago, and it bothered me that I had to cut off these friendships—bang!—just like that."

"Debbie and I tossed this problem around quite a bit," Kevin said. "We found we had similar feelings about it. So we chose the sexually open marriage by mutual agreement. But we knew that to keep our marriage intact, which was very important to both of us, we had to pledge ourselves to two guidelines. First, we agreed to keep each other fully informed about our affairs and especially about our feelings toward extramarital partners. Second, we agreed that our personal relationship would remain *number one* and that any other relationships would be secondary to it. These form the keystone of our sexually open marriage.

"Don't think we didn't have problems," Kevin continued. "This is no easy solution to the traditional marriage bind, believe me. If a one-to-one relationship is tough to handle, think how much tougher multiple relationships can be! Suspicion! Fear of loss! Jealousy! Our agreement to be open with each other headed off some of this, but not all of it. Take my male chauvinist attitude that I 'owned' my wife and that her body 'belonged' exclusively to me. That feeling was deeply embedded—it comes from way back—and I kept banging into it within myself. When Debbie had her first two affairs, I had a brief but bloody war with my emotions. Another man embracing my wife! Another man lying with her and invading her body, having oral sex—and she *letting him do it*! Intolerable! Wicked! My instinct was to fight! I was back in the cave." His eyes blazed as he recalled the old feelings. Deborah nodded sympathetically.

"I knew he had these feelings," she acknowledged. "I could sense the struggle inside him. But he has another quality that quickly cooled his hot temper. He understands *me*. He knew what had been going on with me. He felt with me my disappointment when we couldn't be together, my loneliness, my temporary resentment at him for breaking our date, my fear of telling him what I'd done. Instead of punishing me, he comforted me." She looked at him almost with adoration. "There never was a man like that," she breathed.

Kevin went on. "I found I could reconcile myself to the fact of Debbie finding sexual enjoyment with another man. What I *couldn't* live with was not knowing what's going on and wondering if someone might capture Debbie's affections and take her from me. I needed constant reassurance on this point."

"So did I," said Deborah. "So do I, still. I know Kevin loves me, but I need to be reassured about it often. And I have to reassure him."

Kevin tapped his pipe and lit it. "A lot of people don't understand us," he went on. "A sexually open marriage sounds to them as if we were hopping in and out of other people's beds all the time. We're not.

Being free to do a thing doesn't mean you're doing it continually. Don't forget we're extremely busy people. I have a business to run. Debbie works part-time in a library and takes care of our sixteen-year-old daughter. (Our son is in college.) This doesn't leave time for constant bed hopping, even if we wanted that—which we don't. All we've done, really, is lift certain restrictions. When Debbie and I are away from each other, such as when I'm on a business trip, we are freer than most married couples. That's what it comes down to."

Deborah interjected, "What flashes across some people's minds is mate swapping, sex orgies, and the like. Those don't interest us. We're both very discriminating people, really. When we have affairs, they are with individuals we like and know well, often with friends of long standing—*special* people. For us, sex is an aspect of a whole human relationship. It's the *relationship* that's important. We're interested in people *as people*, not as sex partners for an evening. Do I make sense?"

"Let me ask you a question," I said. "Your own relationship with each other is number one, as you've said. Why, then, do you have affairs? Why is there need for them?"

"They add another dimension to life," Kevin replied. "They're fun. They're exciting. Every new affair is a new experience. Debbie isn't always available to me, but even if she were, I'd want some other experiences from time to time. People are fascinating. I meet charming women. Why need I exclude them from my life?"

"Does what he says frighten you?" I asked Deborah.

"Sometimes," she responded. "When Kevin comes home and tells me what a captivating woman so-and-so is, I get a twinge." She gave Kevin an impish look, and he grinned. "I'd like to be assured *I'm* captivating, too. But we work through these things. I have to remember that I can't be everything to Kevin any more than he can be everything to me. Trying to measure up to that requirement is too great a load to carry.

"I'd like to tell about the man I'm dating now," Deborah went on. "About a year ago I met a man who in certain respects is almost Kevin's opposite. For me, he supplements Kevin in several remarkable ways. Kevin is energetic and dynamic. This man is quiet and contemplative. The personalities of the two men are completely different. Kevin likes strenuous sports like tennis, but I can't play tennis with him—he runs me all over the court till my tongue hangs out. I need a gentler form of outdoor sport. The man I'm referring to offers me one: sailing. Once a week he and I go sailing on the bay in his twenty-four–foot sloop. I've learned to handle the Genoa jib, and I can do a fair job of tacking upwind. Sailing doesn't appeal to Kevin—if he's on a boat he wants to go fast, plowing the water and stirring up a tremendous wake. But for me, sailing is perfect. It's busy, yet relaxing. It has moments of excitement. It's close to nature—I feel a part of the wind and water. We sail for a couple of hours, then anchor in a cove somewhere and do something else I like very much. My friend brings delightful books—he's an English professor—and reads aloud to me, or I read to him. Kevin is fond of books, too, but he and I never read aloud. For him that's too slow; he likes to devour a book in one sitting.

"What I'm telling you is that my new friend adds another dimension to my life. He doesn't replace Kevin. He supplements him."

"How about that?" I asked Kevin. "Does it bother you, what she just said?"

"No," he said. "A few years ago it would have. For a long time we bought the idea that each of us had to be everything to the other, and the strain of trying to do it nearly broke us up. Debbie is right. We finally learned, by knocking our heads together, that no one—I mean *no one*—can be everything to another person, especially one who's growing. I'm me. I'm what I am. But I'm changing. Debbie appreciates me. But she gets something from her English professor, who is what *he* is. And what he is is different from what I am. Not better, not worse, just different. And Debbie is what *she* is. And she's changing. When we stop expecting each of us to be *everything* to the other and to stay the same forever, we can relax and enjoy each other for what we are and what we are becoming. That's a tremendous relief! I think it's great that Debbie has her sailing friend."

"Do you make love with your friend in the boat cabin?" I asked Deborah.

"Occasionally," Deborah answered. "For most of the summer all we did was snuggle close while we read aloud. He's a very reserved person sexually. And also, he didn't want to cheat on his wife. The reading aloud was satisfying enough—for a while. But we both felt sexual stirrings, and we had complete privacy and were in bathing suits. One day the book he brought was a book of erotic love poems. I guess he knew what he was doing. The bathing suits came off." She flashed a smile at Kevin.

"Do you ever feel jealous?" I asked Kevin.

"Yes," he said. "Sometimes jealous as hell! I'm human, I'd like her all to myself. But I know I can't have it both ways. I've learned to live with jealousy. I know I'm still number one with Debbie and she's number one with me. If we both can hang on to that, it's all that really matters. And I think we can."

"Absolutely," agreed Deborah. "Our marriage is rock strong. Isn't it?" And she looked at Kevin as if seeking assurance. "I'd be an idiot to leave Kevin to live with my professor," she went on. "I wouldn't think of doing it, and both men know it and it relieves both their minds. And, frankly, I think Kevin would be a damn fool to leave me." Both laughed.

"But suppose you fell in love beyond your control?" I pursued. "Are you sure you can keep your emotions where you want them?"

"Yes," said Deborah. "I've experienced love enough to know its power and its limits. In a way, I'm in love every time I have an affair. But I never harbor the thought of running off to live with somebody else. I'm not so stupid. Kevin and I have an emotional investment in each other that no one else could replace. We've lived not only with the moonlight and roses but also through hardships and rough spots. We know what it is to wonder, misunderstand, worry, and argue. We've been agents of each other's personal growth. We've comforted each other in times of trouble and suffering. Each of us knows that when one of us is in need, the other will be there. Each of us is the other's best friend. We have many things we love to do together: dance, attend plays and concerts, travel (when Kevin can get away), discuss ideas, work on joint projects—and have great sex. That's why peripheral affairs can't tear us apart."

"Do you think a sexually open marriage is a possible answer to the strains of modern marriage?" I asked.

"No!" Kevin's answer was definite. "You have to have a strong marriage first before it's even possible. The average marriage couldn't withstand openly acknowledged affairs. They'd clobber it. There is no shortcut to building a stable, satisfying marriage. By the time that's accomplished, the partners may no longer want to have affairs. A sexually open marriage happens to be a workable pattern for *us* because of who *we* are. But we don't see it as a general solution for unhappy or disintegrating marriages."

"How about the people you have affairs with? Are you a threat to their marriages?"

"Perhaps in some cases. On the other hand, I honestly think many of my affairs have *helped* marriages. I've had women say to me, 'Kevin, you've helped me understand my husband for the first time.' Or, 'Kevin, you've helped me see what's wrong with my marriage!'

"I don't tempt women away from their marriages. My women friends are fully aware that their relationship with me is one of friendship only, and I let them know from the start that I don't intend to become bound by any fixed arrangement. This understanding relaxes both of us. I find, over and over, that my affairs relieve women of tensions and frustrations that had been playing havoc with their marriages and with their relationships with their children! Through an affair I've seen sour-tempered women become sweet-tempered, irritable ones grow more tranquil, nervous ones calm down. Husbands ought to appreciate what I'm doing for their wives—and for them, too. But I don't count on it!"

"There's a lot to what he says," Deborah interposed. "Kevin does help people. He's an attentive, considerate listener. But, Tom, I think I often help the marriages of *my* friends too. I think this is true of my sailing friend. I believe, through me, he has come to understand women better, and this is helpful to his marriage."

"How do your affairs affect your children?"

Said Deborah: "We're careful never to let our affairs result in neglecting the children. But also we're careful not to let our children dictate our life-styles. The children know we date a lot. We don't hide this. Our boy—now in college—knows we have extramarital affairs, and I think sometimes it bothers him. Children like to think their parents are models of conventional behavior even if they themselves are not. But on the other hand, I believe our son appreciates our being honest with him. Our daughter, sixteen, takes our way of life in stride. She's doing some sexual experimenting herself and has told us about it. We've made sure she has enough knowledge not to get caught in a pregnancy or lose her head over some kid."

"She's willing to confide in you, then?"

"Yes, and we're greatly pleased. It's one of the products of openness in family relationships. If Kevin and I don't hide things from each other, our children don't feel they have to hide things from us."

"Isn't your way of life risky?" I inquired. "Mightn't it even yet destroy your marriage?"

"It's conceivable," said Kevin. "All adventure is risky. Look at the risks skiers take on mountain sides and glaciers. Racing-car drivers— imagine the hazards they face! Having affairs is risky, sure. But, hell, not having them is risky too. Suppose I had said to Debbie after her first two affairs, 'If you have another affair, our marriage is finished!' Do you imagine *that* would have cemented our relationship? I think it's safer to give both partners full freedom. If marriage is a prison, the prisoners will always try to escape. If it's not a prison, who needs to escape? Debbie and I know what love is, and I doubt very much if some openly acknowledged sexual variety will destroy what we've built together."

5. *Fulfillment*

i know something special
*   that i haven't told you yet*
*   or maybe you know*
*   and haven't told me that you do . . .*
*   even so . . . . . .*

i want to tell you how i feel
*   but i can't . . . because*
*   i don't want to frighten you . . .*
*   or me . . . by something that i haven't*
*   sorted out yet . . .*

but if i tell you what it is
*   you've got to promise*
*   not to laugh . . . or cry . . .*
*   or run away . . . because i'll die*
*   inside me . . .*

and when i tell you . . . remember
*   that it comes from me . . .*
*   it's not a plea to you to be . . .*
*   or say . . . or do . . . whatever's not you*
*   for me . . . . . .*
*   you see . . . .*
*   i love you*

THE URGE TO FULFILLMENT

An extramarital affair, like a marriage, is a human relationship. It deserves respect for this reason alone.

Warm, healthy relationships with emotional content offer the gifts of personal growth and fulfillment. If the world were orderly, if marital partners were well chosen and there was adequate training for marriage and parenthood, perhaps marriage and parenthood would be the most fulfilling relationships, and extramarital affairs would not be. But in the real world it is quite often the other way around.

What is personal fulfillment?

There is, I think, a basic underlying force that each of us shares not only with other human beings but with all living things. It's an urge to become what the living organism was meant to be. It's an urge to fulfillment.

A seed wants to grow. A seedling wants to become a mature

plant and will grow out of a crack in a rock. Fish swim upstream through rapids and leap dams to reach spawning grounds. Everywhere the urge to fulfillment—toward living out what one was meant to be—manifests itself.

What is a man or a woman meant to be? The patterns of fulfillment are endlessly diverse. We fulfill ourselves when we develop our capacities and talents, when we grow and become more mature human beings, when our lives and relationships are enriched. We do it in many ways: in our arts and crafts, our literature, our work, our play, our houses and cities, the flower baskets we hang in our windows, our inventions, decorations, dreams, thoughts, human relationships, and other ways too numerous to mention.

But many of us block ourselves in. We may be musicians who never learned to play, artists who never learned to paint, poets who never learned to put feelings into words, scientists who never learned to think, husbands and wives who never learned to love and nurture their relationship. We may sink into apathy or fall prey to restlessness and discontent. We may be sidetracked into blind alleys offering temporary escape but not fulfillment: alcohol, drugs, gambling, street fights, passive entertainment, hasty marriages, unsatisfying love affairs, and much more.

The drive toward personal fulfillment is altering human relationships on a grand scale. Not everyone thinks it's a good thing. The drive has been accompanied by confusion and unrest. Some see dire effects on family life by putting too much emphasis on *me* and *my* wants instead of on family needs. Parents are criticized for seeking personal satisfaction instead of caring adequately for their children. But there is another view: that fulfilled individuals at peace with themselves and making full use of their capacities are likely to be better parents and better husbands and wives than unfulfilled or half-fulfilled ones.

There's no shortcut to fulfillment. Every achievement has to be worked for. The musician must learn to play his instrument, the scientist to think, the artist to paint, the writer to master the use of language. But also the bride and groom need to learn how to live together and enrich each other's lives, and parents how to nurture children; these skills also are a part of personal growth. To be truly fulfilled, you need to develop yourself on *all* levels: Sharpen your intellect, free your imagination, give scope to your creativity, train and nurture your emotions, become more aware of your own and other people's feelings, keep your body active and fit, and build rewarding relationships with people. For these are all aspects of a whole human being, and to neglect any of them is to remain partly unfulfilled.

It's in human relationships that our failure to find fulfillment seems to cut deeper than anywhere else. We are taught that marriage and family life form the base upon which human relationships are built, and it's assumed that fulfillment is found there. We expect marital partners to be congenial companions, loyal coworkers, efficient homemakers, capable breadwinners, nurturing parents, and delightful lovers. The lover relationship is, by tradition, exclusive; no one else may share it. And it is assumed that the marital relationship will contribute to nurturing the personal growth of both partners—for many years or for a lifetime.

But does it? Can it? Are we demanding the impossible from marriage? We referred earlier to Dr. Birdwhistell, who has made a pioneer study of nonverbal communication. He believes that because of losing the lateral support of family, other relatives, neighbors, and friends, marriage has turned in upon itself and become a "closed dyad"—an unnatural social form.[1] Closedness, in his view, is the inability to make valid social contacts with other people. According to Sheehy, who interviewed him, he has called this form of marriage "a snake eating its own tail." Neubeck puts it this way[2]: "That marriage should serve all the needs of the spouses is built into our marital expectations, yet anyone who examines this proposition realistically is struck with its impossibility."

Sally, a woman of about forty who is in her third extramarital affair, writes about this: "I've been thinking—if I had a really good relationship with my husband—suppose I married a second time, for all the *right* reasons this time—say, he gave me a lot of personal space—sex was terrific— we made special times for sexual encounters, as in an affair—I was attracted to him and little things didn't disgust me (body odors, sloppy habits, etc.)—I could share leisure activities like jogging, reading, tennis, a spa—I was able to respect and admire him—I really enjoyed being with him even in the same room doing different things—his work fascinated me and mine fascinated him—we could really relax together—take long walks or bike rides or horseback rides—comfortable in silence or in excited sharing—if I could collaborate with him on some life work—Damn! *I wouldn't dream of having an extramarital affair!* I know that's true for me—or would be for quite a long while. But what about for twenty years? Maybe Margaret Mead and her serial monogamy is the answer. If I can't have serial monogamy, I don't want marriage. *It has to be possible.* Anyway—I know that two people cannot meet *all* each other's needs. I have an enormous personal need to be left alone at times—to run or just lock myself in my room. But there's no reason why a person couldn't have that freedom in a marriage. . . ."

She goes on: "Deep down, the built-in guides I have for my conduct say, 'Marriage is, or would be, the best choice (with the right person).' But then immediately my experience says—how many people pick the 'right' person at twenty? I *want* marriage to work—I'm hurting in a way because mine couldn't. I didn't know at twenty what I would want or need or *reject* at forty."

Sally obviously does not think of either her marriage or her extramarital relationships as permanent. She doesn't seem to want them to be. She can't even conceive of her "ideal" marriage as lasting "twenty years." She sees herself as continually changing and growing. Even if she has a good marriage, she may someday want a still better one. Can she herself be sure that a relationship that satisfies her now will still satisfy her twenty years from now? On the other hand, is it reasonable to ask whether her affairs have helped her find true fulfillment or whether they are, like alcohol or drugs, mainly an escape? Could they perhaps be both?

Traditional marriage, which proved stable for a very long time, functioned in the context of the extended family, which now exists in limited form. The extended family was a mutual support system; the husband and wife weren't expected to be everything to each other. There were relatives and neighbors in easy reach, providing many opportunities for human inter-action. People could drop in for tea or a chat, give a hand on some project, feed the baby, stay for dinner, talk about their problems; or they could argue and get annoyed with each other. But either way, they interacted. And people remained in the same locality long enough to build deep, loyal friendships.

But what have we got now? Married couples, as Birdwhistell points out, are often isolated units with little, if any, support structure to help hold them steady. They hardly know their next-door neighbors. They have lost the habit of visiting. They are forced in upon each other as few married people ever were in the past. Many couples don't stay in one place long enough to develop enduring friendships. What they have is a kind of imposed togetherness. And togetherness, without true intimacy and the skills of interaction, can lead not to cohesion but to rupture.

As the extended family lessens and married couples become isolated and thrown too exclusively on their own resources, they often become mutually dependent, possessive, defensive, and fearful. Instead of letting there be spaces in their togetherness, they cling ever more tightly. For to allow spaces requires inner security and deep trust. How can you say to your spouse, "I want you to find your fulfillment," if you are obsessed with fear that anything your spouse gains through a relationship with someone else is at your expense? To find or to help another to find new paths to growth, it is sometimes necessary to free and *let go*. Wise parents know there's a time to let go of their children, to free them to make their own lives. It's harder to acknowledge that there may also come a time when it is necessary to let go of a spouse or a lover.

HUMAN INTERACTION: KEY TO PERSONAL GROWTH

Without human interaction, personal growth is hampered, if indeed it takes place at all. I knew a young man who wanted to become a great poet. He secreted himself in an attic studio and, for a year, scarcely ever went out. He thought uninterrupted privacy was all he needed for great poetry to flow out of him. He was wrong. It didn't. Creative effort is stimulated by human interaction.

Talented writers, artists, and businessmen interact continually, with each other and with the people around them. As a group, artists and poets have a reputation for numerous love affairs, but many are also known for fights and disrupted marriages. Their lives are hardly tranquil. They seem to need human interaction, loving or otherwise. When such people fall into quiet routines, their creativity may wane.

If we look at the emotional and psychological reactions that take place in extramarital affairs, we may better understand how human interaction contributes to personal growth and fulfillment. Creation of any artwork or the blossoming of any talent is a multifaceted activity, taking place on many levels. A meaningful human relationship also develops on a number of levels.

Consider what knowledge can be gained in a qualitative extramarital affair. In it, a person has an opportunity to learn what he or she might have learned from marriage but did not. An affair, potentially, is a school of human relationship, usually functioning under protected and favorable conditions. Distractions are reduced to a minimum. The extramarital partners, while together, can give full attention to each other. Maybe the attention is mainly sexual, but it is still attention and carries with it strong emotional impact. For individuals in midlife, the experience can be rejuvenating, carrying them emotionally back to youth. Partners in an affair often work at the relationship with an intensity they never thought of bringing to their marriages. Partly this is because the extramarital partners have limited time together and little to divert them; they must "make hay while the sun shines." Also it is because they dare not take each other for granted if they want the relationship to continue. So they give special care to their relationship, learning from each other, discovering what makes a relationship succeed and what smothers or disrupts it. And working at an intimate human relationship is a powerful stimulus for personal growth.

IMPACT OF INTIMACY

Earlier in this chapter, I mentioned how even seemingly superficial human interactions may contribute to personal growth, creativity, and fulfillment. How much more significant are such gains when the interaction becomes more qualitative through intimacy! By intimacy, I do not imply that the relationship is developed only through an affair. Instead, I am referring to any close relationship—either in or outside of marriage, and either between people of the same or of the opposite sex.

Whether or not you are able to share intimacy depends primarily on how you feel about yourself. If you really like yourself and feel good about yourself you can more easily accept and cherish the good feelings that come to you from another person. Consider how difficult this might be if you were to think harshly, repudiate, reject, or punish yourself by maintaining distance from others. In that case, you might not be able to accept intimacy.

The opportunities to develop qualitative relationships with another human being can occur in four major areas of human functioning. First, you can turn on to the other person through *intellectual intimacy* by sharing observations, ideas, concerns, and insights. A second way is through *emotional intimacy* in which feelings are exposed and explored. The level of trust you build through a close relationship minimizes the risks of revealing your private self. Feelings and emotions are an integral part of your makeup. Intimate relationships provide the climate which can encourage you to open up and share your inner world.

Nonsexual physical intimacy is a third aspect of intimacy. Hugging, holding, and touching offer stimulating dimensions for closeness. Husbands and wives—and lovers—to whom sexual intimacy is readily available, often overlook the warmth that can be generated and transmitted through touching without sexual involvement. Touching invites a contact with another human being that transcends words. And touching can cement a bond of intimacy without genital involvement . . . proving that men and women *can* be intimate friends without having to be lovers.

The fourth area is *sexual intimacy*—not the mechanical lovemaking that marks the deterioration of many marriages or extramarital affairs, but an intimacy built upon the joy of giving and receiving pleasure in the most human of ways from someone whose closeness you prize highly—and who prizes you in the same way.

Intimacy can be relatively short-term—two people brought together for a brief time through business or social situations. Or it may be long-term; some intimate relationships are sustained for most of a lifetime. But the depth and condition of intimacy is alterable—it can be more intense at some times than at others; it may surface only occasionally in some relationships, more frequently in others.

How, specifically, can an intimate relationship between two people contribute to their growth and fulfillment? When you interact with another in ways that involve, simultaneously, your mind, emotions, and physical body, you experience what I describe as *coming fully alive.* To be *alive* is to be awake, to respond, to vibrate, to feel, to think, to be turned on, to be exhilarated at times, to experience a full range of human emotions, to work enthusiastically, to laugh, to play—to fulfill your potential. A person who is fully alive can appreciate his own uniqueness, is able to love and be loved, to be involved, devoted, share closeness, be nurturing, and experience the full richness of a human relationship.

It's an ever-widening circle—the more an intimate relationship encourages a person to become fully alive, the more receptive he becomes to intimacy. People involved in intimate relationships are open, non-defensive, comfortable. They develop greater understanding and appreciation of other people's thoughts, feelings, values, and actions . . . more accepting of differences. They gain more confidence and self-esteem.

As I noted earlier, the personal growth and fulfillment which I have attributed to intimacy need not take place through an extramarital affair or even a close friendship. It can be had through a vital, dynamic marital relationship. In a successful marriage the spouses, no matter how busy, make sure they devote a few hours a week exclusively to each other. They may go out for dinner, send flowers, give gifts, say complimentary and encouraging things, tolerate shortcomings.

Unfortunately, not enough of us take seriously the continuing need to nurture and work at a marriage. We settle too easily into sameness and repetition. We call this settling down. Doing the same things every day. Seeing the same people (but not being close to any). Rehashing the same old arguments (or, more likely, virtually ceasing to converse). Retreating into safe, secure routines. Having sex always in the same way, in the same place, and letting the act become mechanical. Letting marriage turn into a "status" (which means freezing it) instead of an adventure. Falling imperceptibly into boredom, though the partners may scarcely be aware they are bored. Eventually getting to seem old hat to each other. When a marriage reaches this state, the temptation to find a new, fresh, exciting relationship with someone else can become difficult to resist. But newness and excitement can wear off, and after a time an affair can begin to go the same way the marriage did.

One of the big plusses of an extramarital affair is the feeling it gives many people that they are important to someone—that they are loved and regarded as special, perhaps for the first time in their lives. Imagine the condition of a person who doesn't feel loved or wanted by *anyone*—the emotional equivalent of being lost in a desert without water. Cuber, in his study of adulterous practices of healthy people, referred to earlier,[3] was "struck by the sizeable group of people who were involved in adulterous relationships of many years' standing, who were enriched and fulfilled through the relationships in much the same way that intrinsically married people are, whose health, efficiency and creativity remain excellent—many of these pairings are in effect *de facto* marriages."

The longing to be loved and wanted is two-way—it's also a longing to love and want someone. A woman currently in an affair writes: "Some extramarital affairs satisfy unmet desires for holding, stroking, being wanted—wanting. People need to desire other people almost as much as they need to be wanted. . . . Needing/wanting someone to say 'You're special and I freely choose you'—in fact, to say, 'I go out of my way to be here—I change my routines, I even go so far as to lie and actually change my values—*that's* how very important you are to me!'. . . . WOW! Does that ever make one feel *GOOD!* . . . But from a spouse . . . would a spouse *DO* it?"

Another woman writes: "I knew years before I started my first extramarital affair that there would be someone, someday, to whom I would feel physically drawn and with whom I would experience my first passionate lovemaking. I knew that making love with a man who turned me on would be one experience I could never turn down. But he also had to be someone I would *respect* and *trust.* When I actually met the man, I knew at once he was 'the one.' As I got to know him better (we went to school once a week and I saw him there), I experienced him as a very supportive, caring, concerned individual."

"I found that fulfilling the sexual side of me was a very, very important reason for an affair." Dee—and extramarital partners

Let's hear from another woman, who speaks even more directly in a letter: "I have had such *positive growth* from my extramarital relationships. They were sometimes painful (as when I found out my lover was involved with someone else). *But the hurt made me feel*—and I learned that I am more apt to value honesty than infidelity. . . . Well, my trust disappeared because he lied—but I also saw that he had lied because he was afraid if I knew, I would leave him, and he didn't want that. The lack of communication was mutual, and I guess we were both responsible. That's a big thing to learn."

Dee continues. "I'm very cautious about the people I select as partners. In each case, I knew the person for many months before the affair began and found him to be mentally as well as physically appealing. In the first affair, I was the initiator (with a lot of messages to 'go ahead and flirt' from him). And in the second, I was literally pursued for a year—he never ever gave up or took 'no' for an answer until I finally could not resist at all. There was a big thrill to that—someone saying, 'It's *you*,' and not giving up for a very long time. I wouldn't have gone after him, either. I had decided after my first affair that I would never have another. An affair seemed too complicated, took too much time, too many hours waiting for him to call, waiting, always wondering.

"But number two was not that way at all. He announced he loved me—spoke to me daily for three years—called from all over the globe— was always in touch—two or three times a day sometimes. We worked together in the same office—shared a dream of a program that meant a lot to both of us. . . . Yet in the end our relationship didn't work out. I found that real people have needs, and in this kind of relationship eventually someone says, 'Make a commitment.' First, I couldn't/wouldn't. Later, it was too late.

"Anyway, why an extramarital affair?" Dee gives this answer: "Because people in affairs are 'dates'—you don't share the laundry, the kids, the thingamajig that doesn't work. You can share ideas and long, *long* hours in bed. (How many married couples spend hours in bed—stay home from work just to make love all day on a rainy day?) In a marriage you start to get away from romance. Mine was a childhood sweetheart romance without sex—and I later found that fulfilling the sexual side of me was a very, *very* important reason for an extramarital affair. In my marriage I had had sex, orgasms, childbirth—but where was the passion? It NEVER was. (And I'll *never ever* enter another intimate relationship in which I could not feel passion—a 'turn on' that envelops my whole being).

"The passion my second affair aroused even now burns inside me when a smell or a sound triggers a memory. We made love a lot, but we also fucked a lot: in parks, in cars, in the woods, on a golf course, in a movie, in an airplane—at every opportunity, including on (and under) his desk and conference table. . . . I was thrilled at being such a 'turn on' for him. He made me feel like what was happening was incredible for him—one erection following another—three or four (or more) orgasms in one night (or day, or both).

"I chose to end the affair when I began to feel my own self-esteem being affected. He wanted me to be in an exclusive relationship with him, yet he would not accept commitment in the same way with me."

Dee says her affairs were "growth experiences." She actually uses the word "fulfilling." Can we take this seriously? A skeptical person reading Dee's somewhat narcissistic account might well react to it as a shameful tale of lecherous irresponsibility and self-gratification. What about the spouse of this adulteress and the wife of her "playboy friend"? Dee doesn't even mention them. And how about her children and those of her lover? I can hear the judgments being pronounced. Can anyone achieve "growth" or "fulfillment" through betrayal of a spouse and lust for sex? These are serious questions that can't be summarily dismissed. Is Dee's claim that this was a "growing experience" mere self-justificaiton? Is Dee confusing weakness with strength?

Dee has asked herself these same questions, and she did not resolve them without intense internal struggle. She felt, for a time, a great deal of guilt. For she knew well enough how her adventure would appear to an onlooker. But Dee feels she did, in fact, grow through her affairs—although she was helped by therapy to consolidate her gains. First she learned to deal with pain and disappointment (the collapse of a relationship that had meant a lot to her) without running away from herself and without bitterness. To accomplish this called for considerable maturity.

Dee was, from one point of view, a victim of a deceiver who had lied to her about his other attachments (though not about his marriage). Dee, of course, was a deceiving wife, so morally she and her lover were on parallel tracks. But the interesting thing is that in Dee's account there isn't a word to suggest that Dee saw herself as a victim. Nor is there a hint of bitterness. She had too much pride to accept a one-sided commitment that would bind her but not him. Yet she gives her lover full credit for the many hours of pleasure she enjoyed with him. She wrote: "My affairs were deliberate decisions I made. I accepted the responsibility, actively wanted the relationships, and, most important, totally enjoyed myself physically and emotionally."

If personal growth means increased capacity to cope with disappointment and pain without turning them inward against yourself or outward against someone else, Dee had made substantial progress. If growth means heightened awareness and understanding of others, Dee had progressed in that, too; she could write, "I . . . saw that he had lied because he was afraid that . . . I would leave him." Then she added, "I guess we were both responsible." If growth means an expanded capacity for human relationships, Dee had moved far in that direction. She had dared to love passionately, to accept love, to be vulnerable, to share her thoughts and feelings, and to be honest with herself and her lover (if not with her husband). These are no mean achievements.

Is the experiencing of high physical passion a kind of fulfillment? When I compare any of the three women I've just quoted with great numbers of emotionally numbed people whose capacity for passion has withered, I have to say yes. Each of these women is vibrant and alive—Dee especially. If Dee's husband could awaken to what she is and begin to appreciate her and turn on to her, their marriage might yet be transformed. Dee could be a better wife than ever before.

Extramarital affairs, like marriages, can be deep or shallow, qualitative or superficial. But to be growth enhancing and fulfilling, an affair needs to have emotional and intellectual depth; it must be a qualitative relationship, a healthy interaction on three levels: emotional, intellectual, and physical. A superficial or merely physical connection contributes little to personal growth.

"With Lisa I redirected my entire life."
Dan and Sylvia—and Lisa and Saul

The fulfillment some find in an affair may go far beyond the discovery of passion or of ways to deal with disillusionment and disappointment. I've seen affairs that led to abandonment of an unproductive style of living and the embracing of a new one in which the individual could breathe, find meaning, and grow. (I've seen the reverse, also. But now we are talking about fulfillment.)

The two couples I'm about to describe are acquaintances rather than people with whom I have worked professionally, but I know their story well. And even though their affairs are "extracouple," not extramarital, they illustrate the point I've just made.

Dan and Sylvia, both in their early twenties, were unmarried and living together. They looked out at life from the windows of a huge featureless apartment complex in Jersey City, New Jersey. In the street, eight floors below, people hurried in every direction, reminding Dan of ants in a disturbed anthill. Automobiles, buses, and trucks streamed by endlessly. A block away, riveters did their noisy work on the steel skeleton of a new building. Two blocks away, freight trains rolled by with horns blasting.

To Dan, this never-ceasing motion and noise was confusing and meaningless. He felt like one of the ants, imprisoned in a tiny cubicle in a vast structure he couldn't understand. To city-bred Sylvia, this was life; the restless activity reflected something in her, and she responded to it.

Though Dan had lived in the city for three years, having come from a small town in the Midwest, he felt increasingly alienated. He had nightmares of cities crowding in upon him; of losing himself in a labyrinth of alleyways dead-ending in blank walls; of being surrounded by armed gangs closing in upon him, and nowhere to flee.

Dan worked in a produce market, where he handled the fruits and vegetables shipped from distant places. And every time he looked at an apple or bunch of asparagus, he had a wistful feeling he couldn't find words to describe. Had he been able to express it, it would have been something like, "I wish I were out where this came from—where things are growing and alive."

When Dan once suggested to Sylvia that they move to a small town where he could get farm work, Sylvia was appalled. "I'd die in a small town," she burst out. Dan pushed the dream out of his mind.

Dan and Sylvia socialized frequently with another young, unmarried couple, Lisa and Saul. The two couples went off together one day on a weekend automobile trip into the hills of Pennsylvania, where they shared a motel room for one night. This was a fun experience. They pranced around a bit in negligees and shorts and enjoyed some flirting and bantering, but didn't swap partners. Dan looked at the farms and woodlands with eyes of longing. So, he noticed, did Lisa.

"Do you sometimes wish you lived away from the city?" Dan asked Lisa when they were alone.

"Do I!" she exclaimed. "I *loathe* the city. I'm a farm girl at heart. Would you believe it? I once milked cows, raised vegetables and drove tractors. It was neat!"

Dan and Lisa began to see each other in secret. An affair developed. Not, of course, an extramarital affair, since neither was married, but an extracouple relationship that, in its dynamic and emotional aspects, was virtually identical to one.

Sylvia began to suspect that Dan and Lisa were more than friends, and confronted Dan: "What are you and Lisa up to?" Shamefacedly, Dan confessed. "Get out of my life!" Sylvia stormed. He did. With a little money inherited from an aunt, Dan bought a small farm and Lisa taught him how to run it.

The next few years brought long hours and back-breaking toil, but both were doing what they had wanted to do. Dan later attended an agricultural college. He and Lisa married and their relationship became strong and close.

When we think of an affair only as a problem of marriage, I believe we are looking at it much too narrowly. Dan and Lisa's affair was a product of changing *relationships*—a new, more fulfilling relationship evolving as an older one declined. So it is with many affairs. It is the reshuffling process we referred to earlier. It can happen whether the original couple is married or not, because human relationships are not static—they are moving.

6. *Guilt*

A lot of guilt was involved, as the whole relationship was totally against my strict religious morals. I was sure to burn in hell! . . . But now, knowing myself better and accepting myself without the horrible guilt and self-condemnation of before, I like myself much better. . . .
    Vicky

GUILT IS WHERE "OUGHT" AND "WANT" COLLIDE

Suppose you are savoring the delights and excitement of an extramarital affair—or you're trying to, or want to. But there's a cloud. Unless your background has been exceptionally permissive, you are doing something you've been taught is wrong.

Maybe this doesn't bother you. Many people engage in extramarital affairs with little or no feeling of guilt. But others, especially when they first begin to have affairs (like Vicky), or when their affairs are discovered, experience overwhelming feelings of guilt, unworthiness, and self-blame. "Ought" and "want" are in collision. And because of this, people may feel not liberated but trapped and hurting.

The conflict between "ought" and "want" is as old as mankind. People always have formulated rules to control their conduct and then striven to break them. In our culture the conflict is especially acute because our society encourages so many wants; trying to satisfy them can cause bewildering struggles with "oughts."

Guilt feelings arise whenever you violate or fail to live up to your own moral standards of right and wrong. Those standards are reflected in your expectations, the rules you live by, and the values you put on things—the dos and don'ts, shoulds and should nots, cans and can'ts. They are basic conceptions that influence how you think, feel, and act. And they were mostly formed in childhood as a result of responses to the requirements, demands, and prohibitions of parents and others. One way of looking at guilt feelings is to regard them as the conscience speaking. And if this is what guilt feelings are, they are as necessary for living in the world as a compass is to a navigator.

But there are two major ways of dealing with guilt feelings: *constructive* and *destructive*. They differ largely in how the feelings are handled. When a guilt feeling stirs you to become a better, kinder, more considerate and understanding person, it could be called *constructive* guilt. The relation of this guilt to the personality is like that of pain to the body: It is a warning signal. It can encourage you to do something you haven't done, stop doing something you are doing, steer a different course, modify your wants, or alter some of your conceptions of "oughts." Working constructively with guilt can be a motivation to change and to grow.

Destructive guilt is another matter. This is the guilt feeling you try to ignore, hide, or suppress, or drown in drinks or drugs, or turn outward against someone else or inward against yourself. It arises when you adopt attitudes of escape, submission, dependence, irresponsibility, hate, blame, or remorse. It can do enormous damage to yourself and others. It can constrict your life, dull your sensibilities, undermine your self-esteem, kill your joy. This aspect is dramatized in Hawthorne's novel, *The Scarlet Letter,* where the minister, Reverend Dimmesdale, who had fathered a child by a married woman, is consumed from within and literally dies of shame. But destructive guilt is most poisonous when a person won't acknowledge it, refuses to take responsibility for it, and projects it upon someone else, holding the other person exclusively at fault.

Many guilt feelings you experience may be inappropriate and unnecessary. You may be punishing yourself for actions committed in the past that you cannot now undo, yet this self-punishment may not help you do better in the future. You may feel guilty about things you cannot help, such as being a member of the white race (because of its past treatment of other races). However, the things you feel guiltiest about are apt to be things you were most criticized for in childhood, such as lying to your parents, concealing your misdeeds, being impudent, cheating, being too aggressive (or too passive), showing disrespect for your elders, using bad language, being lazy, being late, failing to achieve high scholastic standards, acting like a tomboy or like a sissy, playing with your genitals, and so on. Yet the same person who feels guilty about some of these things may not feel at all guilty about shoplifting, drawing up a misleading accounting statement, or endangering lives by driving recklessly after a few drinks. Some people inflict hurts and damage on others' lives with very little compunction, sometimes justifying their actions on the grounds of serving some higher cause, such as victory in a war or revolution.

Guilt feelings clearly need to be looked at, which means confronted, felt, acknowledged, thought about, and worked with. Not run away from. And never laid on someone else. Many of us are victims of unnecessary or destructive guilt and need to work to free ourselves. Or maybe we don't feel enough guilt; maybe we are insensitive to the consequences of our actions.

A lot of guilt feelings have to do with sex, and not all of these are rational. Slowly our society is emerging from the conception of sex itself as sinful, but our obsession with sex shows that we remain very much entangled and confused. Many people are still uncomfortable with sex unless it is tied strictly to marriage and is limited to so-called acceptable forms. We are indeed far from a general acceptance of sexually open marriage such as that of Kevin and Deborah, described earlier. Our reluctance is understandable. Consensual adultery (adultery by mutual consent of the marital partners) violates too many social, cultural, and religious taboos and is too personally threatening to be easily managed by most of us.

Piled-up guilt feelings can bring acute distress, anxiety, a sense of unworthiness, self-blame, worry about what others may think, self-imposed restrictions, self-punishment, conflict, fear of retribution, psychosomatic illness, failure on the job, withdrawal, excessive aggression toward others, and sometimes severe depression. It is too distressful a feeling to sustain for long. You have to do something to ease it. But what?

One way of dealing with guilt feelings, of course, is to stop whatever it is you feel guilty about. This means accepting the verdict of your conscience without inquiring whether the teachings that gave rise to your guilt feelings were valid or are appropriate to your present condition. As a child, for example, you may have been forbidden to cross the street, but it would not make sense to feel guilty about crossing it now. Of course, the advice to stop doing what makes you feel guilty is no help in relieving you of guilt feelings about past behavior, thoughts, or feelings (such as wishing your parents were dead), or about activities of the larger society of which you are part (like fighting a war).

The old cure for wrongdoing you may have been taught as a child was to confess your misdeeds, expect punishment, punish yourself if others don't punish you, feel badly about yourself, say "I'm sorry," plead forgiveness, promise never to do it again (or even to think or feel such a thing), and try—if you can—to make restitution to anyone you have hurt. All the self-abnegation you go through in this process is supposed to make you a better person. Usually it doesn't. Except for the confession and restitution, this whole sequence may be counterproductive. It is unlikely to contribute to personal growth because thoughts and feelings are not worked with or essentially changed. It may not long restrain you from repeating the "bad" actions, feelings, or thoughts. And it can leave you with damaged self-esteem, which can hamper you all your life.

The key to dealing constructively with guilt, as with any strong emotion, is first to acknowledge it, feel it, face it. That's the "confession"— you confess to yourself if to no one else. Without this, you'll look for an escape that solves nothing: drink, drugs, burying yourself in frantic activity, blaming someone else, martyrdom, or a symbolic cleansing such as vomiting. The principle of the confessional is sound: You have to face who you are and what you have done. And you have to seek forgiveness within yourself.

But confession, too, has its pitfalls. If you have an urge to confess to the person affected by your action, search out your motivation. Are you trying to unload the guilt on someone else, saying "it's really your fault"? If you had an affair, would confessing it to your spouse hurt your spouse? Some unfaithful partners do this intentionally to make the spouse feel bad or even to destroy the marriage. Often part of the motivation for confessing an infidelity to a spouse is to get the spouse to assume a portion of the guilt, thus easing the guilt felt by the person in the affair. The aim may even be to get the spouse to forgive the infidelity, thus releasing the unfaithful partner to do the same thing again and again. This sets up a manipulative, game-playing cycle not unlike that of the alcoholic or the chronic gambler.

Once your guilt feeling is acknowledged and faced, you can begin the real work of exploring and evaluating the background and meaning of your guilt feeling. What early teachings gave rise to it? Are those teachings still valid for the person you now are, in the situation you now are in, here, today? You may recognize some of those teachings as outdated, or as appropriate for a child but not for an adult. If so, ask yourself if you want to hang on to them. Does clinging to outworn teachings limit your life? Do you want your life to be so limited? By reevaluating the ideas upon which a guilt feeling is based, you may draw the fangs of that particular guilt. On the other hand, if you feel that the original teachings were right and you should live up to them, make up your mind to do so and associate with like-minded people, but don't torture yourself with past mistakes.

You may need help with all this, for without feedback from other people, you are in the position of using your own value system to appraise your own value system. Getting feedback can lead to new insights, new ways of looking at life, a willingness to experiment, to learn, and to enjoy. This approach does not subjugate "want" to "ought" or "ought" to "want," but permits a creative interaction between the two, as symbolized in the Chinese Tao's yin and yang—the interpenetrating opposites. "Ought" and "want" are both valid. We would not choose to crush or eliminate either.

This is a process of personal growth. Through it, the individual comes closer to being in charge of his life. Whether it leads necessarily to a sounder ethical position is arguable. In some cases there is risk that it might simply weaken the "ought." Vicky, a woman in her midthirties who was quoted at the head of this chapter, had this to say: "If you had asked me a few years ago about my personal values, I would have said extramarital affairs are taboo, against all my moral codes, especially religious. After being involved twice, I can no longer feel this way. I think now that if two adults feel strongly drawn to each other and they don't hurt anyone in the doing and feel justified in the relationship, why it's OK. A 'wrong' in my eyes would be the exploiting or hurting of someone through the affair." She assumes the spouse isn't hurt if he doesn't know about it. But how can she be sure he will never find out? And what if he does? Who is hurt then?

Following are accounts of three extramarital affairs in which guilt feelings were a major factor. In the first, these feelings were constructively handled. The extramarital partners were dedicated people who believed deeply in the sanctity of marriage. They felt guilty before God; their struggle to find peace of mind is worth telling. In the other two cases, guilt feelings turned to destructive channels with appalling consequences.

"My priest is a beautiful soul."
    Eva and David—and Father Gordon
    This is the story of two people, honest to the core, who were drawn together into a secret, illicit love against the teachings in which both

believed. The agony of their lonely struggle with their consciences brought them both to me.

Eva is a warm, loving, nurturing human being—the kind of person to whom anyone in trouble instinctively turns. All her life she has been the rescuer, the one on hand when a friend or stranger needs help or a listening ear. She has taken innumerable bowls of chicken soup to sick people, visited the old and lonely, organized a group to work for prison reform, counselled with young drug addicts, etc. She's been a tower of strength in her church; she, in turn, draws spiritual sustenance from a strong faith in God.

Father Gordon was, for a long time, her priest and confidante. He loved her, and she him. They had worked together in the Lord's work for a number of years. Eva had come to occupy a special relationship with the church-affiliated school which included all levels from kindergarten to eighth grade. Eva was not the administrative head of the school. But she was, in a sense, its spiritual mentor. She stood in an unofficial position as the one to whom everyone—teacher, pupil, and principal—turned for help in untangling the knots of human emotions and behavior. And her priest, Father Gordon, had turned to her for help on innumerable occasions as he encountered daily the perplexities and afflictions in people's lives.

Eva was married. And for a long time Father Gordon and Eva were scrupulously careful not to overstep the bounds of propriety in their personal relationship. The Father was keenly aware of the church's teachings on the sanctity of marriage. None knew them better than he, or believed them more completely. And Eva knew and believed them with equal fervor—or thought she did.

But these two people were experiencing a growing emotional attachment, and had begun to feel stirring within them forbidden thoughts and urges. They sensed they were in moral danger in the light of the teachings of their church, and they tried to stop seeing each other. Yet the need to work out solutions of the church's problems kept throwing them together. And each time they were together, they found it harder to part. One night, after a difficult and stormy committee meeting that left them both emotionally exhausted, they looked at each other, and were overwhelmed. They fell into each other's arms. "We're lost," they said. "I can't live without you," Eva cried. "Nor I without you," mourned Father Gordon.

They meant never to cross the forbidden barrier of sexual relations, and for more than a year after their declaration of love they held the line. But they couldn't refuse each other the comfort of being in each other's arms or of expressing the emotions that welled up in them. Each was deeply troubled in mind and spirit. They wanted tremendously the support of one another's love and strength. They began to meet in Father Gordon's private quarters. They hated sneaking and subterfuge, but they had to take exceptional precautions to avoid arousing scandal. They suffered through many sleepless nights. Even though they were not committing adultery, they knew they were violating the spirit of the marriage sacrament. The love and comfort they were giving each other belonged, by church law, to the separate relationships of Eva with her husband and Father Gordon with his church. They were commanded to stay strictly within those limits. And they were not doing so.

The fact was, however, that Eva had not for years been able to find any love or comfort in her relationship with her husband, David. Nor could Father Gordon find it solely through the impersonality of an institution—his church. Both longed for a close *human* relationship in which they could give fully of themselves. In theory, God's love was supposed to be enough for them both. In practice, they weren't able to achieve such dizzying spiritual heights, though they tried. They yearned for human love, too. The conflict left them bewildered and depressed. It seemed to them they were being forced to choose between human love and divine love, and they couldn't do without either.

Eva, in the impulsiveness of her youth, had made a sad choice of a husband. Wisdom grows slowly; for how often does a girl of eighteen have the discernment to pick a man who will meet her emotional needs sixteen years later—to say nothing of twenty, thirty, or forty years later? Eva had grown and matured over the years, while her husband had remained immature and stagnant. Marriage, in many ways, is a lottery. Not knowing what the future will bring, a young person takes a chance.

Eva's parents hadn't been fortunate in their marriage, either. In marrying David, Eva seemed to have been repeating her parents' pattern.

"I never understood my father," Eva said to me. "I longed to be close to him, but he never would let me. He'd just stand at a distance and find fault with everyone. As a little child, I looked on him with awe; he seemed almost godlike. I think that David, my husband, must have attracted me originally because he seemed so much like that 'god,' my father. Maybe I thought that by getting close to David I was, in some way, getting close to Dad. I misunderstood both of them completely. I know now that neither is godlike; they're just cold and out of touch with themselves. That's an awful way to talk about my father, isn't it? And my husband, too. But how can you reach out to a man who builds a wall around himself?

"I think the barriers my husband and my father put up against my love were part of the reason I went in so strongly for good works. A person has to have an outlet for love. Some people pour out their love on pets. I poured it out on my children, on sick people, on the lonely and oppressed. And on my church. And especially on my beautiful, beautiful priest! It's been satisfying. I've had a good life even though my husband drew further and further apart from me. Since David shares almost nothing of himself with me, I've long ceased trying to share my feelings with him. The church says marriage is a sacrament. But how can it be so when a husband and wife don't build a relationship with each other? A marriage sacrament that isn't a relationship seems meaningless to me.

"Actually, the kind of God-centered relationship I'm supposed to have with my husband I now have with my priest. Isn't that ironic? I love

Mike—Father Gordon—so terribly I can't sleep at night. He's full of feeling, he's aware, he's sensitive, he's lovable, he understands me. I want to give myself completely to him. And he wants that too, but can't bring himself to it. I never in my life would have dreamed I'd contemplate being unfaithful to my husband. The idea was unthinkable. And Mike and I have still held off from sexual relations, thank God! But we've come awfully close. And, when alone at night, I've sometimes thought the unthinkable. Remember what Jesus said about the person who has committed adultery in his heart? I've done that. *Real* adultery couldn't be much more of a sin, could it?"

Eva described the struggle she and Father Gordon went through when they felt they were separating themselves from God. "Mike was more troubled than I," she said. "Because he had never had the experience of marriage or any intimate relationship with a woman, his notions of marriage were otherworldly. The realities of marriage, as he learned about them from me and from others he counseled, troubled him deeply. And he was troubled also for himself. He had dedicated himself to a lifetime of service to his church and to God. He felt he was compromising himself and being unfaithful to his vows. He felt that by loving me, he had become a party to the violation of my marriage vows. He knew he could not reconcile this with his faith. Over and over, we found ourselves locked together in each other's arms, aching for a complete union, and then at the last minute we'd spring apart. The frustration was almost unbearable."

When, finally, the barriers were broken and the couple completed the sexual act, the father notified his superiors that he could no longer function as a priest. He ceased being Father Gordon and became plain Mike Gordon, a teacher. He and Eva then went into a full-fledged affair, seeing each other almost daily and growing closer and closer physically, mentally, and emotionally. They finally worked through their struggle with themselves and attained a new level of self-knowledge and understanding.

"I haven't lost my faith in God," Eva told me, her eyes shining. "I love God more now than I ever did. So does Mike. Somehow, human love and love of God seem necessary to each other. I don't know why, and it doesn't fit church doctrine, but so we've found it. Perhaps it's because, as human beings, we feel God's love through other human beings. God's love for me shines through Mike—he's the conduit. And I've always been a conduit through which God's love flows to Mike. I know the church says I must stay with my husband and forbids me to love Mike as I do. But the heart doesn't always pay heed to doctrines, does it? Since following our hearts, Mike and I have been much happier. Our hearts say we were right. Anyway, we'll soon make it right. We're going to be married when my divorce comes through." And she did a little dance.

Some people, at some time in their lives, need a slow buildup to sexual intimacy and love, and are wise enough to choose it. When guilt is strong and intimacy and love progress slowly, there is less likelihood of an affair becoming destructive. Eva and Mike had plenty of time to work with their feelings.

"It's too bad, in a way, that it had to be through adultery and divorce—both condemned by our church—that we experienced the completeness of love," Eva reflected. "But I'm not sorry now. I feel that God understands. I know I led Mike on, and I'm not ashamed of it. I had to— Mike was adamant about not yielding to what he always had thought to be 'animal' impulses. I knew the only way Mike could find out that sex is beautiful in the context of love would be to experience it. I had to be his teacher." She gave a shy smile. "I played Eve to his Adam, you know. When he finally realized I was ready for full sexual union and wanted it very much, he yielded—I think for my sake. Our union was too beautiful to describe."

"Then came the expulsion from Eden?"

She laughed joyously. "Mike expelled himself. I told him he didn't need to—he was a marvelous priest, a beautiful soul. But he felt that to stay was two-faced. He was right, of course. You can't preach one thing and do another. He's happier where he is.

"His withdrawal from the priesthood worried me very much at first. I thought—someday he'll regret having cut off his chosen career and will blame me for it. I finally told him of my worry. 'My sweet Eve,' he said, 'you can put it out of your mind. I'll never blame you. I had been thinking of leaving the priesthood for several years because I wanted a personal life of my own. I just hadn't brought myself to act on it. Loving you made me actually do it. I'll *thank* you rather than blame you.' Wasn't that a lovely thing to say? Can you imagine the biblical Adam saying such a forgiving thing to the other Eve?"

David, Eva's husband, was slow to wake up to the fact that Eva was moving out of his orbit. When he realized he was losing her, he was upset and wanted to retrieve the marriage. For him it had been a comfortable marriage, and Eva had been a devoted wife who had served him well. But he was too late.

The affair has changed Mike and Eva in perceptible ways. They are softer and sweeter than before—less officious, less self-important, more understanding of human weakness. They have the serenity and strength of mature and fulfilled people.

The kind of guilt Mike and Eva felt when their affair blossomed was a *constructive* guilt. It forced them to think through where they stood in their relationship to their church, to God, and to each other. They accepted responsibility for their guilt; they didn't lay it on anyone else. They discovered that their love for each other had become paramount in their lives. And they found they could love God just as deeply in spite of their profane love. Their capacity for both kinds of love had been, if anything, enhanced. They could not feel this to be wrong. They decided that adherence to doctrinal rules about marriage was less important to them than obeying the dictates of the heart. Whether the decision was right or wrong is arguable, but they made it, accepted it, and are at peace with themselves.

Not everyone succeeds so well in dealing with guilt. The following two cases illustrate different forms of destructive guilt.

> *"I knew my affair was wrong, and it ended with a crash."*
>   Daisy and Jack—and Fred

Meeting Daisy on the street, you'd see a middle-aged woman who looks like somebody's grandmother—which she is. She has four grown children and five grandchildren. For much of her life she has followed comfortable routines: cooking nice meals for her husband, going to the supermarket, working in her flower garden, watching TV, welcoming her children when they came home to visit. Yet when you draw her out, she is startlingly witty, and her wit has a slightly risqué flavor. You might suspect she has a hidden side. She does. For more than three years, alongside her conscientious service to her family, she carried on a torrid sexual affair with a married neighbor.

Daisy was involved with her husband's best friend, whose wife had been her own best friend. For many years the two couples had gone to the shore together, shared numerous weekend camping trips, and taken their vacations at the same resort. Daisy came to me after a terrible accident and a period of hospitalization during which her affair had collapsed in ruins.

"I'd had nearly thirty years of a dull life with an unresponsive husband," Daisy explained. "Jack is an accountant, he works with figures all the time, and I don't think the guy ever *sees* people. He sure never saw me. I'm the woman who got his breakfast every morning and his dinner at night, and I used to bet if somebody else took my place at the table he'd never even notice. I wanted to put a dummy there sometime to see if he would react. Jack's only interest is sports. He can't bear a conflict or confrontation with anyone; he just wants to be left undisturbed. He wriggles out of problems and leaves them for somebody else to solve—generally me! Whatever disciplining the kids got I had to give them myself.

"I think Jack's avoidance of conflict and the fact that I didn't mean much to him except as a doer of chores explain why my lover, Fred, and I found it so easy to carry on our affair. Jack *had* to know something was going on if he'd half an eye. Look, Fred telephoned me almost every day. Jack was there many times and answered the phone. Any normal man would have wondered why in hell Fred was always calling *me*. But Jack never asked. I'd take the phone and Jack would resume watching TV. Several times a week I'd slip out of the house after supper to be with Fred, and Jack never once inquired where I was going or why. I don't think he even missed me. Can you believe it?"

"How much do you think he knew?" I asked.

"Oh, he must have suspected," she replied. "But we never talked about it. In a way, I can understand why. Jack is a poor sexual partner and knows it. He's had trouble with impotence for years, but even before that he was so unsatisfying sexually and emotionally that I began dreaming of a lover. I wanted a *man* who would function as one. And I wanted to be loved as a woman, not just taken for granted as a housekeeper. When Fred and I began our affair—which started as a lark on a dull Sunday afternoon—I discovered to my amazement that Fred had wanted a woman as much as I had wanted a man. And that woman was *me*! I could scarcely believe it. I thought I was too old and unattractive. But *he* said I was the girl of his dreams. Sounds silly, doesn't it?

"Pretty soon we were wild with each other. My sexual hunger had been dammed up for years. Fred's a lusty guy and I'm a robust woman, and our temperaments just matched. But I was bothered about hurting Fred's wife, Martha, who is one of my favorite people. Fred kept reassuring me: 'Relax, baby! Martha knows my sexual habits, though she doesn't know about you. She and I hardly ever have sex.' 'But what if she finds out?' I asked. 'She won't,' he said. 'She doesn't want to know what I'm doing. She's been shutting her eyes to it for years. I've never pretended to be sexually faithful.' So I tried to forget Martha. But when Martha and I met, I could see in her eyes that she knew. An invisible coolness rose between us. Yet I couldn't give up Fred. You see, I'd found in him what I had wanted for so very long! Our sexual passion got more and more exuberant.

"There's something you should know about Fred," she went on. "He has a terrible fear of growing old and dying. To him, sex is a symbol of life—it means youth and renewal. 'I hate thinking of the hereafter,' Fred told me once, 'because they tell me there won't be sex in it. Sex means *this* life to me, and I want to grab as much of it as I can while I'm still alive.' In a way, I felt like that too. I'm over fifty and I didn't see too many years left to me, either. Fred showed me what a lovely thing it was just to let my hair down and my clothes off and be free as a bird with someone who liked me.

"It was good exercise, too," she added with a laugh. "Kept my weight down."

But Daisy had suppressed her feelings of guilt. She had been strictly brought up by now-deceased parents whose memory she cherished. She had kept close ties of affection with her children. She felt especially badly about hurting her best friend. She was afraid to admit her guilt feelings to herself, fearing that if she did she wouldn't be able to continue the affair that meant so much to her. Actually, she wasn't too bothered about her infidelity to her husband. There had seemed to be an unspoken agreement between them that he wouldn't challenge what she was doing. She was concerned, though, about her relations with her children. She would have been heartbroken if they had learned of her affair. And then there was her mother, who was still alive in her memory. Daisy had loved her mother, and her mother had taught Daisy to be a good, moral woman and a faithful wife. Daisy knew she had let these teachings go down the drain. Yet her affair with Fred had developed intense emotional ties. She had, for the first time in years, begun to feel like a woman.

One day Daisy, who was ordinarily a careful driver, lost control of her car, struck a tree, and was hurled through the windshield. She was in a hospital for six months and came out with a ravaged face and crippled body. Unknown to her, Fred had begun a new affair with one of Daisy's married friends, who joyfully took up where Daisy had left off. Fred rarely visited Daisy after her accident. He couldn't bear to see the wrecked body and face of the woman with whom he had shared his passion; it reminded him too painfully of his own fears of death. When Daisy learned of Fred's new affair the bottom dropped out of her life. That was when she came to me. Yet she also felt a strange relief, as if a curious kind of nightmare had come to an end. She's back to square one with her husband, and what remains of her life she will have to work out with him. Or find another partner, if she's able.

Daisy's affair, like most affairs, was more than just sexual. Fred and Daisy had a close relationship they both wanted. But the affair cost her a valued friendship and undermined her feelings of personal integrity. Daisy had come to despise herself. Her reaction to guilt feelings had always been to punish herself; in this situation she nearly took her own life. There had been a lot of hidden hostility in the Daisy-Fred affair that finally emerged in the accident and in Fred's consequent abandonment of Daisy. Probably part of Daisy's trouble was that she had too narrow a circle of friends. Had she been acquainted with more men, she might sooner have recognized Fred's superficialities and limitations and perhaps not have picked him as an extramarital partner. It is as if, at an unconscious level, she created the pattern that nearly destroyed her. She chose a course that produced feelings of unworthiness, anger, and guilt, and forged this into a weapon directed against herself.

Now we look at a tragic affair in which the guilt feelings of the *spouse* of the participant in the affair were projected upon the participant (Frank) and damaged everyone in the family.

The wreck of a "perfect" marriage
Frank and Rosalie—and Norene

Rosalie had a "perfect" marriage (she kept telling people). She had reason to believe this. She had a husband who cared about her. He cared about most people. Frank is a brilliant, imaginative architect who heads his own firm. Busy as he is, he managed to set aside some time every day for his wife and three children; he paid attention to them, was unfailingly warm and affectionate and considerate of their feelings. He is the sort of man who remembers his wife's and each of his children's birthdays and never forgets an anniversary. Everyone loves him. His family (until the disaster) idolized him. Women can't stay away from him.

Rosalie basked in the glory of this paragon of a husband, and her refrain to everyone was, "Frank is super-wonderful. We have the most perfect marriage in the world." Rosalie is an attractive woman in her late thirties, with smooth skin and delicate features, but there is a look about her—perhaps her tightly compressed lips—that suggests she can, at times, be difficult. Beneath a deceptively soft exterior she is rigid, critical, and disapproving. Her head is full of audio tapes about how marriage "should" be, how people "should" feel and "should" act. She believes wrongdoers "should" be punished. She has deep feelings of inadequacy, but generally hides them from herself and others by disguising unpleasant realities behind a romantic glow. When her rose-colored glasses fail to cover up the smudgy spots, she switches to her "dirt-colored" ones that make things look worse than they are.

Frank, unknown to her, was having a pleasant but (at first) not too serious extramarital affair with Norene, an architectural assistant in his firm, who was several years older than he and twice divorced. Of the many women who find Frank attractive, Norene is the only one who enticed him to be more than just a friend. She's a lively, beguiling woman, far less inhibited than Rosalie. One day she invited Frank to her apartment after they had been enjoying each other's company with a few cocktails at lunch. Dropping into her apartment at lunchtime for "a little more" became a frequent practice after that, and these romps had been going on for about a year when suddenly, without warning, their fun house exploded.

The collapse occurred just in time to prevent the Frank-Norene relationship from becoming a deeper entanglement. The two were growing rather too fond of each other, and Norene's feelings about Frank were akin to hero worship. But the affair was more a sexual match than a true love match.

To both Frank and Norene the affair, in its early stages, had seemed simply an enjoyable way to spend part of a two-hour lunch. They felt a little naughty and Frank had some guilt twinges, but he convinced himself the game was harmless. Nobody was being hurt. Frank saw no likelihood of the escapade threatening his marriage. Norene's apartment was private; the chances of discovery seemed small. He felt he was a good husband and father; he still carried out all his responsibilities faithfully. The affair was, to him, just some ice cream on the marital pie.

Rosalie, though she didn't admit it to herself, shared a good deal of responsibility for Frank's adventure. She was a tight, restrained sex partner who rarely satisfied Frank fully. She had some very fixed ideas about what was proper or permissible in sexual relations, and these restrictions rather annoyed Frank. Norene had fewer inhibitions. Yet Frank was loyal to Rosalie and at no time contemplated leaving her.

Rosalie was not a very perceptive person, for had she been sensitive enough, she would have suspected much earlier. She had convinced herself that her "ideal" husband would never "descend" (as she put it) to having sexual relations with another woman. But one unhappy day she discovered in Frank's desk a receipt for a jade necklace. "Who's *that* for?"

she demanded. Frank was dumbfounded; he hadn't realized he had left such a piece of damning evidence lying around, and he could think of no convincing words at that moment to explain it away. (He wasn't a quick-witted liar who could have said, "Why, I bought it for *you* for your next birthday.") Rosalie saw through his stumbling evasions and went into a blind rage. In one flash, she lost all her illusions about Frank and about men in general. She switched from her rose-colored to her dirt-colored glasses; her marriage changed instantly from perfect to abominable. Frank was no longer "that wonderful man." He had, overnight, become a "filthy deceiver, liar, sneak, animal, beast!"

Frank was terribly ashamed and contrite. He saw at once that his affair wasn't worth the destruction of his marriage, and he wanted to make amends: to take Rosalie on a long trip (like a second honeymoon), turn over a new slate, ask her forgiveness, give her gifts. He broke off his affair at once. But Rosalie rebuffed every overture and shut Frank out of the house. She refused to talk to him either directly or on the phone. She made alarming noises about killing herself and the children. Frank was frightened. He wondered if he should remove the children from her for a time for their safety, but she guarded the house like a sentry and he couldn't get near them. He tried to talk with Rosalie on the sidewalk in front of their home. She slapped his face and screamed, "Help! Police!"

Frank came to me in terrible distress, feeling himself to have been a failure as a husband and as a man. Rosalie later came to me, full of bitterness and finding herself unable to cope with the problems facing her. About Frank she was implacable. "He's no good," was her verdict; nothing could shake her of this conviction.

To gain any comprehension of Rosalie, it's necessary to know how her view of men and of all human relationships had been shaped. She had grown up in the turmoil of wartime Germany. Her father, a former Nazi officer, was a martinet whose view of life was dominated by the command-obey pattern. He forbade Rosalie to have any contact with boys during her teen years, perhaps remembering what soldiers had done to young girls during his war service. When Rosalie protested, her mother told her, "Don't trust boys, dear. They'll always take advantage of you if you let them." This bit of adult "wisdom" slumbered for two decades in the back of Rosalie's mind, exploding like a bomb when she discovered Frank's affair. She seemed to hear her mother's voice: "Never trust a man! He'll let you down every time."

What Frank had done seemed to Rosalie unforgivable. If something is unforgivable, you can't forgive—obviously. Apologies are dismissed as insulting. Rosalie had only contempt for Frank's contrite pleadings ("the spineless double-crosser! I'd like to spit in his face!").

They divorced. That was more than two years ago, and Rosalie is as bitter as ever. She broke off therapy because it was raising in her mind questions she did not want to face. She lives alone with the children. She says, "I'm through with men! Never again! They're animals!"

Frank, for more than a year, was a stricken man, overwhelmed by guilt feelings and not knowing how the damage he believed he had done to his wife and children could ever be made right. "It was a sad mistake, that Norene affair," he confessed to me. "I liked Norene—I still do—but Tom, I'd never have taken up with her if I'd known it would wreck my marriage. When Rosalie uncovered my affair, I felt like a worm. I'd have done almost anything to set it right with her. And with Norene, too. Norene cried when I told her our affair was ended. I felt like crying myself. I realized I'd ended up hurting two women. But Rosalie took full measure of revenge. She devastated me by calling me a beast and liar so that I nearly fell apart, myself. For at least a year I was miserable. The worst thing was being separated from my children. Rosalie claimed I wasn't fit to be with the children and refused to let them come to see me. That hurt! I could have sued legally for visitation rights, I suppose, but with Rosalie in the mood she was in, I didn't feel like pushing things that far. Maybe I should have.

"But I can't understand Rosalie. Why does she stay so unhappy and so bitter? She's made me pay fifty times over. We had a good marriage for almost eighteen years. She was happy with it, or said she was. Then she finds out about my hanky-panky during a few lunch hours—which had really never affected her in any way up to then—and she throws the whole marriage out. Eighteen good years down the drain! It makes no sense. Why do people do things like that? Of course, I have to ask myself why I had the affair. That didn't make sense, either, did it?"

Frank and Rosalie both need to get in closer touch with their feelings, Rosalie especially. Her continued bitterness is a denial of one of her deepest feelings, which is love for Frank. She still loves him, and it tears her apart. Her parents, looming out of the past, have terrorized her into trying to throttle this love she has always felt for him. She was deathly afraid of reestablishing communication with Frank, for fear he would reawaken her love and cause her to weaken. And her martinet father, whose image she always carries within her, demands that she punish her husband and herself. He scorns "weakness," which to him is willingness to listen, negotiate, and forgive. Rosalie has adopted his pattern. She strews guilt in everyone's path. This is sad for her children, who hear her call their father a beast, whereas to them he had always been a gentle, loving parent. They are desperately confused.

Rosalie seems doomed to a bitter and lonely life unless she can learn to respond to her own feelings instead of living out the frustrations and hatreds passed on to her by her parents. Frank, on the other hand, is opening up and getting in better touch with himself. He's asking himself some basic questions now: Was I wrong to have had the affair? Would it still have been wrong even if the affair had never been discovered? Are affairs always wrong? Did my affair ruin my marriage, or was it Rosalie's reaction to my affair that ruined it? Did she have to react as she did? Could she have handled the matter more constructively? Could I have? Was the guilt I felt my own, or was I suffering from guilt feelings put upon me by

Rosalie? (There's one of the key questions.) And how great was my own guilt?

When Frank has faced all these questions and dealt with them honestly, he will have made significant progress in working through his guilt and it will cease to have power over him.

Rosalie, unhappily, is refusing to acknowledge any responsibility and puts the total blame on Frank. Her unbending stance, which is really a living out of her parents' hostilities, has cost her her marriage (which otherwise could have been preserved), has driven out of her life a man she really loved, and has doomed her (if she continues in this course) to a lonely isolation for the rest of her life. It greatly hurts her children, who are being torn apart by her rancor against their father. It hurts the two teenage boys especially, who are keenly feeling her condemnation of the entire male sex. It hurts her twelve-year-old daughter, who is being given a distorted conception of man-woman relationships, just as Rosalie herself had been emotionally damaged in her own youth. It hurts Frank through his children. He's strong enough now to shrug off the accusations she hurls directly at him. But he can't shrug off what she's doing to the children, influencing them to hate their father (and perhaps eventually both their parents).

"She once threatened to kill them," Frank mused. "Now she's doing something even worse. She's undermining their capacity to meet life. I can't stop her. She can't seem to stop herself. Is there no hope?"

Only Rosalie has the answer now.

One of the problems of identifying and dealing with guilt is that it is always mixed with other feelings in varying proportions. Father Gordon's guilt was mixed with disappointment in himself, fear of sex, fear of scandal, and many other emotions. Daisy's guilt was mixed with repressed anger, self-pity, pity for Fred with his fear of death, and embarrassment at what she was doing to Fred's wife, etc. Frank's guilt was mixed with concern for his children, compassion for Norene, loss of self-esteem, etc. Rosalie's guilt had turned into burning hatred and fear that consumed a love she had long cherished. Guilt feelings are not simple; that is why they call for exploration and confrontation.

Each person has to come to terms with himself, either through obedience to his conscience or through reevaluation of the appropriateness of his guilt feelings.

7. *Why, Oh Why?*

I need to feel special
That no one else will do
Frightened someone else could do
Frightened you'll want me too much
Needing to know you want me
Afraid you do

Wanting you
Touching you in my mind
Needing to call
>   *to hear your voice*
>   *saying nothing at all.*

So like me
So unlike me
To want someone like this
Sometimes glad
Sometimes sad
Sometimes scared

Wanting more of you
Unable to let go
Loving to feel wanted
Wanting to feel and feeling
>   *desire*
>   *desired*
Mutual need

Enjoying you
Enjoying us
Enjoying feeling special
Afraid we'll stop
Afraid we won't.

MARRIAGE: PROGRAMMED FOR FAILURE?

Why do people have extramarital affairs? Each individual has his own private reasons. Few things in life are so personal and intimate; few are more resistant to open investigation.

But we know this: Affairs, looked at broadly, are an offshoot of marriage. And marriage has been studied forward, backward, and sideways. Restrictive, inflexible, unsatisfying marriages that inhibit personal growth are an invitation for affairs. We call these closed marriages, and we know a great deal about how they come into being. William Lederer[1] has observed that the conditions leading to eventual marital incompatibility are present long before a couple commit themselves to the marriage. Unrecognized emotional difficulties, destructive behavior patterns, and unreasonable expectations often predispose a person carried away by emotion to make an inappropriate choice of a marital partner.

These destructive patterns may be visible enough even during courtship, while the engaged pair is trying to pretend they don't exist. Thus a woman who divorced her husband because he was a "mama's boy" (he was always leaning on her emotionally, trying to make her mother him) remembers now that he showed evidence of this tendency long before they were married, but—like lovers the world over—she paid little attention to the warning signals.

Patterns that eventually destroy a relationship usually have their origins in childhood. Our "mama's boy" had a mother who waited on him, solved his problems, and spoiled him. Many people, when under severe and prolonged stress, instead of being able to adapt their behavior to the needs of a real situation, tend to mimic (unconsciously) the behavior of someone in their original family when under a similar stress. In this state, they lose their autonomy—they function with a built-in pattern from the past. And it can be a troublemaker.

It is in childhood, therefore, that many bad marriages are born—and, eventually, extramarital affairs. The child has been taught myths having little to do with reality, such as the romantic-love myth and the marital-bliss myth. And when a child's unmet needs, longings, dreams, unfulfilled wishes, deprivations, and hurts are not successfully worked with in the early years, but are left to simmer and perhaps fester unattended, a process is set going that in later life can result in a poor choice of spouse, a disastrous marriage, and an affair. This is the basis of my earlier statement that yesterday's child is the architect of today's affair.

THE INCLINATION TOWARD AFFAIRS

The reasons for affairs are by no means as obvious as they seem. Take Becky's case (the woman with the crippled husband whom we met in Chapter 3). If there was ever a situation where the reason for an affair was self-evident, it should have been this one. A lonely woman tied to a mean, repressive husband. What more need be said? But this still doesn't explain Becky's choice of an affair instead of some other solution. For example, a great many people in equally unpleasant marital situations, instead of having an affair, become emotionally deadened so they scarcely feel anything. That's a common form of defense: apathy. So we have the question, Why did Becky choose an affair instead of, say, apathy? The same kind of question might be asked about any extramarital affair. But let's stay with Becky for the moment.

Offhand, I can think of at least nine alternatives (besides apathy) to having a secret affair that an individual in Becky's situation might have chosen, and there are probably more. The fact that Becky didn't choose any of these, but instead had two secret affairs, was evidently a result of the particular set of circumstances.

Another wife in Becky's position might have done any of the following:

1. Stayed loyally with her husband and tried to build a better marriage. (But Becky had lost hope that this was possible.)

2. Walked out on her husband and sued for divorce. (But Becky didn't have enough self-confidence or financial independence to strike out on her own. Also, she felt some responsibility for the care of her husband.)

3. Given her husband a tongue-lashing when he got abusive. (But Becky didn't like conflict; she shrank from a verbal or any other kind of fight. Besides, Reggie was better at this than she was.)

4. Clouted him. (But Becky wasn't violent by nature, and Reggie had twice her strength.)

5. Suggested to her husband that they both have affairs. (But Becky wouldn't have dared suggest this to Reggie. His reaction would probably have been violent.)

6. Found an absorbing interest to brighten her days. (She did— her extramarital affair. But it might have been something different like volunteer services, adult school, or church work—there are endless possibilities.)

7. Developed a talent or engaged in a creative activity like music or painting. (But Becky had not yet learned what her personal talents are; her life had not yet opened up.)

8. Cultivated friendships without sexual involvement. (But Becky wanted sexual involvement, too.)

9. Sought solace in faith and prayer. (But Becky was not a deeply religious person.)

These surely don't exhaust the list of alternatives for dealing with Becky's predicament. But they illustrate the fact that when a person has an extramarial affairs, and current opportunities. Becky found the solution that personality characteristics and emotional needs, early teachings, religious beliefs, education, marital satisfaction or dissatisfaction, social and community position, work situation, previous experience in premarital and extramarital affairs, and current opportunities. Becky found the solution that seemed most satisfying *to her*, being the person *she* was. Someone else might have chosen differently.

WHO ARE MOST LIKELY TO ENGAGE IN EXTRAMARITAL AFFAIRS?

If Becky had all these options and, because of the kind of person she was and the situation she was in, chose an extramarital affair, the same could be said of anyone having an affair. There are always options. No one has to have an affair. My observations in clinical practice indicate that certain personality characteristics are more likely than others to incline a person toward an affair.

But it is necessary to approach this kind of generalization with caution. It would be a mistake to assume that possession of a "pro-affair" characteristic (if there is such a thing) means that the possessor is likely to have an affair. It only means that the possibility of an affair is somewhat greater than would otherwise be the case.

What follows is based not on any comprehensive study or survey, but on personal impressions derived from working with many people in affairs.* The personality characteristics which I have encountered most frequently are these:

1. *The adventurous,* with their itch for excitement, adventure, intrigue, discovery, new experiences, meeting new people, etc. They are willing to take reasonable personal risks and may have a strong desire to experiment with life. Some individuals with this quality are highly attractive, interesting, creative, inventive, and alive. They are often curious about affairs and wonder what it would be like to have one or more lovers. Some do get involved and even bring back experiences from the affairs that enhance their marriages. They may have grown up in families that did not repress their childhood curiosity or curb their investigative tendencies, or they may have had a very strict, repressive upbringing against which they are rebelling (like Charlotte and Monica, Chapters 3 and 4). To some, sexual adventure may be a natural part of their outreach into the unknown ("I wonder what so-and-so would be like in bed?"). Their extramarital affairs tend to be passionate and sometimes stormy, but also can be very satisfying.

2. *Warm, friendly, loving, open people* whose nature it is to form close, affectionate relationships and who do not shrink from intimacy. Some are capable of and comfortable in loving more than one person. They are likely to have grown up in families in which affection was openly expressed and at least one parent gave a good deal of love. This quality of reaching out to people (which is also a quality that makes for a good marital relationship) does not, by itself, produce affairs; but if combined with strong dissatisfaction with the marital relationship, it can make affairs a possibility (as with Eva and her priest, Chapter 5). Such affairs can be caring human relationships that sometimes develop into true love unions.

3. *The strongly sexual,* for whom sexual involvement is extremely important. Some may not be sufficiently satisfied sexually in the marriage (like Daisy, Monica, and Dee). Others may feel acutely sexually deprived for one or more reasons: The spouse may have little interest in sex, or be dull or inadequate in making love, or may have a disabling physical problem (e.g., a cardiac problem or severe asthma) or a sexual dysfunction (e.g.,

---

Impressions developed in this and other chapters in the book will, it is hoped, give some direction for more needed research on extramarital affairs.

impotence, frigidity, chronic infections), or may often be away on extended business trips or in service in the armed forces. The strong sexual urges of these deprived people may be a result either of sexual repression or of exceptional sexual freedom in childhood. Through sex, these people may develop emotional closeness with their extramarital partners. In some cases, however, the sexual desires are compulsive and not accompanied by strong affection. In others, the sexual episodes may be an unending search for an emotional satisfaction they never quite find. A satisfying sexual affair can reduce marital antagonism and tension caused by unsatisfying sex.

4. *The rebellious and self-willed,* who tend to ignore rules and restrictions and want untrammeled freedom to do as they please. Some are in revolt against the restrictions imposed by traditional or closed marriages. Some women are in protest against the double standard; they want to assert the same privileges men have claimed in the past. People like these may have grown up in strict, rule-oriented, authoritarian families against which their rebellion is directed, and may still be fighting their parents (like Monica). Others may have grown up in an excessively permissive atmosphere in which an early tendency to rebel was never redirected or curbed. Affairs give such people a feeling of asserting their individuality and of not letting themselves be hemmed in.

5. *The highly suggestible.* We are all suggestible to some extent. Otherwise, the advertising profession would go out of business. We are constantly exposed to newspaper accounts, movies, TV shows, plays, and books about extramarital affairs, and these can have an effect even on those of us who put up strong sales resistance. But some people are especially vulnerable to suggestion. They are easily influenced by people they meet or by what is being done in their circle. They may, for example, be persuaded that an affair is the approved thing to do, especially under such circumstances as parties, conventions, and vacations. They may be excessively willing to please others, so that they acquiesce too readily to sexual overtures or become involved with people who take advantage of them. They may have been overdirected or overprotected as children and not encouraged to think or act on their own. The resulting affairs are often spur of the moment and poorly prepared for, and may lead to unhappy consequences such as discovery or unwanted pregnancy.

6. *The excessively impulsive,* who act without much thought of consequences. As children they may have been too protected from having to take the consequences of their actions. They may be subject to temporary infatuations and fall quickly into and out of love. They may tend to be irresponsible. Their affairs are likely to follow repetitive patterns and lack enduring satisfactions.

7. *The bored and lonely.* Everyone feels bored or lonely on occasion. But some people are more susceptible to this state of mind than others. They may be individuals who, in their growing up period, did not develop wide interests or a variety of inner resources. In some cases, they may have come from families where the parents either had a narrow range

of interests or were preoccupied and didn't share much of themselves with their children. Not having developed satisfying outlets through reading, arts, crafts, sports, or the like, these people tend to grow restless when, for example, they find themselves alone for an evening, so they go looking for excitement. Many find outlets in gambling, drinking or entertainment. Some get into extramarital affairs. Such people may include bored housewives (like Daisy, Charlotte, and Monica), businessmen or businesswomen away from home (like Sydney, who found his Barbie), people who for various reasons have to live in different localities or take vacations at different times, and many others. Affairs for such people sometimes bring renewed animation and excitement into an otherwise dull existence. There are certain individuals, however, who are bored by almost any human relationship after the novelty wears off and get into the habit of constantly seeking new partners. The affairs of such people tend to be superficial and experimental, and partners are not always wisely chosen.

8. *The troubled and anxious.* All of us feel troubled and anxious at times. But some are in this emotional state habitually and almost continuously. They yearn for temporary relief from worries, responsibilities, fears, irritations, painful emotions, etc. They may be suffering from loneliness, depression, feelings of worthlessness, anger, resentment, hostility, rejection, failure, etc., or they may have a low tolerance for frustration and feel unable to cope with the responsibilities and pressures of marriage, family life, or work. The affairs are an escape—a temporary release—but may play an important part in holding the person together emotionally, as in Becky's case.

9. *The self-doubting,* who crave ego bolstering through frequent assurance that they are attractive, lovable, and sexually potent. Such doubts may arise especially in midlife, when many people worry about the aging process and fear that life is passing them by. Such self-doubt often has its origins in a pattern of put-downs and discouragement in childhood where a child gets to feel he's of little worth; such feelings can persist throughout life. The affairs of these people tend to be experimental and sometimes have a wild, desperate quality. But their affairs also may help relieve doubts and help restore their lost confidence.

10. *People who fear closeness, intimacy, and emotional involvement.* Some people seek physical relationships without strings because they can't bear the sustained intimacy that marriage or real love affairs demand, yet they want to enjoy sex with new people. In childhood they may have had unloving parents, or suffered the loss of someone they loved deeply, or been rejected by a person they loved, so that they have come to associate love and affection with pain. They tend to withdraw from any partner who shows signs of seeking emotional closeness.

11. *People with unresolved traumas and problems from childhood.* They may have experienced conflicts with parents, loss of a loved one, abandonment, family disintegration, etc. The affairs are an attempt (usually unconscious) to find a solution to these unresolved problems; the extra-

marital partner may have been chosen because he or she reminds the person of a parent or someone else in early life with whom the person still longs to relate. The resulting relationship is not a fully adult one and can involve excessive dependency or conflict between the extramarital partners.

12. *The emotionally dull and withdrawn,* who communicate poorly in the marriage, do not express much affection and are often preoccupied with outside matters such as business or sports (like Jimmy, Monica's husband). They generally are people who grew up in families where there was little demonstration of affection and poor communication of feelings. Often a person with these characteristics is so unsatisfying to his spouse that the spouse is the one more likely to have an affair (as in Monica's case); but emotionally dull people (like her husband, Jimmy) sometimes seek affairs too, in an unending search for a meaningful human relationship. The search is frequently a disappointment because the same personal characteristics that make the person's marital relationship unsatisfying are likely also to undermine the extramarital relationship. An emotionally dull, routine-oriented person is likely to feel uncomfortable in any situation where real emotional involvement, intimacy and spontaneity are expected. People like this sometimes go in for mate swapping, orgies, and other sexual adventures in which personal feelings are minimized or can be disregarded.

13. *People lacking moral or ethical values.* These are people with a poorly developed sense of right and wrong, for whom marital bonds and commitments mean little. They are unable to forego present pleasures for future satisfactions or long-term goals. They act impulsively and may have a propensity for excessive alcohol or drug use, sexual irregularities, cheating, lying, or sometimes even criminal behavior. They can turn themselves into charming, ingratiating personalities when this is what is required to get their way or to manipulate someone. When they get into trouble, they blame others. They have no close friends. They often come from homes in which they were either rejected by a parent or smothered by parental overconcern and overindulgence—sometimes both at once. Their affairs are apt to be spur of the moment, devoid of affection, and exploitive of the extramarital partner, often leaving the extramarital partner hurt and disappointed.

It may seem surprising that some people with opposite characteristics—such as the warm, friendly, and open on the one hand and the emotionally dull and withdrawn on the other—both may be inclined toward extramarital affairs, although for opposite reasons. The kinds of affairs these two types of people have, however, are poles apart in quality.

WHO ARE LEAST LIKELY TO ENGAGE IN AN EXTRAMARITAL AFFAIR?

Some of the people least likely to engage in extramarital affairs, in my view, are these:

1. *The very happily married* who love each other, feel committed to each other, find satisfaction with each other, give encouragement to each

other, and would not consider doing anything that they believe might hurt their marriage. These are people who take their marriage and its commitments seriously, enjoy living together, and work continuously to keep their relationship alive and growing. They are not thrown into panic or estrangement by temporary differences or difficulties, but strive to work them out. Their interest in affairs is much less than that of a majority of married people. However, it was pointed out earlier that affairs sometimes can happen even in happy marriages under certain circumstances; and there are sexually open marriages, like that of Kevin and Deborah, where affairs are mutually accepted and are out in the open.

2. *The devoutly religious,* who strongly believe in basic scriptural or spiritual teachings and sincerely try to live by them. Adultery to them is a forbidden practice. Here again, however, sincere religious faith may not insure against having an affair, as the Eva-Father Gordon affair shows. Love is a powerful force too, and it's not necessarily confined to the marriage.

3. *People who live by strict ethical principles* such as fidelity, commitment, truth, loyalty, and obedience. They are often devoutly religious as well. But these people have thought out their ethical positions rather than taking them from scriptural or other authority. Adultery violates a number of these principles (such as truthfulness and faithfulness to a commitment) and is therefore avoided.

4. *Conformists to conventional standards,* whose conformity is not so much to principle as to public opinion—to what neighbors and relatives and friends are likely to think. They are concerned about their reputation and image, about what "is done" and "isn't done." If public opinion about affairs changes, their views will change too.

5. *People with little interest in sex,* who for various reasons have an exceptionally low level of sexual desire (like Jack, Daisy's husband). The causes may be physical or emotional, but the absence of sexual desire makes them unlikely candidates for extramarital affairs. They may, however, be so unsatisfying to their spouses that their spouses have affairs (as in Daisy's case).

6. *The very low in self-esteem,* such as those who grew up to think of themselves as unlovable, unattractive, or ugly. They don't believe other people like them and so tend to be self-depreciating and to withdraw from social contacts. Such people often dress unbecomingly, pay little attention to their personal appearance or hygiene, and may develop unattractive or offensive mannerisms. They are not too likely to become involved in extramarital affairs.

7. *The very shy,* who feel embarrassed and awkward with people, though some cover this up successfully. They would like to feel closer but are afraid to make the initial advances. They tend to withdraw into the shelter of their own marriages, families, or small circles of friends. Even with friends they may be reserved and untouchable. They are unlikely to have extramarital affairs, although under certain conditions and stimuli,

shy people do sometimes break through the barriers they had created for themselves.

8. *The solitary,* who are not lonely but are solitary from choice. They enjoy solitary pursuits such as reading, study, writing, painting, collecting, and research. Even their sports or physical activity may be solitary: running or jogging, hiking, bicycling, swimming, body building, yoga, and the like. They may not dislike people, but they are most comfortable as loners living in a world of their own personal choice. Affairs may not attract them; they may be more interested in ideas or inanimate objects. But if they are too solitary they may neglect their spouses, and the spouses may be tempted to have affairs.

9. *The extremely dependent,* whose marital relationship is often very closed. The husband may feel dependent on his wife to take care of his physical needs, keep his house, prepare his meals, raise his children, and supply some of the emotional elements (such as warmth and affection) lacking in his own makeup. The wife may feel dependent on the husband for problem solving, decision making, and economic support. She may have few or no skills she can sell in the marketplace to support herself. Such people tend to be locked together in a marriage of mutual bondage, clinging to their marriages as shipwrecked sailors do to a lifeboat. This is an unhealthy kind of relationship because the partners are hindered from achieving their full potential and the marriage becomes almost a kind of prison. If they are helped through therapy to reduce their mutual dependence, the unsatisfying quality of their marital relationship may become apparent to them; this sometimes results in one or both having affairs.

10. *The unsociable,* who don't particularly like people and tend to keep them at a distance. They form few close relationships of any kind, in or out of marriage. Their friendships may be shallow and lack warmth. Their satisfactions come more from preoccupation with work, ideas, problems, and inanimate objects.

11. *The routine-bound,* who are most comfortable with settled routines and dislike anything that might upset the regularity of their existence (like David, Eva's husband). Extramarital affairs would disrupt their work and leisure pursuits and might interfere with their weekly tennis game and regular bridge night. These are not generally very stimulating or interesting people to live with, and sometimes the spouse of such a person longs for some new stimulation and may try an affair.

12. *The very busy and hardworking,* who are totally absorbed in their work ("workaholics") and have neither time nor energy for extramarital affairs (like Richmond, Chapter 3). They may be driven by ambition or by the work ethic, or they may use work as an escape from having to deal with people or with their own feelings of pain or inadequacy. They may be using work in the same way some people use affairs (e.g., as solace). It often happens, however, that these busy people don't have much time for the

spouse, either—a condition that may drive the spouse into an affair (as in Diane's case).

It is obvious from these "who" lists that we cannot categorize people who do not have affairs as emotionally healthy and those who have them as emotionally unhealthy, or vice versa. And it would be foolish to label the people who do not have affairs good and those who have them bad. Those are not valid or useful categories.

WHY DO PEOPLE ENGAGE IN EXTRAMARITAL AFFAIRS?

There are three major theories about why people become adulterous:

1. They are naturally *polygamous*. Monogamy, in this theory, is a social construct imposed upon human nature and in basic conflict with biological urges.

2. They are adulterous because of *personality problems* such as those arising from childhood experiences that leave them unable to form committed relationships. (Otherwise, they would be monogamous, according to this theory.)

3. They are adulterous because of the *situations* they find themselves in, such as unusual opportunities for affairs, or marriages that do not meet their desires or needs. (Otherwise, they would be monogamous, says the theory.)

Each of these theories has its advocates, but none can be convincingly demonstrated. The idea that humans are "naturally" polygamous is impossible to prove, and, in any case, is irrelevant to real life because there is no society without some social controls. The idea that personality problems are responsible for adultery is the basis for two of the myths discussed in Chapter 2 (numbers 5 and 6). Clinical experience suggests that emotional instability and other personality problems produce some affairs, but by no means all. We emphasized earlier the importance of *opportunity* as a contributing factor in affairs; but it cannot be taken to be the sole factor, as the third theory would imply. People who want affairs badly enough obviously make their own opportunities.

The complexities of human motivation make the construction of simplistic theories an academic exercise. Work with actual people shows clearly that the motivations for extramarital affairs arise from a complex blend of mental, emotional, biological, environmental, social, religious, educational, and historical factors—which is to say that no one is in a position to construct an authoritative theoretical structure that would neatly explain all extramarital affairs.

REASONS GIVEN BY PEOPLE IN AFFAIRS

Let's turn, then, to what the people in affairs actually say about why they engage in them. Some of their statements have to be taken, of course, with a grain of salt. Many, obviously, are excuses or rationalizations. Some people attempt to put the blame on others, especially the spouse. Some argue that the affair was really an accident. (Yet we know that no affair is an accident.)

The motivations for beginning an affair are often quite different from those that keep the affair going after it has started. For example, an affair may begin as a seemingly casual dalliance, as Sydney's did with his associate, Barbie, and Frank's did with Norene—maybe as a temporary relaxation from business tensions. But so-called casualness is an illusion: No affair is casual. And the waves even a one-night stand may set in motion can travel far and wide. What looks like a purely sexual contact can be much more. Many extramarital sexual experiences, even brief ones, involve positive qualities such as sensitivity, support, warmth, mutuality, respect, and consideration—that enrich a human relationship.

The reasons people give for their affairs generally fall under four headings: (1) their personal patterns of feelings and reactions, i.e., how they feel about themselves and about events in their lives, and how they tend to respond; (2) dissatisfaction with their marriages; (3) frustration with their family life; and (4) the special attraction of their extramarital partners.

1. *Reasons relating to personal patterns of feelings and reactions.* These are reasons that are closely related to the personality types listed earlier in the section *Who Are Most Likely to Engage in Extramarital Affairs?* To list many of the reasons people give (like "I love the excitement and adventure of an affair") would be to duplicate much of that material. But some of the variations on this recipe add to the flavor. Said one woman, "It's exciting to delight, charm, fascinate, and captivate someone." (She might have added, "And to be delighted, charmed, fascinated, and captivated.") Some get a thrill out of making new conquests. Some enjoy the risks that an affair involves; the danger of discovery is part of the fun.

Warm, friendly, open people sometimes have affairs simply because they are warm, friendly, and open. But we get a closer glimpse of the reactions of some of them when they report the "wonderful feeling of being desired, loved, held, stroked, and cuddled." An affair helps people like this to feel happy and alive. Some long to feel close and intimate with another person with a continually growing depth of understanding and companionship.

Strongly sexual people (another category) are not always forthright about admitting that sex is what primarily draws them into affairs. Yet some are quite frank about it. ("It's fascinating and great fun to feel a new body with its structural and tactile differences . . . and its unpredictable reactions. I never tire of this.") Probably some of the people who give other reasons for going into affairs have a similar feeling but do not admit it. Some people say the reason they engage in extramarital sex is that they enjoyed a variety of sex partners before they married and don't want to give that up.

Other personality types, of those discussed, give the kinds of reasons one might expect; I will not explore them separately here. These include the rebellious and self-willed; the highly suggestible; the excessively impulsive ("I just don't know how it happened"); the bored and lonely; the troubled and anxious; the self-doubting; the people who fear closeness, intimacy, and emotional involvement; the people with unresolved problems and traumas from childhood; the emotionally dull and withdrawn; and people lacking moral and ethical values. What these people say about why they went into affairs does not add much to what we already know about them.

The self-doubting are an important group. Their drive is to recover some lost self-esteem and sense of personhood. Among them are the people in midlife referred to earlier who are wondering if they still possess the power to attract a person of the opposite sex. Some of them say they want a last fling before they lose their youth and looks. There are also people for whom an extramarital affair is a challenge; they have to prove they can do it. Or they need to convince themselves they are not prudes or squares. Some fear they might be homosexual and seek an affair to prove they are not.

A variety of other motivations also emerge. Some people have affairs because of curiosity to know what an affair is like. Some maintain that an affair helps them be better people, less frustrated, easier to live with. ("If I hadn't had an affair, I think I would have taken it out on somebody.") These people claim the broadened experience helps them grow as persons. And finally, there are those who insist their affair was entirely unintentional and blame circumstances or the easy availability of extramarital partners.

2. *Reasons relating to dissatisfaction with the marriage.* In comment after comment, it is implied that the relationship with the extramarital partner offers something the marriage does not. The question keeps recurring: Why does marriage offer so much less than many people want? Or, put in another way, why are so many people dissatisfied with what marriage *does* offer? And even more basic, why can't marriage supply the satisfactions that some people now get from extramarital affairs? We've suggested some answers already, but now we will examine how these questions are viewed by the people in affairs.

A number of them (some of whom we have met earlier) report that their marriage is dull and boring. ("I love to go out but my spouse just wants to look at TV.") They consider their relationship with their spouse humdrum. Others feel "smothered and hemmed in" by their marriage and want to be with "more interesting, stimulating people." Some say they can't talk to their spouse; they look for someone they can talk to who would understand them. Some say their spouse is so preoccupied with business (or a career or sports or the children) that they feel like outsiders. ("He/she is always too tired or busy.") Some of them say they don't get much love, affection, or sex at home and look for it outside. A common report is "We don't love each other any more." Some say of their marriage, "We are drifting apart, have increasingly different interests and friends, and no longer enjoy the same things." Said one, "My spouse has changed and is no longer the person I married." Said another, "I'm changing and becoming a new person myself, but my spouse just wants to stay in the old groove."

Some comments reflect strong hostility, feelings of rejection, or dislike of the spouse. Words like "selfish," "inconsiderate," and "a slob" are used. Some individuals are angry because the spouse doesn't fit their idea of what a good wife or good husband should be. ("My wife is a poor house-keeper and a lousy cook." Or, "My husband never helps around the house. He expects me to do all the work.") Some say the spouse drinks too much, gambles, takes drugs, or has some other bad habit. Some say their affair was intended to shake up the spouse and make him/her "straighten out," or that they wanted to break up the marriage. And some are having an affair as retaliation for a spouse's affair. A number of these complaints boil down to: "I want out of the marriage." And some say, "I didn't want to have an affair, but my spouse pushed me into one," and then add, "I'll bet he wanted an excuse to have one himself."

A number of comments blame the marital relationship for the affair rather than the spouse as a person. A common remark is, "I didn't know marriage would be like this." The problems and responsibilities of marriage seem too much for some individuals, and they seek a relationship free of such burdens. Some affairs are attributed to frequent absences of the marital partners for extended periods. Some individuals have an affair to escape the constant arguing and hassling at home. Some say, "My spouse and I just can't get along." And then there is the very common complaint, "My marriage doesn't satisfy me emotionally or sexually." This includes cases where the marriage is fairly good, but not considered good enough as was discussed earlier. Many of these people have an affair to supplement their marriage and contend that the affair enables them to remain in the marriage.

3. *Reasons relating to frustration with family life.* Frustration with family life is not quite the same as frustration with the marriage. It has more to do with the burdens, the restricted life of a mother of young children, the demands on a husband, the responsibilities, the noise and confusion, the financial strains, the endless work as some parents see it. One significant note here is that the extramarital affair begins to emerge as an alternative to divorce. I hear comments like: "I need to get away sometimes. Life at home is such a hassle." Or, "My kids drive me up the wall! I have to escape where I don't hear 'Mommy this,' 'Mommy that' all day." Or, "I get so tired of no one to talk to but the children."

I also hear comments like: "Without the relief affairs give me, I'd be a lousy parent and a poor marital partner. I'd be like a cat tied by the tail." "Affairs make it possible to continue our marriage. I can't afford divorce and I don't think I could raise the children alone." And, "I think my affairs do less harm to the children than a divorce would. Children need both a father and a mother."

There is not quite the antagonism expressed here that is so

obvious in some of the complaints about the marriage and the spouse. None of these comments say, "I hate my family." No doubt many people would be ashamed to admit such a feeling even if it were true.

4. *Reasons relating to the special attraction of the extramarital partner.* What follows could be called the "pull" reasons—the pull of the extramarital partner—as contrasted with the "push" reasons: the dissatisfactions with marriage or family life. Both, of course, operate at the same time in many affairs. But the emphasis can shift. An affair originally begun because of dissatisfaction with the the marital or family situation can move toward a love affair. The attraction of the extramarital partner then may become a sufficient reason by itself.

The extramarital partner is often seen and experienced as a very special person ("He/she is warm and wonderful. We love being together." Or, "We are great companions. We stimulate each other, and we like the same things." Or, "He/she makes me feel I'm attractive, exciting, intelligent, and sexually alive." Or, "I'm much more comfortable with him/her than with my spouse." Or, "We are in love.") Many report better communication than in the marriage. ("We understand each other. We can share with each other our feelings and experiences. We can be open and honest.") Sex is often more varied and exciting than with the spouse, and there is fascination with physical, intellectual, emotional, and social differences. Some people report solace in an affair. ("We both have a lot of troubles and are a comfort to each other.") Some feel that their extramarital partner has virtually rescued them from depression and despair.

Some individuals report that their affair developed originally out of work the extramarital partners were doing together, and feel that working together provides a valuable element of mutuality in a relationship. But others report that an affair interferes with working together and say that, because of this interference, they had to break it off. Some people in affairs feel that the relationship they have with the extramarital partner is much healthier than the one they have with their spouse. Some say they love both the extramarital partner and the spouse and do not want to hurt or give up either.

But there are also people who exploit the extramarital partner, are dazzled by the partner's wealth or importance, and are thrilled by being taken to glamorous places and given expensive gifts. Some women, for example, are attracted to prominent political figures, and some people of either sex are drawn to individuals in the entertainment world. Some claim that the extramarital partner enticed them into the affair.

In certain cases, the extramarital relationship is a homosexual one that an individual is pursuing to supplement his or her marriage. ("I want both kinds of sex.")

These statements help us understand and appreciate the enormous variety of reasons why affairs occur.

SELDOM ACKNOWLEDGED MOTIVATIONS FOR AFFAIRS

The preceding four sets of reasons spread out a virtual panorama of the human condition in the area of couple relationships. There's hardly one of us, whether engaged in an affair or not, who could not have made some of these comments at one time or another. Yet often, behind these relatively surface reasons, are deeper ones of which the individuals themselves may not be aware. Or if they are aware, they may be reluctant to speak of them. Frequently they emerge as a result of insights developed through therapy and come out indirectly through dreams, slips of speech, clinical hypnosis, and in other ways.

I have divided these seldom-acknowledged motivations into two categories: those arising from personal patterns of feelings and reactions, and those arising from dissatisfaction with marriage and/or family life. Many people are, at first, not consciously aware of these reasons; discovery of them can come as a shock.

1. *Seldom acknowledged reasons arising from personal patterns of feelings and reactions.* These are reasons or inner drives, often deeply buried, that reflect the ways in which people react to the circumstances of their lives. They have great variety because the psychological-emotional patterns of people are so diverse. Some are as follows:

Certain people have a low self-concept and need the frequent reassurance of others (such as in an affair) to convince them they are lovable or worthwhile. Some never had enough affection shown them as children and still experience the child's deep longing to be touched, caressed, held, hugged, and kissed. Some feel superfluous in their everyday roles and have an excessive desire to feel needed and wanted. ("It feels so good when a person dares take great risks just to be with me. Then I *know* I'm loved and wanted.") Some pursue sex for itself—its excitement and physical pleasure—and don't much care with whom they have it; but they refuse to admit their promiscuity to themselves. Some, without realizing it, keep their extramarital partners at emotional arm's length because of fear of emotional involvement, and find an excuse to break a relationship that threatens to get too close or intimate. Some have affairs to escape the responsibilities of marriage and family life, but do not recognize this as the true reason.

Some use an affair to gain temporary relief from such feelings as worthlessness, abandonment, chronic anxiety, depression, boredom, restlessness, inadequacy, anger, resentment, frustration, shyness, excessive irritability, failure, unhappiness, etc., but they do not recognize consciously what they are doing. Some, because of weak egos and unrecognized feelings of helplessness, have an urge to dominate and exert power over other people and use affairs for that purpose. When combined with sadistic, masochistic, or paranoid urges, such dominance seeking can be very damaging. Some use affairs to express arrogant, vengeful feelings for which they have few other outlets. Some have deep-seated sexual conflicts such as excessive preoccupation with sex and pornography, fascination with kinky sex, a compulsion to have many sex partners, or an unhealthy infatuation with much younger or much older people.

It is common in affairs for people to use the affair to work out, at an unconscious level, traumas or problems carried over from childhood and never resolved. We have seen how an affair is sometimes used as a way of defying parents with whom the person was in serious conflict (as in Monica's case). We have discussed how an affair may be an attempt to relive the past with an old love, a parent, a sibling, or someone long gone. Or an affair may be a living out of bad childhood memories of marriage and family life. An affair, for some, may be an unadmitted attack on all social order and authority, just as a frustrated child may flail about him with his fists. Or an affair may reflect a feeling that "I have a right to do as I please." Some people have affairs because they are excessively suggestible, but do not realize that this is so. Some have lost the capacity to get joy or pleasure out of anything and look to an affair to recover what they have lost.

2. *Seldom-acknowledged reasons arising from dissatisfaction with marriage and family life.* These reveal much about the "underside" of marriage and family-life. Few married persons are ready to admit that they probably got married in a fit of what Lederer calls "temporary insanity." They try to think up justifications for an act that, deep down, they know was idiotic. Few admit that they were persuaded or coerced by social, religious, and family pressures into a marriage they really did not want. Few admit that they made a bad choice of spouse, or that they married for the wrong reasons (e.g., money, social position, pretty face, attractive body, athletic prowess, etc.). Few admit that they never loved their spouse. (They like to pretend they once did, even if they do not now.) Still fewer want to admit that they never wanted children or don't like children, although their actions and words make this obvious. Not many people want to acknowledge that the failure of their marriage was, to a large extent, their own doing. And people run away in panic from facing the fact that they actually hate their spouse and are using an affair to hurt him or her.

Living in a world of illusion and fantasy is often easier than struggling with the real world; hence, people deceive themselves. But it is not only their weaknesses, foolishness, and faults that they flee from admitting. Many also refuse to acknowledge their own good qualities and the values and strengths that exist in their relationships. Their marriage may not be as hopeless as they think or feel it is. Possibilities of improving, enriching, or rebuilding it may be much greater than they imagine. They may underestimate their spouse's capacity to respond to new initiatives. The spouse may have greater flexibility and capacity for personal growth than they have believed. They may be better people themselves than they think they are; low self-esteem is a widespread curse. Their extramarital affairs may not be as wicked as they think or as damaging to the marriage as they assume. Even their fondness for sex may not be quite as shameful as they have been taught to believe.

WHY PEOPLE CHOOSE NOT TO HAVE EXTRAMARITAL AFFAIRS

Many people choose *not* to have extramarital affairs even though opportunities are plentiful. What holds them back? Many of the reasons are evident in the discussion of personality types in the section *Who Are Least Likely to Engage in Extramarital Affairs?* The happily married, for example, have a clear reason for not engaging. Said one, "I am a one-to-one person and so is my spouse. I love my spouse and have no desire for anyone else." Said another, "I feel my marriage gives me more than I could ever hope to get from an affair. I believe that true love deepens with each passing year." Devoutly religious people and people devoted to ethical principles may have clear-cut reasons, also. One said, "I would feel guilty and ashamed to engage in an affair. It would undermine my good feelings about myself." A father said, "I want to serve as a good example for my children. I don't want my children brought up in an atmosphere of deception and infidelity."

Some refrain from affairs because of the risks and problems involved. Said one, "My marriage is very important to me and I feel too much is at stake to take chances with it." Said another, "I couldn't live with the anxiety, lying, cheating, maneuvering, and sneaking around that would be involved in an affair. I would hate the feelings an affair would arouse." Some people fear they could not keep an affair secret and dread what would happen if it were discovered. Some dislike the idea of multiple relationships with the possibility of jealousies, rivalries, hostilities, and suspicions. Some fear falling in love with (or being loved by) an extramarital partner and the complications this could cause. Some are afraid they could not make a good sex-love relationship with anyone other than the spouse. One said, "I'd be simply too embarrassed even to talk about an affair with a person of the opposite sex."

Other reasons mentioned by people include not wanting to spend the time, energy, or money an affair would demand. Some people are too busy. Some are just not interested. And some fear venereal disease or possible pregnancy.

GOING IN BLINDFOLDED

If people enter marriage blindfolded, as Lederer argues that many do, how equally blindly do people go into affairs? Few are prepared in advance to deal with the negative or even positive consequences of affairs. Only those with previous experience are likely to enter them with their eyes open. People too often let themselves be drawn in, moved by feelings they neither fully understand nor are equipped by experience to handle successfully. They are likely to bungle their affairs as they bungled their marriages, and for many of the same reasons. For both are human relationships; if a person is clumsy at one, he's probably clumsy at the other unless he learns from the experience and allows himself to change. Even people of mature years sometimes don't face up to the fact that they are about to have an affair and that a mishandled affair is capable of brewing a storm that could blow up their marriages and perhaps injure their careers as well. Their plight seems not unlike that of hapless teenagers who engage in sexual intercourse without contraceptives, not because they are ignorant of biological processes, but because neither participant wants to admit they are about to do the forbidden. So they do it anyway and the girl gets pregnant. Most married adults know how to avoid pregnancy, but how to avoid emotional turmoil, marital disruption, and other possible effects of affairs is another matter. That's why coping with affairs becomes a major issue to which we will devote attention in later chapters.

8. *No Two Alike*

. . . It is like playing God. I feel as if I am holding a life in each hand—in one hand is my wife and in the other is the other woman, and the decision is mine. No matter what I do, someone will be hurt—including myself. The past several months have been nothing short of torment—and that, I feel, is only a prelude of things to come.
    Randy

THE VARIETY OF AFFAIRS

Randy is despairing. He is torn apart by his affair. But another person describes her affair as "a rejuvenation of feelings buried since adolescence." And a third writes unblushingly, "I'm doing it because it's fun, it feels damn good—and I like being involved in other people's lives." Yet all these contrasting feelings could exist at different times in the same individual, or even be felt simultaneously. Affairs can produce the whole gamut of emotions of which the human being is capable.

But because people are different, the way these feelings combine is different in every case. This leads to a bewildering variety of kinds of extramarital affairs: simple one-to-one, multiple one-to-one, group sex; secret versus consensual; short-, moderate-, and long-term; heterosexual, homosexual, bisexual, and nonsexual; marrieds with singles and marrieds with marrieds. Within each of these broad categories there is an immense variety, depending on the emotional and other motivations that underlie the affairs.

Some extramarital affairs herald the breakup of a marriage. Some are only incidental to the marriage. Some supplement it, compensate for its defects, or even strengthen it. If you are in an affair or if you suspect or discover your spouse to be in an affair, it can be very helpful to know which kind it is and to understand what it means.

The reactions an affair arouses in the people affected are often a much greater danger to the marriage than the affair itself; for a marriage, in many cases, can survive an affair or even thrive in spite of affairs. But can it survive the emotional disruption that an affair can trigger? Or the interference of parents and in-laws?

A person discovering a spouse's affair needn't assume that the marriage is doomed. Rather, an affair often calls attention to something that needs to be done to help a troubled spouse or to revitalize and enrich a dull or failing marriage.

ONE-TO-ONE AFFAIRS

There are some fourteen basic types of one-to-one affairs that I repeatedly run across in my practice. Each type involves a somewhat different kind of person and affects marriage in a somewhat different way. While any of these might challenge a marriage, the type likely to pose the most direct threat is the fully developed love affair, because it sets up a serious long-term rival for the partner's affection. But even a true love affair may not necessarily destroy the marriage, for various reasons that we'll examine.

The fourteen types of affairs fall into two groups. The first nine are what I call *relationship affairs;* they grow out of a developing relationship between the extramarital partners. The relationship may have come about because of an unsatisfactory marriage, but it is primarily the attraction between two people that leads into the affair and keeps it going.

A particular affair may have the characteristics of more than one type, or may evolve from one type to another. But thinking in terms of types can help overcome the false belief that all affairs are alike and equally challenging to a marriage.

1. *Fully developed love affairs* (e.g., Eva-Father Gordon; Diane-Andy; Sydney-Barbie). When this kind of affair develops, the marriage may be in real trouble. The spouse is threatened by a rival. But not every affair is like this, for not everyone is ready for a deep love commitment or wants one. To engage in a full love affair involves an awareness of one's feelings; a fondness for warm, intimate human relationships; a strong desire to love and be loved; a willingness to give of one's self and to accept the demands that love makes and to take its risks. These are characteristics of a loving person—one who, if the marital relationship supplied enough affection and love, could be a faithful husband or wife; but who, if the marriage doesn't supply it, may transfer his or her affection to an extramarital partner. A fully ripened love affair might, of course, lead to a breakup of the marriage and to the extramarital partners living together or marrying each other. But that's not inevitable. It also may happen that the affair supplies the love and affection the person is not getting in the marriage and thus makes continuance of the marriage possible. The person in the affair may choose to stay in the marriage because of children, affection for the spouse, or for economic or social reasons, etc.

2. *Infatuations*—short-lived passions. ("I'm crazy about so-and-so.") These affairs occur most often with people easily attracted to someone of the opposite sex. They seek attention and enjoy the feeling of being wanted and adored, but do not desire (and may not be capable of) deep emotional ties or long-term involvement. Emotionally, such affairs are not unlike the crushes adolescents have. The same qualities that make these people unfaithful to a spouse are likely also to limit the depth and permanence of their extramarital relationship. An infatuation at its peak can be a threat to a marriage, but since it is apt to be a temporary con-

dition, the marriage has a good chance of outlasting it. However, infatuations can become a repetitive pattern with some people, and a succession of such affairs can severely strain the marriage.

3. *Affairs mainly for sex* (e.g., Daisy-Fred and Monica-Slim). Most affairs are sexual, but these affairs exist *primarily* for sex. Some people, of course, engage in them simply for fun and physical satisfaction—an evening of pleasure. Others rebel against parental upbringing or authority and convention and have strong sexual urges and few inhibitions. Also, there are people unsure of their sexual capacities who want to test themselves with someone other than the spouse. Or, in still other cases, the habit of a variety of sexual partners had been established before marriage and is continued thereafter. Such affairs are frequently a result of neglect by a preoccupied or sexually unresponsive spouse. They are not necessarily incompatible with marriage. By becoming a more loving person and a better sex partner, the spouse might reduce the other's desire for an affair.

4. *Fun-and-adventure affairs,* including flings and one-nighters (e.g., Deborah's two affairs before her marriage with Kevin became sexually open). These are apt to be lighthearted and usually short-lived. The affairs are more a product of the situation people find themselves in than of a particular psychological type, although fun-loving, easygoing, gregarious people may be more likely to have such flings than withdrawn, rigid, or hostile individuals. Affairs of this type often take place at resorts, or during or after parties, or while traveling. They may be very sexual, but their main motivation (at least in the beginning) is to have an adventure. If the affair is not long continued, a marriage will likely survive it.

5. *Affairs incidental to business or other relationships* (e.g., the Frank-Norene affair, which broke a "perfect" marriage). These affairs occur in business, professional groups, clubs, churches, relationships between professionals and their clients, teacher-pupil relationships, and many other situations where people of opposite sex are closely associated in their work, social life, or recreation. Such affairs are not limited to any particular type of person, although warm, outgoing, gregarious people are more likely to get into them than cold, withdrawn, rigid, or hostile ones. Attraction and propinquity bring on the affair; but the affair is likely, if it persists, to move toward one of the other types. These affairs are not necessarily incompatible with marriage, but sometimes they develop into full love affairs, which can be threatening.

6. *Friendships and mutual interest affairs* (e.g., Henrietta). These are intimate, qualitative friendships. Although they may include sexual relations, sex is not a primary reason for the relationship. Such affairs are often based on a mutual interest such as music, art, politics, church work, outdoor sports, etc. The mutual interest draws the people together, and the pleasure they get in sharing this interest may result in their becoming very close. An example might be two people who love to play music together and meet frequently for this purpose. Such an affair may threaten a marriage because the spouse feels left out; or it may supplement a marriage

by supplying an element lacking in it (as when one spouse loves, say, dancing, and the other does not). This can even preserve a marriage that might otherwise fail. A less qualitative kind of "friendship affair" occurs in certain social circles (as in some sections of the counterculture) where having an affair is part of the social scene, like smoking pot.

7. *Companionship affairs* to assuage loneliness and keep in touch with people (e.g., Henrietta). The people who get into these affairs are not usually ones whose loneliness is due to psychological withdrawal, but rather people whose life situation has isolated them in some way (e.g., as a result of prolonged separation from a spouse or a move to a new location) and who are unwilling to accept solitude or sexual continence for very long. Such an affair may be a result of neglect by a preoccupied or absent spouse. They are not necessarily incompatible with marriage. By paying more attention to his partner, the spouse might reduce the other's desire for an affair.

8. *Affairs to relive a relationship from the past.* The driving force for these affairs is an unresolved problem of relationship with a parent, sibling, or other close person, usually having its origin in childhood. We have noted earlier how a person may be drawn to someone who reminds him or her of a parent or sibling, producing a mother-son, father-daughter, or sibling type of relationship in the extramarital affair. Affairs where the partners have wide age differences are especially apt to be of this type.

9. *Compulsive and pathological affairs.* Some people, like the Dr. Jensen referred to later in this chapter, have a compulsion to have sex with many constantly changing partners. Others may engage in sadomasochistic practices in which receiving and inflicting physical pain heightens the sexual enjoyment. These are pathological conditions calling for treatment.

All the above come under the heading of *relationship affairs.* The next five types I call *reactive affairs* because, instead of arising from a relationship between the extramarital partners, they occur originally as a reaction to a crisis, a quarrel, or an unhappy situation in the marriage. They may subsequently change into relationship affairs as the extramarital partners develop a closer relationship. The escape-and-solace affair and the restorative affair are especially prone to turn into relationship affairs, the latter sometimes becoming full love affairs. Reactive affairs are often symptoms of an already troubled marriage.

10. *Affairs resulting from exasperation with an unsatisfying marital situation* (e.g., Charlotte and her rock singer). The people who engage in these affairs are often ones whose value systems would ordinarily keep them faithful, and who resort to affairs only because of provocation by an insensitive, unaware, or indifferent spouse. The marriage is threatened if the spouse remains insensitive, unaware, or indifferent; but if the spouse reacts more positively and seeks to understand, an affair is less likely to occur.

11. *Affairs undertaken in anger or revenge.* These are cases where the affair is a reaction to something the spouse did (such as having an affair) and is intended to inflict pain and arouse anger. The people who engage in such affairs may have a pattern of harboring hostile, unforgiving, or vengeful

feelings; or may act suddenly on impulse; or may simply be driven almost out of their minds by a difficult marital situation. This kind of affair may take the form of going to bed with a stranger, or with a person of different social status or race, or with someone hated (or loved) by the spouse. It may be deliberately initiated in order to break the marriage or to force a major change in it.

12. *Affairs to gain power or advantage.* Some individuals seek power over others and use an affair as a device to gain it. One form of this is to try to force some kind of change in the spouse. ("If you don't do such-and-such or stop doing such-and-such, I'll go out with somebody else.") Some use an affair for sexual or other exploitation of the extramarital partner or even for blackmail. Violence can result. Both the extramarital partner and the spouse may be victims. There was a hint of this in Slim's relationship with Monica, which came to light when she showed signs of wanting to end the affair.

13. *Escape-and-solace affairs* occur to escape from family or business pressures, or to offset a miserable personal situation or feelings of depression, etc. (e.g., Becky). The people in these affairs often feel harried, frustrated, troubled, and miserable, but they are also people who are open enough to share their feelings with others—in many cases with the extramarital partner. Closed people, on the other hand, tend to keep their feelings and troubles bottled up. These affairs are not necessarily incompatible with marriage. If the partners worked to improve their marital relationship, the desire for this kind of affair would diminish.

14. *Restorative affairs* seek to overcome dullness and boredom and recover emotional vitality missing in day-to-day life. Some people turn to this kind of affair in midlife, when they feel their youth slipping away and wonder about their ability to attract someone of the opposite sex. Such self-doubt can afflict almost anybody, but the kind of person most apt to translate it into an affair is a gregarious person unwilling to settle for boredom who looks outside the marriage for a new, refreshing, stimulating experience. Often this kind of affair revitalizes an individual and enhances personal growth by drawing the individual out of a condition of stagnation. This might help a marriage if the spouse can accept the situation or does not know of the affair. But there is also the possibility of the affair developing into a full love affair.

Any of these types of affairs may be either secret or known to the spouse, may be either with married or with unmarried partners, and may be either heterosexual or homosexual. Some, like the fully developed love affair, tend to be long-term. Some, like the infatuation and the fun-and-adventure affair, are usually short-term.

HOW DO PEOPLE MEET AND AFFAIRS START?

Before an extramarital affair can begin, people have to meet. Merely smiling and saying hello isn't meeting—it's only a ritual. Our modern world combines unprecedented mixing of the sexes with unprecedented loneliness and emotional isolation.

Clearly it takes more than surface contacts to produce a qualitative affair. It takes an interest in people, a willingness to open up, to risk rejection, to talk, to listen, to feel, to wonder, to respond with warmth and affection. These are all *healthy* qualities; each is a characteristic needed for a good marriage. So the dilemma we face is that some of the qualities that make for a good marriage are the same as the qualities that make affairs possible. Conversely, the remote, cool, withdrawn, extremely private individuals (like Francine, Sydney's wife) are not likely to get close enough to anybody to have an affair. But this kind of person also may have difficulty holding a spouse.

A situation where many people meet is the workplace. Co-workers are apt to have a common interest, a legitimate reason to be together, and may get to know each other very well—sometimes better than spouses do. The work situation also offers a convenient cover for an affair ("I have to work overtime tonight, honey." Or, "All next week I'll be at a conference in Denver.")

Many affairs are with social acquaintances who have met at parties, banquets, dances, or other gatherings. We noted one affair (Daisy's) that was with a spouse's best friend—a not unusual situation, for best friends are apt to have mixed socially with spouses over a period of time. Two affairs (Becky's and the Monica-Slim affair) were with neighbors. Some affairs are with former boyfriends or girl friends, or even with former spouses—for although a previous marriage may have broken up, the emotional and sexual attractions may remain.

There are also many other situations in which people become close enough to have affairs. Physicians sometimes have affairs with patients, lawyers with clients, teachers and professors with students, and students with each other. Professional associations and clubs bring together men and women of parallel interests; this is becoming increasingly true as women enter jobs, professions, schools, and clubs previously reserved to men. The increased participation of women in sports such as jogging, golf, tennis, and swimming provides still further opportunities for meeting. In addition, there is that most ancient institution through which, for generations, men and women have met one another: the church. Many churches have choir, theater, and couples' groups. The Eva-Father Gordon affair, coming about through mutual interest in church work, is far from unique. Affairs occur between residents in boardinghouses and apartments and even in senior citizens' homes. And finally there are affairs with strangers encountered in restaurants, planes, trains, hotels, and resorts.

It has to be acknowledged that in a society where men and women mix in great numbers in almost every aspect of their lives, some connections that are *more than friendships* are bound to occur. This unquestionably is a challenge to marriage. Can marriage adapt itself to this fact of modern life? As a woman with considerable experience in extramarital affairs put it to me: "There are some very exciting people around, and if your inner rules of conduct permit you to have affairs or if you have a sexually open marriage, the *people themselves* become the primary motivating factor." Sometimes an affair blossoms suddenly between people who have known each other for a long time, but not in the capacity of lovers. Sometimes an affair develops quickly between individuals who have only recently met (as with Diane and Andy, who met at a party and were in a passionate affair within a week).

HOW DO FRIENDSHIPS BECOME AFFAIRS?

Many extramarital affairs start out as simple friendships or working associations that, in some way not always understood, cross a boundary (usually sexual) to become *more than friendships.* How does this happen? Is it an accident? Or does it happen by design?

I've referred to the reluctance of many people, especially in a first affair, to crossing the sexual barrier, and to the irrevocability of that action. When it happens, the relationship takes on a new character. This fact may cause us to hang back, particularly if it's a friendship we prize. But the pressures toward sexual involvement can be great.

"I didn't know I was going to spend a night with Barbie," Sydney said. "I didn't want to cheat on Francine. I consider myself an honorable man. But I found myself wanting Barbie terribly, and I discovered that she wanted me. We looked into each other's eyes one evening over our scotch and sodas and an instant knowledge passed between us. Without our saying a word, we both knew it was going to happen. And it did—that night. But I also know we both were ready for it. There was a kind of inevitability about it. Somewhere deep inside us we had made up our minds." He sighed. "After that night, we couldn't stay apart."

Monica said of her first meeting with Slim: "I didn't start off with any idea of a sexual relationship. It's just that Slim aroused my interest and curiosity—I'd never met anyone like him. He reminded me of one of those villains in an old-time silent movie—the kind that was always trying to take advantage of the heroine. Looking back, I realize I was fully ripe for an affair—but at the time I didn't consciously recognize it. When Slim began pressing me for sex, I played games with him, holding sex just out of reach but teasing him with it. I knew this was just a game, and *he* knew it was, and the end was a foregone conclusion."

Not everyone, of course, plays games in their affairs. Eva and Father Gordon did not. They were fully open with each other.

When people say "It happened by accident," they show simply that they are unaware of the inner processes going on within them. An affair comes about because at some level, conscious or unconscious, the people involved *want* it to happen. Human behavior is purposive. Consider Deborah's experience early in her marriage. She went to the shore without her husband (who had called off their date because of business pressure), met an old flame she had known before she was married, and spent an evening talking over old times. "By the end of the evening," Deborah said, "we were both turned on and didn't want to separate. As a joke, Vern said, 'I wonder what you'd be like in bed.' And as a joke, I replied, 'There's only one way to find out.' So we kidded and laughed and spent the night together. Only these quips weren't jokes. We pretended they were but we both knew they weren't. We wanted each other that night. We were inseparable for the rest of the week. Then we drew a curtain over the entire episode and returned to our spouses. We knew we had to cut it off dead or we'd both be in trouble.

"I admit this wasn't an accident," Deborah mused. "Running into Vern was an accident, of course. But having the affair with him was not. I'd had a soft spot for Vern ever since college days, and if circumstances had been a little different I might have married him. Our little affair was a kind of finishing up of something we had once begun but left dangling. It was great to be with him again. But neither of us wanted to disrupt our marriages."

A person who doesn't want a friendship to turn into an affair can handle the matter forthrightly, as a married patient of mine did. "He wanted me to have sex with him," she said. "I simply said, 'Look, Billie, I prize your friendship but I prize my marriage, too. If you want to be just friends, fine. If you want sex, go after somebody else.' We're very good friends now, and he's stopped trying to entice me into an affair. There's no reason why an intimate friendship between a man and a woman need go the sexual route."

MARRIED-MARRIED VERSUS MARRIED-SINGLE AFFAIRS

A great many intimate friendships, nevertheless, do go the sexual route. Consider affairs between extramarital partners *both* of whom are married. These affairs are not quite the same as ones between a married and an unmarried partner. The atmosphere tends to be different. An affair between two married persons is faced with the fact that two spouses (and perhaps families) are in the background instead of one; this, among other things, complicates the problem of getting together in secret and of finding ways to take time off without arousing the suspicion of one or the other spouse or a family member. There is not only increased risk of detection when both are married, but also a greater possibility of trouble and pain if the affair is discovered. Two marriages may hang in the balance instead of one. In this kind of affair, there may be greater fear of discovery because more is at stake. The extramarital partners are, in a sense, members of the same club—marriage—and are therefore coconspirators in a special way. They may also be on a more equal basis with respect to their age and life experiences.

In contrast, a single partner in an affair is often younger than the married one and may be of a different generation, although there is a wide variation in these situations. The unmarried partner is likely to be more available than the married one and may, too, have a place of his or her own where the pair can meet with minimum danger of discovery. Sometimes an unmarried partner presses for an exclusive relationship in the affair, which could only be achieved at the cost of the other's marriage.

FIRST AND SUBSEQUENT AFFAIRS

Of the twenty-five extramarital affairs (or sets of affairs) described in detail in this book, about half were *first and only* affairs. Seven persons had two affairs each and five had more than two. It is hard to say how typical this is of the general population.

In none of these cases, except that of Dr. Jensen, whom we will meet shortly, was more than one affair being carried on at a time. The popular picture of extramarital affairs as a promiscuous activity is not borne out by most case studies in my files. Affairs, with the exception of some one-nighters, are not usually gone into lightly; and when an affair takes place, it is more likely than not to be the only affair the person is engaging in at that time, and often the only one ever.

A first affair generally has somewhat different characteristics than a second or subsequent one by the same person. Many people are more reluctant to enter upon a first affair. But once they do, it can be tremendously exciting and lead rather quickly to infatuation or love. It also can lead to a greater inner conflict than a later affair; the guilt may be more keenly felt. So may be the frustration at not being able to meet easily or often. The extramarital partners, after the crumbling of the sex barrier, may become so entranced with each other that they want to meet constantly, which is generally impossible. This emotional intensity may keep the relationship on a high for a considerable time. Or it may undermine the relationship, especially if felt more by one than by the other.

In my work with people in affairs, I find that the likelihood of a second affair is influenced by two major factors: (1) whether the first affair was basically a positive or negative experience; and (2) whether the personal, marital, or other conditions that led to the first affair remain the same, have improved, or have deteriorated. If this formula is valid, then a person who has had a very positive experience in the first affair and is experiencing a deteriorating marriage may very possibly have a second affair. On the other hand, a person who has had a disappointing first affair and is experiencing improved satisfaction in the marriage is much less likely to have a second affair.

When a second affair is undertaken, there may be fewer extravagant expectations than in the first. And it is entered upon with less trepidation. People experienced in affairs seem to recognize each other and come together with more conscious awareness of the forces working upon and between them. The sexual barrier is easier to surmount and sexual relations are less inhibited. The emotional involvement, on the other hand, may be less intense than in a first affair. The person experienced in affairs may try to avoid deep love entanglements, feeling that they endanger the marriage too much and may bring too much pain when the affair ends. Yet these affairs are not unemotional by any means, nor are they exclusively sexual. It is simply that the more experienced person in affairs is less likely to be completely carried away.

FREQUENCY OF MEETING

One of the frustrations for people in affairs is the difficulty of getting together as often as they'd like. If they meet frequently, such as more than once a week, their difficulties multiply and the risk of discovery grows. Very frequent meetings can lead to early satiation and an end of the affair, as happened with Monica and Slim, who saw each other almost daily for some time (made possible by the disinterest of Monica's husband). Monica got too big a dose of Slim. Too frequent meetings also may cause diminution of the capacity or desire to have normal sexual relations with one's spouse. Also, pressure by one partner for more frequent meetings, as we discussed earlier, can sometimes drive the other partner away.

On the other hand, very frequent meetings could result in a person spending more time with the extramarital partner than with his or her spouse. The relationship could become closer than the marital relationship and be, in effect, a parallel marriage—a kind of unofficial bigamy. But the affair may begin to suffer from the same problems of day-to-day coping that the marriage does. Two concurrent marriages can be several times as difficult as one alone.

If meetings are spaced more widely—say, once a month—the affair may either ripen into a long-term relationship or decline because of lack of enough stimulation to keep it going. Some affairs, however, thrive in spite of widely spaced meetings. The play *Same Time Next Year*[1] is the story of an extramarital couple that come together once a year at the same time and place—a long-standing ritual leading to a lifelong friendship.

DURATION OF AFFAIRS

Often, what determines whether a marriage can survive an affair is how long the affair lasts. The duration of most affairs is much briefer than that of most marriages, for an affair operates under several handicaps from which a marriage is free. The biggest handicap is the lack of a clear long-term goal. The extramarital partners, unless they plan to divorce their spouses and marry each other, may have little to look forward to over a long period; they just live from day to day. And without a common objective as a glue to bind them together, they eventually begin to move in different directions and drift apart. Marriage, on the other hand, has the goal of providing and maintaining a home and (in many cases) a family. A person worried about a spouse's possible affair might be less frightened if this fact is kept in mind.

Another handicap of the extramarital affair is its need (under present cultural attitudes) for secrecy. Extramarital partners often do not dare telephone or write each other or even give each other gifts because of the risk of discovery. This undermines communication in the affair itself as well as in the marriage. To the spouse of a person in an affair, it may look as if the extramarital relationship has all the advantages and the marriage all the disadvantages, but in general the marriage, if at all sound, has a much better chance of surviving, especially if the marital partners are stimulated to work constructively on their marriage.

Yet in spite of all the difficulties faced by people in affairs, some affairs do last a long time—some even for years. I have worked with situations where affairs had gone on undisturbed for ten years or more. A few have lasted, incredibly, for as long as *twenty years*. In such cases the extramarital partners have what amounts to a second marriage coexisting with the legal one(s), each relationship supplying elements lacking in the other(s). Thus the affair may supply missing emotional and/or sexual elements, while the legal marriage provides the children and security.

There's a great difference between short-term and long-term affairs. A short-term affair, such as a one-nighter, is mostly a here-and-now experience. While it involves no permanent commitment, it can have great intensity while it lasts. Any affair, even a one-nighter, is a human relationship with multifaceted aspects. When two people meet, reach out to each other, share with each other their mutual desires, decide what they will do together and how, where, and when they will do it, they form a relationship, however temporary. As they move into physical intimacy, there is a ceaseless flow of emotions, thoughts, questions, wonderings, and fantasies. The pair may be curious about each other, excite each other, and become high with each other. Although they may never see each other again, their brief contact may leave indelible memories and emotions—pleasant or unpleasant.

The partners in a short affair are free from concerns that often arise in long-continued affairs, such as "Why didn't you call me last night?" or "Where shall we meet next week?" There's less fear of discovery, since getting away for a single afternoon or evening is much easier and arouses less suspicion than getting away regularly for a long-continued series of contacts. The short affair offers fewer opportunities for the partners to irritate or misunderstand one another; each simply accepts the other as he/she is (or appears). Their fantasies about each other are not challenged. There are no problems of termination; the affair terminates itself since there is usually a tacit understanding that the relationship will be temporary. The short affair is an *interlude* in a person's life, not an altered life-style, as a long-term affair tends to be. The long-term affair may be in serious competition with the marriage and may threaten to supplant it, whereas a short-term affair needn't be such a threat unless its discovery upsets the husband-wife relationship. It was because Deborah's early affairs were short-term (by her deliberate intent) that she and her husband were able to reconcile them with their marriage. Had she permitted herself to get involved in a long-term affair at that stage, the marriage might not have survived.

An affair that lasts a number of years is likely to be a very satisfying one, with many of the same qualities as a good marriage. Such an affair may have, in Cuber's words,[2] "strong emotional and sexual bonds, continuity in the relationship, monogamous sentiments, intense sharing of a variety of ideas and activities, and mutual emotional supports." However, this is not true of all long-term affairs. An affair also can become stale, as we've said, and fall into sterile routines just as a marriage can, and for many of the same reasons. The extramarital partners may not be fully aware of how dull it has become—routines can be comfortable. And even if the partners are aware, they may not know how to end it gracefully. Consider the situation of a spouse who has been seeing the same extramarital partner, say, every Tuesday afternoon, always doing the same things, for the past six years. The experience is all too likely to have lost its freshness. Each partner may be wondering how to bring it to an end without hurting the feelings of the other. Both may hesitate to broach the subject; it's easier just to coast along. So they continue, perhaps more because of inertia than real desire.

Hazards, however, tend to build up as an affair goes on. If the affair is secret—as most are—the longer it continues, the greater become the chances of its discovery and exposure. This is true for several reasons. First, when an affair becomes routine, the participants may get complacent and careless, as Diane did. (Earlier in her affair, she would not have left incriminating material where Richmond could find it.) Second, it's virtually impossible to conceal an affair that goes on month after month (to say nothing of year after year) if the marital relationship is at all close. When a long-continued affair remains secret, the reason almost certainly is that the spouse of the participant is either very uninvolved in the marriage (like Jack, Daisy's husband, or David, Eva's husband) or doesn't want to admit the possibility that an affair exists. But this mood of ignoring what's in plain sight can change abruptly. When a spouse is confronted with evidence he can't ignore, as Richmond was, the whole thing may explode. And the exposure of a long-continued affair can be a far heavier blow to the self-respect of a spouse than the discovery of a brief affair.

A person in an affair who hesitates to end the affair for fear of hurting the extramarital partner may be greatly increasing the chances of hurting the spouse. This raises a question few of us want to face: If somebody's going to be hurt, who shall it be? With despair written over his face, and gesturing with outstretched arm, Randy (quoted at the beginning of this chapter) expressed the dilemma he was in: "I'm holding a life in each hand—my wife in one, my mistress in the other. I don't want to hurt either. What shall I do?"

SECRET AFFAIRS AND THE EFFECTS OF DISCOVERY

The fear that an affair arouses in a participant's spouse is the fear of the unknown. "I could stand it if I *knew* he loved someone else more than me," a wife said, "but I can't stand the uncertainty, the wondering, the imagining." That's one problem with secrecy. It's not knowing. And secrecy is rarely absolute secrecy. Unless a spouse is deaf and blind, he or she is almost sure to suspect something, and the pain that the secrecy was intended to avoid may already have begun—secretly!

A secret extramarital affair is quite different in character and mood from one that has become known. A man whose secret affair was later exposed described the difference in this way: "As long as my affair was secret, it was a private experience protected from outside intrusion. We could forget our family problems, our children, housekeeping routines, business worries, and what our spouses might be doing or thinking. We focused completely on each other—enjoyed the thrill of being alone together; the delight of sharing thoughts, feelings, and bodies; the love and warmth we felt for each other; the closeness and trust; the wonderful sex. I learned so much about myself. As you know, I had always been a person who had difficulty getting close or intimate with anyone. Yet in my affair I was open in a way I never had been with my wife or children. That was part of my trouble at home, no doubt. Strangely enough, I felt almost no guilt. The affair was an indescribably beautiful experience, and I savored every moment of it. We two had entrancing dreams and fantasies about each other. We thought nobody else in the world had ever felt about each other the way we did. We were taking big risks for each other, too, and this bound us together with special closeness. We lived an unreal, enchanted life. Then one day it all collapsed.

"As we walked out of a 'no-tell motel,' totally absorbed in each other, we practically bumped into a neighbor of mine who's an incurable gossip. She must have burned the telephone lines for hours. The news spread all over town. My wife, of course, heard about it. Our beautiful dream vanished like a punctured soap bubble. What had been a lovely private experience became public knowledge and drew ugly disapproval and sneers. Our children (both mine and hers) made scornful comments like, 'What got into you two old fools?' My wife withdrew into hurt silence. My girl friend's husband threatened divorce. We both felt guilty and humiliated. I could hardly look my family in the eye. My girl friend and I both had to face questions we had hitherto avoided, such as 'Do we want to save our marriages?' and 'Shall we terminate our affair?' Misunderstandings flared up between us. I got blamed for the exposure. (Why hadn't I seen the neighbor first? Why hadn't I dodged behind a post? And so on.) I suddenly discovered that my dream girl was a rather ordinary woman. Why had I thought her like no one else on earth? The conspiratorial secrecy that had bound us so closely was stripped away. We couldn't meet or talk on the phone any more without arousing suspicion. We couldn't comfort or strengthen each other. Each of us felt isolated and alone."

The urge to secrecy is more than simply a reasonable protection against hurting a spouse and damaging a marriage. Often, it has a childhood origin. As Lake and Hills put it,[3] affairs are secret often for the same reasons adolescent sex explorations were secret. "Similar feelings are experienced," say the authors: "The dramatic fallings in love, the consuming guilt, the same rebellious thrill, and the counting of scalps as a badge of achievement." The marital partner is not told for the same reason parents were not. The child knows the parents would have felt letdown, shocked, angry, and hurt. So secrecy, too, has multiple motivations. Some people find secrecy exciting; others say it "drives them mad."

CONSENSUAL ADULTERY

Some people circumvent the secrecy by engaging in what is called consensual adultery. A couple makes an agreement that when they engage in adultery, they will do it with each other's knowledge and consent. Henrietta's affairs, as I pointed out earlier, were encouraged by Harry, perhaps to assuage his feeling of guilt about his own affair. There are a number of forms of consensual adultery, including mate swapping ("swinging"), triads, group sex, and orgies in which both spouses participate. Also the sexually open marriage we described in Chapter 4, which invites more selective, freely chosen, and qualitative relationships.

An advantage of consensual adultery is that it doesn't go on behind a spouse's back. "It's not infidelity as most affairs are," says a man who is enthusiastic about mate swapping. "My wife and I don't lie to or cheat on each other. It's all done in the open. We aren't betraying our mutual trust. So it doesn't hurt our marriage." The story his wife gives is a little different. "I'm not crazy about it," she says. "I didn't really want to do it in the first place, and it still makes me uncomfortable. My husband kept bugging me until I gave in. Personally, if I'm to have an affair, I'd much rather choose the man myself and not be put in a position where I'm expected to take the husband of a woman who catches my husband's fancy. Someday I'll have a *real* affair with a man I can love and respect and feel close to. Or I may leave my husband." Obviously, mate swapping works out poorly if one partner or one couple finds the switch more agreeable than the other.

Some couples, on the other hand, enjoy the freedom of this lifestyle. It gives them sexual variety without the burdens of secrecy and guilt. New partners can be intriguing, and if they are not always good lovers, not much is lost. A person can stand a single boring night with a dud. There may also, however, be a risk of some very unpleasant experiences with unexpectedly crude or unfeeling partners.

When several couples do this together and exchange partners

repeatedly during an evening, the experience is called an orgy. The sex under these circumstances is often casual and mechanical, and the emotions accompanying a real personal relationship are likely to be missing or minimal. Feelings may become hostile if a partner is using sex as an ego booster or a power play. Avoiding close personal attachments is, in fact, one of the purposes of these kinds of experiences, for if someone were really to fall in love with one of the participants, the result would upset the entire system of consensual adultery. It would switch into a sexually exclusive one-to-one affair. In some cases, the repeated separation of physical sex from affection and love can damage the capacity of the individual to grow into a whole person.

It's doubtful if either mate swapping or group sex are fully satisfactory solutions to marital boredom. When spouses make an agreement to engage in mutual adultery, they probably aren't enjoying a fully satisfying relationship with each other; there's a good chance that one or the other spouse is feeling a hidden, unexpressed hurt because of this. One spouse might consider the other's permission for him/her to have an affair as saying, in effect, "I don't care about you," for caring usually means being concerned about what the other does. It is interesting that in *Time*'s opinion survey[4] referred to in Chapter 2, the exchange of partners by couples drew more condemnation than simple adultery by either husband or wife; eighty-one percent of the respondents condemned it. Leon Salzman has pointed out[5] that, in spite of the agreement of the partners in advance, consensual adultery can result in disruptive jealousy, rivalry, and open hostility, which makes this kind of arrangement highly unstable. Ronald Mazur[6] reports a contrary view that consensual adultery can sometimes add a rich, new dimension to the lives of couples. It is possible that both views are correct, but for different people.

SUCCESSIVE AND MULTIPLE AFFAIRS

In addition to simple one-to-one affairs, there are also multiple affairs, where a spouse either has a succession of brief one-to-one affairs or engages in several affairs simultaneously. Some individuals don't fit well into a one-to-one life-style; they have a roving eye, they are attracted to a number of different people at different times (or even at the same time), they enjoy the differences in personalities and physical characteristics, and they want a variety of sexual as well as social contacts. They refuse to stay put either in a marriage or in a long-term one-to-one affair. In the past, this kind of restlessness was generally found only among men—and a minority of men, at that. Women were expected to hold the home and family together. But today we observe a significant number of women, too, seeking this untrammeled freedom to experiment and sample. If the itch for excitement can lead to a single affair, it can just as easily lead to two—or a dozen.

A hundred affairs—Dr. Jensen

The desire for numerous partners can become a compulsion resembling an addiction. Dr. Jensen, a prominent dentist specializing in oral surgery, is married and the father of four children. He has engaged, he claims, in about a hundred extramarital affairs over the past fifteen years. During that period he kept a changing roster of seven or eight women with whom he constantly carried on simultaneous affairs. His sexual capacities are something to marvel at, for he often had intercourse with one of these women in the afternoon and then with his wife at night, week after week and year after year.

Women patients love him because he pays close, personal attention to them, listens to their troubles, and is gentle, understanding, humorous, and compassionate. He's the person everyone dreams about and rarely finds—a dentist who conveys the feeling of really caring about his patients. The nurses he works with also admire him; some sleep with him. He's a fascinating talker, is widely read, and can discourse on any subject. Naturally, he's enormously successful. And it is remarkable that none of his multiple affairs have gotten him into trouble with angry husbands, with the women themselves, with his wife (who suspects his habits), or with the hospital administration (which doesn't). The women keep their secrets faithfully long after his affairs with them have ended. He makes no time, love, or marriage commitments to anyone, yet each woman feels she was very special to him—which she was, for a time. Instead of resenting his fickleness, the women cherish the memories of the lovely times they had with him—bright spots in lives otherwise rather humdrum. He is expert in choosing women who would feel this way and avoids ones likely to give him trouble.

Though he is a conscientious and able professional, he has never experienced real love involving the whole of himself. He keeps love at arm's length. Many of the women, however, fall in love with him; as soon as he recognizes the symptoms, he finds an excuse to terminate the affair and moves on to someone else.

He recognizes his incompleteness and knows that something is missing. He has no close friends, because instead of participating fully in human relationships, he tends to manipulate them. Yet he doesn't believe he's using or exploiting these women. "I give them something they've been yearning for," he explains.

His background illuminates the reason he pursues this way of life. "My mother was the dominant figure in our family," he says. "My father stayed in the background. Mother was self-centered, complaining, suspicious, very money-conscious, and saw everything as it related to her or to the pocketbook. We all circled around her, though at times we hated her. She wasn't loving or affectionate. But she admired men who were sexual athletes—maybe because my father was not one. In any case, my brothers and I all got the idea from her that having extramarital affairs was admirable and expected of a man. I think all my life I've wanted love, though I didn't know this. But I also was afraid of love. So in search of love I've had affair after affair. Yet in fear of love I've rejected the women who wanted to love me."

Through therapy, as the dentist gets in touch with his feelings and comes to understand and work with who he is and how he got to be who he is, his compulsion to have affairs decreases and the quality of his marriage and family life improves. For the first time, he is getting close to his children and discovering a basic affection for his wife.

HOMOSEXUAL AFFAIRS

Since homosexuals ("gays") have been coming out of hiding in recent years and demanding public recognition of their right to their sexual preferences, the incidence of homosexual affairs seems to be rising. In any case, we are hearing more about them.

Because heterosexual marriage is the only type of marriage that is socially acceptable and legally valid, some homosexuals have married persons of the opposite sex for reasons of appearance and convention, but live their sexual life clandestinely with homosexual partners outside the marriage. In such a case, the heterosexual spouse also may turn outside the marriage for sexual satisfaction, since he or she can't get it with the marital partner. In some cases, a person who thought himself (or herself) to be heterosexual experiences homosexual urges after marriage and finds more satisfaction in a homosexual connection than in the marital one. "I got so I couldn't stand sex with my husband," said Lillian, a young lesbian. "I thought I was sexually frigid until I met Rosanna, and then I discovered that sex could be gentle, beautiful, and delightful—not rough and pushy as it was with my husband. Now I've left my husband to live with Rosanna."

The case of Lillian and Rosanna sounds idyllic until you meet the family and discover the complications. Both women had husbands and children. Both marriages had collapsed. Lillian's husband, unknown to Lillian, had engaged in two extramarital affairs before she left him. Rosanna's husband had already separated from her, leaving their two teenage daughters with the mother. When Lillian went to live with Rosanna, she took with her her own child, a boy of nine. The children did not get along; they fought and bickered continually and began to get into drugs. The strains of being in a socially unacceptable type of relationship, plus trying to be both mother and father to three rebellious children, have been so disruptive that all relationships in the household came close to total disintegration. It is not certain that the lesbian orientation of these two women was the root cause of the present difficulties, although it undoubtedly contributed to unsatisfactory sex relations in both marriages. More likely what destroyed the marriages were temperamental incompatibilities, conflicts of values, and the inability of the spouses to maintain a mutually rewarding interaction. The greatest sufferers in this case were the children, for children often have difficulty fitting into the framework of a "gay" primary relationship.

Some people are bisexual and can enjoy sex either with persons of the same sex or with those of opposite sex. A homosexual affair of a bisexual spouse may merely supplement the marriage rather than be a substitute for it. "I like both kinds of sex and companionship," said a married bisexual. "I can't see why I have to limit myself to sex in the marriage. To me, life would be poorer if I had to limit myself to either one alone." It may be rather difficult, however, to convince a heterosexual spouse of the validity of this argument, for society's attitudes toward the homosexual have been so negative for such a long time that homosexuality still seems an intolerable deviation to many people.

THE "OTHER WOMAN" (OR "OTHER MAN")

No matter what variety of affair you're trying to understand and cope with, an inevitable concern arises. Who is the "other woman" or "other man"? Is she or he the conscious destroyer of marriages that the popular stereotype portrays? In the case of the "other woman," is she the single woman of dubious reputation and unscrupulous morals who maneuvers to grab somebody's husband? Or the "gay divorcée" out for a good time at some poor wife's expense. I hope we have seen enough of the human side of extramarital affairs to know that she usually is not. But as I pointed out when discussing one of the myths, the double standard has resulted in the "other woman" being commonly more blamed than the "other man." This may be changing now as more extramarital affairs are involving wives; the husbands are beginning to view the "other man" in much the same light as wives in the past have thought of the "other woman."

The "other woman" and "other man" may indeed sometimes mimic the traditional image. Either may appear aggressive, insensitive, conscienceless, not caring who gets hurt. In most of the affairs I have studied, however, the "other woman" and "other man" do not fit this image.

Consider the "other woman." She could be married or unmarried. If she's never been married, she might be looking for a husband, or she might be quite content with her single status. Even if she is hoping to meet someone with whom she can settle down, that person may not necessarily be the one she is having an affair with. However, their experiences together might help give her insight into the kind of man she *would* like to marry. If she has chosen to remain unmarried (at least for the time being), her relationship with a married man could have the additional advantage of being "safe"—he's already attached and she can stay "free."

Divorcées and legally separated women might have other reasons for involvement with a currently married man. Like the never-married woman, they too might be broadening their range of experiences by forming relationships with a variety of men. If they had married young, it's likely they hadn't had much opportunity to meet many different types of males. Then too, the reasons for their original marital choices may be completely different from the qualities they now seek in a mate. They may feel a need to find out what they really want by experimenting, to guard against another wrong decision that could imperil their future. Then there's the possibility that because the first marriage was a negative experience, they may choose to remain unattached through maintaining relationships in which there is no long-term commitment.

When the "other woman" is currently married, a wholly different set of motivations may apply. If she's reasonably content with her marriage, with no thought of ending it, she may choose to develop relationships with other males as a means of supplementing her marriage or enriching her life. If her extramarital partner is also married, both may feel they can share in this process with no threat to the marital status of either. Some even encourage their extramarital partners to improve and revitalize their marriages. In addition, either or both partners may find their decision to remain married reinforced by the knowledge that "there's nothing out there better than what I already have at home."

That realization may do a lot to strengthen a shaky marriage if the wife (or husband) is unsure about the future of the marital relationship and tries an affair to see what it's like to be with someone else. On the other hand, the experience with an extramarital partner, if it's positive, may be the deciding factor in ending a bad marriage. In situations of this type, the "other woman" may have embarked on an affair to help clarify her mind about what could be a painful decision. In the event that she finds an extramarital partner with whom she feels there is a potential for a future alliance, she may choose to end her marriage in favor of the new relationship. If not, it is possible that she will continue looking for such a relationship before she severs her current marital bond.

For some married women, the success or failure of an extramarital affair has no bearing on the future of their marriage because they've already decided to sever their marital ties. For them an affair may be the salve needed for a bruised ego or the reassurance that they are still sexually attractive. With their minds already geared for divorce, these married women might be willing to take greater risks than others—both with their own future and with that of their extramarital partners.

Of course, emotions have a way of upsetting even the most carefully laid intellectual plans. No matter how nonthreatening the "other woman" may have intended to be, no matter what her original reasons (if, indeed, she had been able to verbalize them), the extramarital relationship could develop more intensity than she (or he) had bargained for, thereby precipitating much pain, frustration, and emotional trauma for everyone concerned. Whether or not the affair leads to the breakup of either marriage and whether or not it is discovered by either or both spouses, this escalation of emotions adds another dimension to the complexity of feelings confronting the "other woman" (and "other man").

The fact is that the "other woman" may be subject to as many emotions of uncertainty, unworthiness, disappointment, fear, anxiety, jealousy, and anger as is the wife—plus the added burdens of lying, secrecy, and perhaps guilt. One of my patients has written about what this feels like:

> *I'm having an awfully hard time handling our relationship. I feel that I mustn't let go emotionally. So I try, although unsuccessfully, to guard and protect myself from wanting too much . . . from the pain of not getting the affection I crave.*
>
> *Sometimes, we're very close. We're friends. We're lovers. We've helped each other to grow . . . to understand ourselves . . . even to improve our relating to others. As I see his life with his wife become better, partly because of me, the friend part of me is glad . . . even proud. But the lover part feels hurt . . . rejected . . . sad. Then I see myself being relegated to only a small private corner of his life . . . cut off from the mainstream of his "real life." I don't like this. I don't want to be a secret . . . a dishonesty . . . a guilt.*
>
> *I wish there could be more balance in our affair. I could handle being only a small part of his life if he could be only a small part of mine. I guess this really depends upon how full and active my own life is and whether I'm happy or not. But, when I am lonely or bored or weighed down by problems, he becomes my only bright spot . . . too important. And I feel too dependent upon him. Then I want so much more of him . . . want to be more important to him . . . want to come first.*
>
> *Sometimes I feel the worst after we've been together and felt close and made love and then part with his saying, "I'll be talking to you." Then I feel abandoned . . . let down . . . expendable . . . only a diversion. And I'll miss him so much.*
>
> *A lot of how I feel about our relationship has to do with the focus of his attentions and time. When he concentrates his efforts on his marriage, I feel really jealous, in spite of myself. Somehow, though, after each bout of sadness and longing on my part, I think I am growing stronger. I readjust my perspective a bit and ask myself what I really what from this relationship. In truth, I guess I'm no more ready to commit myself to him than he is to me.*

In spite of psychological evidence to the contrary, the so-called wronged wife may still see the "other woman" as evil. ("If I could get my hands on her, I'd . . ." etc.) What the wife's anger blinds her from seeing is that by hating the "other woman," she is hating someone with whom her husband has chosen to share some of himself. Is the wife's anger really directed at herself for some imagined failure at keeping her husband's interest? Is it guilt at having taken him for granted or remorse for having shown less interest in him sexually than he might have wished? Does she attempt to blame the other woman instead of taking a closer look at the kind of relationship she has with her husband? There may be no need to blame herself, her husband, or anyone else if she can appreciate and understand her husband's yearning to experience another person besides herself. Can she turn the situation around so that it might be advantageous to her—help yield new insights, new awareness of her husband's needs and her own needs? This is impossible as long as she focuses on the "lousy bitch who grabbed my husband."

The "other woman" actually may have a more difficult role to fill than the wife does. She often is far less certain of her position and of the true nature of her relationship with the man. After all, she is likely to have only a limited part of him. It is to the wife that he goes home following one of their meetings, and it is probably the desires of the wife and the responsibilities of his family that will take priority over his relationship and available time with her. Logically, then, you might expect the "other woman" to be more jealous of the wife than the wife is of her.

Sometimes she is just that—jealous, resentful, insecure, hating. She might be responding to negative information about the wife fed to her by her lover to rationalize his guilt. ("My wife doesn't understand me.") Or she might be influenced by her own expectations for the affair. If she had fantasies of moving in on the wife's territory, she'd be much more apt to view the wife as an adversary. Feelings of competition inevitably lead to feelings of jealousy, especially when she fears that the other has scored points.

But not all "other women" are caught in such a tug-of-war. Some are content to enjoy what they have and live day by day. Some would not accept marriage with their lover if he offered it to them, for many of the reasons I have already cited.

Another patient writes about how she has resolved some of the emotional conflicts aroused by her affair:

> I had never planned to be "the other woman." My image of such a person was the familiar one of intruder, home wrecker, loose, irresponsible, adulteress. Besides, I knew I was probably setting myself up for painful disappointment because "most married men don't plan to leave their wives" . . . and where does that leave me?
>
> Yet I didn't really feel all those negative, self-punishing, moralizing things. Why? Was I only rationalizing to keep my conscience quiet? "Who am I in this relationship?" I asked myself again and again. Then the answer came to me: I am "another woman" . . . significant in the life of a married man; capable of giving and receiving love from another human being; aware of making each time together an experience of now, not a future dream; having the opportunity to feel fully alive during those stolen moments when we are together. And loving the feeling of aliveness!
>
> I hold in my possession the privilege of choice . . . either to feel guilty, self-condemning, teased and tantalized by unreal expectations, or

*to feel caring and cared about, sharing a slice of someone's life which it is
my happy fortune to be able to experience.*

*Pain, hurt, disappointment, anger, fear, blame, jealousy, rage . . .
I have known all these. That's why it matters all the more that I
understand that life offers me the chance to choose how I will experience
my relationship with a married man. However it turns out in the end, it
will be forever a treasured part of me.*

Much of what has been said here about the "other woman"
applies also to the "other man." There are some differences. The "other
man" may perhaps be less likely to be using an affair to capture a wife. He is
more likely to have entered the affair for reasons of sexual attraction,
enjoyment, excitement, fondness for women, and the like. But the possibility of arousing a husband's jealousy and anger is nevertheless very real.

THE OTHER "OTHER WOMAN" (OR THE OTHER "OTHER MAN")

If the "other woman" can come to terms with her status in the
extramarital relationship and recognize the wife's rightful claim, what
happens when her lover is involved (as Dee's was) in more than one outside
relationship concurrently? Such a situation creates a new and more complicated set of interrelationships.

Complicated indeed! Her lover is now *directly* involved in three
sets of triangle relationships and, *indirectly,* in a fourth. The diagrams below
illustrate the inter-relatedness between husband and wife (the primary
relationship represented by a solid line); husband and lover(s) (the extramarital relationship(s) represented by a broken line); and wife and her
husband's extramarital partners (represented by a dotted line). (Code:
H=husband/lover, W=wife, OW="other woman," OOW=other "other
woman")

The man (or woman) involved in such multiple relationships has
a whole new set of problems with which he (she) must cope both mentally

Direct involvement

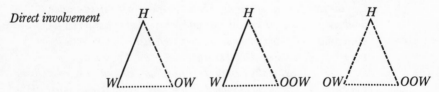

Indirect involvement

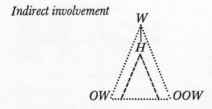

*Triangle Relationships Created by
Single and Multiple Extramarital Affairs*

and emotionally, not to mention sexually and logistically! Keeping two or more women—plus his wife—happy can be no small achievement. Can he handle the added strain? And can they? Even if each extramarital partner is not aware of the other, and the wife is similarly in the dark, can he continue to cover his tracks with so many pairs of eyes following him?

And what about the other "other woman" caught up in this situation? What is her status in terms of her lover's other relationships, as well as in terms of his wife? All the emotions already generated by an extramarital affair are now intensified. While she may be tolerant of the position occupied by his wife, can she be so accepting of a rival extramarital attachment? Can she compete for his time, attention, and love while maintaining her own equilibrium? Can she comfortably accept third place, if need be?

One of my patients, in just such a relationship, had this to say:

> *I guess you might call me the* other *"other woman"—an extra addition in the proverbial "eternal triangle." Which means, of course, that my extramarital partner (who's married) is also involved in an affair with somebody else besides me. Now, there's a new kind of triangle to be dealt with—his wife, his other friend, and me—in which he's not directly involved. I suppose to his wife (if she knew) and to his other "friend" (I think she suspects) I'm "the other woman." But to me, the other person he's involved with is "the other woman"—my rival! I don't see his wife that way. She "belongs" with him and I don't feel at all threatened by her existence. After all, I'm married, too, and will probably stay that way.*
>
> *But "the other woman" isn't. And I guess I do feel threatened by the potential for their relationship developing further than mine with him is likely to. In addition, my available time with him is restricted by my marital obligations. She's free to see him as often as he can manage it. Which, of course, creates another problem for me—he's sharing his limited time (and his body) with both of us as well as with his wife. Maybe less for each of us all around!*
>
> *Even though I've been involved in extramarital affairs before, this situation is new for me—creating within me feelings of jealousy and insecurity that I've not had in the past. Intellectually, I can accept and appreciate his need to experience and enjoy many people on many levels—as I do. And I know that his other "friend" has a lot of beautiful qualities which are quite different from mine. Together we are able to enrich his life in many ways that neither of us could do alone. Yet, on an emotional level, I still have that fantasy that I'd like to have him all to myself.*
>
> *Dealing with all the aspects of this situation has certainly been an educational experience for me—and that's a real plus. I'm learning to look at parts of myself that I never had to face before. And I'm really growing . . . I can feel it. I guess there's a bonus in being the other "other woman" after all.*

ENDLESS VARIETY

The variety of affairs is, indeed, endless. Do some seem far out? To you and to me, perhaps, yes, for most of us grew up with cultural conditioning in which deviations from a conventional marital relationship were not considered permissible. But in a world of change, today's "far out" can become tomorrow's commonplace. The constant that seems likely to prevail through all cultural changes is the deep human desire for continuity in meaningful relationships—especially those providing affection, nurture, and love. Marriage, when it works, supplies this. When it doesn't, where do we go?

9. *Commitment, Fidelity, and Trust*

While under light sedation, being prepared for drastic surgery, I groped for the phone and placed the call. If this was the end, I felt the need to thank him for what he brought into my life. . . . I realized how grateful I was to have had five whirlwind years of love. No longer did I doubt that it had been worthwhile to go through the constant anxiety, lying, conniving, disguising, the disrespect of parents and the disapproval of my best friend.

Yet, I reflected, everything could have been honorable if I'd only had the strength to end a loveless marriage. But I was too frightened and weak, and I believed so in love, marriage, children, and happy endings. I worked hard to achieve a closer feeling relationship with my husband of twenty years. Perhaps, even yet, it will come. But whether it does or not, I'm not sorry that I experienced what openness can be. I've been close to another human being. I have loved and been loved. It may never happen again.

Suzanne

COMMITMENT IN MARRIAGE

Marital vows appear to be changing. In conversations with a number of married couples, I've observed that the meanings they attach to the commitments originally made to each other have changed over time. It is not that the commitments have ceased to be operative. It is rather that the emphasis has shifted away from marriage as a *bond* and toward marriage as a *relationship,* good or bad.

More recently my attention has been drawn to several remarkable alterations in wedding vows by couples who, in consultation with an understanding church pastor, essentially wrote their own vows. In one case, the young couple pledged themselves to a life together of "loving, learning, laughing, and living." Avid for life as they are, and intent on fostering each other's personal growth, they see marriage as an opportunity for deepening an already established relationship, but not primarily as a restrictive bond or a set of directives concerning duties and obligations.

In a recent Quaker wedding, the traditional pledge to be faithful "as long as we both shall live" was altered to read "as long as we shall live together." At first glance this modification seems to take all the meaning out of the pledge, since at any time the couple could cease to live together. But the Quaker couple defended their decision in this way: "We take our affirmations seriously. It isn't honest to make a promise we might someday have to break. We love each other and expect our marriage to last. But how can anyone undertake a lifetime commitment in today's world? Our separate careers or missions might take us to opposite ends of the earth. If so, wouldn't it be hypocrisy for us to bind ourselves permanently as if change could be stopped dead in its tracks?"

Not many couples, as yet, face so squarely this fact of modern life: that personal growth and continuance of the marriage could, at some future time, collide. In the past, when this happened, the wife nearly always yielded. If the husband's career, for example, called for a move to a different locality, his wife quit her job, if she had one, and tried to find work in the new location. But what happens when the wife regards her self-development and her career as of equal importance with his? There may not be an opportunity for her kind of work in the new area; if there is not, the couple has three options: The husband sacrifices, the wife sacrifices, or they separate. Before jumping to the conclusion that it is always the wife who must yield, it should be remembered that she may have spent a number of years preparing for a specialized professional career. So, of course, may the husband. The problem may be complicated by children. The outcome could be separation, with each ultimately finding a new partner.

The shift in the meaning of marital commitments is subtle rather than overt, yet nonetheless real. No one to my knowledge is giving up the idea that marriage calls for faithfulness of some kind. People who do not intend to be faithful would have little reason to marry. But what people mean by faithfulness could well be changing—and I think it is. New concepts of fidelity and commitment, while not necessarily replacing the old concepts, shift the emphasis to the *nurture and enrichment of the marital relationship* as long as the relationship has vitality and meaning. They say less about duties and obligations. Partly this is because the duties and obligations of marriage are much less clear than they once were. Formerly the husband had the acknowledged duty to support and protect his wife and family, but today wives often share in the support of the household and may feel less need of protection. Wives formerly had the duty to bear and care for children and to maintain a home for the family; but many marriages today are childless and many others continue for decades beyond the child-raising period. And in some marriages the husbands share in the home-making duties.

The one commitment that remains valid and meaningful in the face of all changes in the nature of marriage is the pledge to nurture and enrich the marital relationship. If the couple ceases to do that, marriage loses much of its reason for being. We have to ask, however: Is this commitment also a promise to remain sexually faithful? Most married people would probably say yes. But some say no. There are people who insist that outside sexual relationships are not necessarily incompatible with nurturing and enriching a marriage. Kevin and Deborah, of the sexually open marriage, made this claim.

Here, of course, is a highly charged issue. A marital relationship cannot be nurtured and enriched unless the partners want it so and are ready to put their marital relationship ahead of all others. Can they—or would they—do this if they had sexual relationships outside the marriage? Differences of opinion on this are strong. There is little or no research to back up opinions either way. My own observation is that it depends very much on the individual couple. There are couples that can reconcile these two things usually assumed to be irreconcilable. And there are couples that cannot.

Let's look at the reasons why many people want commitment in a marriage.

1. They want the feeling of stability and relative permanence in a long-term relationship. They don't like the uncertainty of wondering whether they will still be together tomorrow.

2. If they have children, they believe a long-term commitment is essential for the children's sake.

3. They want to build a future for themselves and their family. They want to establish a new home and make long-term plans.

4. They want the economic security and the social and community status that comes with an acknowledged long-term relationship.

5. They want to be able to depend on each other for mutual care, help, and support in times of need.

6. They feel special to each other. They don't want to share this special relationship with anyone else.

7. They want to continue to feel accepted, loved, and wanted by each other. Their commitment says to each, "I accept, love, and want you."

8. They want continued comfort and contentment with each other and hope for a long-term ripening of their love.

9. They don't want to return to the anxieties, uncertainties, and heartaches of a search for a new partner.

None of these reasons implies that the commitment must be for a lifetime or that it must override everything else. *Long-term* does not necessarily mean forever. Nor does such commitment mean that two married people are constrained to avoid all other intimate relationships, or that they must continue to live together if the marital relationship has lost its meaning for them. True commitments are made in the heart. Vows, in the end, have little effect if the heart has turned in a different direction. As Jerome Weidman put it in his book *Your Daughter Iris:* "Human beings do not obtain possession of each other when they marry. All they obtain is the right to work at the job of holding on to each other."[1]

COMMITMENT TO CHILDREN

Marital commitment is one thing; commitment to children is another. For children are vulnerable. In a sense, we all are vulnerable, but children are immensely more so. What, then, can be said of the impact of extramarital affairs on children?

Uncomfortable as it may be to reveal an extramarital affair to a spouse, how much more difficult is it to reveal it to a child! Should a child be told at all? If so, at what age? Under what circumstances? Should both spouses be present? How much information should be given or withheld? Should all or only selected children be involved? What happens after the telling?

Children have little or no experience with the tempests of adult love triangles. And especially difficult is the situation when a child accidentally discovers the secret affair of a parent.

Fifteen-year-old Carin had such an experience. She told me this story: "My father was away on an extended business trip. We kids had all gone to bed. I couldn't sleep, and finally I got up and started downstairs for a glass of milk and some cookies. Halfway down the stairs . . . God! . . . what I saw I couldn't believe! There was Mom on the couch, her clothes half off, and she was embracing and kissing Mr. Harper, our next-door neighbor, who is Dad's best friend. I choked back a scream! Half paralyzed, I crept silently back to my room, threw myself on the bed and pulled the covers over my head. I repeated to myself, It can't be. It can't be. My mother, *my* mother with Mr. Harper!!! I thought, My God, what if Dad had returned early from his trip? Or what if my younger brother or sister had seen what I saw? . . . Worse than a nightmare!"

Carin was crying now, and finally resumed: "I was furious at Mom. I could have killed her! How could she cheat on my Dad this way? The thought tore me up. Oughtn't I tell Dad? Then I realized that if I told him, he'd be so mad at Mom their marriage might break up. If they divorced, it would be my fault. Then what would happen to us kids? That would be the end of our home. I didn't sleep a wink that night. In the days that followed, I had a terrible need to talk to somebody. But I couldn't say anything to either of my parents, or to my teachers or friends. A kid can talk to other kids about a divorce—lots of my friends have divorced parents—but about my *mom* making out with another man? I couldn't mention *that* to *anybody*! It just piled up inside me until I thought I'd go crazy! I felt totally alone for the first time in my life."

Carin, of course, had a built-in conviction that an affair is a betrayal. And she might be right; her father might indeed have felt betrayed. But Carin probably had no conception of the emotional and sexual pressures that brought her mother into Mr. Harper's arms: of the slow-growing sterility of a marriage that looked sound on the surface, but had lost its vitality underneath; of the divergence of interests and life-styles of her two parents; of their increasing sexual dysfunction and frantic attempts to remedy it; and of the growing emotional attraction between her mother and the next-door neighbor, whose wife had recently left him. What the girl saw, disconnected from its emotional context, was mystifying and horrifying.

What can torture a child about a parent's affair is that it's a locked-in terror, it's unmentionable, the child is alone with it, and no social machinery exists to help a child manage it. The unspoken torments and moral bewilderment are far worse than the fact of divorce itself. I've known children to simply deny the existence of an affair and go about trying to live as usual. Some children get caught up in an unbearable conflict of loyalties, begin to spend less time at home, lose interest in schoolwork, have frequent nightmares, become sullen and withdrawn, and may develop psychosomatic problems such as headaches, nausea, and stomach pains. Some show their feelings by becoming excessively dependent on a parent or by angry outbursts or by running away from home. Yet, on the other hand, some children develop closer relationships with parents as a result of discussions and involvements about affairs. A few assume a role of marriage counselor for their parents. In the case of Carin, after opening up and working constructively with her feelings during therapy, she became a significant source of encouragement to her parents to try to bring their marriage back to one of excitement and joy.

If a parent is unwilling or feels unprepared to confide in a child, then great care should be taken to avoid the possibility of the child's discovering the affair. Some parents are willing to level with their children about the state of their marriage and their feelings of satisfaction and dissatisfaction with it. This preparation can greatly modify the tornado force of a sudden revelation.

If, as a parent, you do decide to reveal mother's or father's affair to your child, it is important to be aware of the risks, responsibilities, and possible consequences. What are your motives for wanting to reveal it? Is it merely to inform? Is it to be honest and open for your child's sake, so you can be available to help him/her understand and cope healthily with the knowledge? Or is it to get back at your spouse? Or to persuade the child to sympathize with you and be on your side? Do you feel prepared to be fair about the issue, to respect the feelings and opinions of your child, and to give as much time as is necessary for follow-up discussions? Do you have the emotional equipment to deal with the consequences of being open?

The commitment of parents to children is, in many ways, more compelling than that of married people to each other, but it is also more limited in duration. Eventually the child grows up and takes responsibility for his own life. Marriage, on the other hand, is open-ended. Traditional wedding vows say "for life."

CONFLICTING COMMITMENTS

Commitments between men and women, of course, are not limited to marriage. People living together without marriage can feel committed too. So, in some cases, can extramarital partners. Take Diane, Richmond's wife, whom he threatened to kill. Said she: "I love Andy. I can't bear to think of life without him." Does Andy ever think of what this requires of him? He loves Diane, and they are blissful in each other's company. But what if Andy should begin to tire of Diane? Suppose something about the way she looks at other men, or gets into down moods, or questions his pet opinions begins to annoy Andy. What if he begins to think about bringing the affair to an end? What would it do to Diane? Would she kill herself? (Actually, she might. It's not an impossibility.) No one knows if any thoughts like these have ever crossed Andy's mind. But they do cross the minds of people when love begins to fade. I've seen many affairs where the question of possible termination throws the partners into emotional turmoil. They believed they had no commitment; and, in formal terms, they did not. But their hearts tell a different story.

Eva and Mike (the former Father Gordon) are more totally committed than most married people are. Without question, they feel themselves united—for life. They'll marry as soon as Eva gets her divorce. It will not be the marriage, however, that seals their commitment. The commitment is sealed already. The marriage will only formalize it.

One of the facts often lost sight of by people concerned with the violation of marital commitments is that marriage is only one of many commitments people make, and is by no means always felt to be the most important one. A man (and today often a woman, too) may put commitment to a career or work ahead of the marital commitment. He or she may be able to combine the two commitments; but sometimes the commitments collide. And consider the commitment of the student: to get through medical school, say, or law school; to master a field or a skill, or develop a talent. I knew a woman preparing to be a concert pianist who practiced six hours a day and continued to do so even after her marriage. Like all who aim for high achievement, she was more than committed—she was *dedicated*. Few marriages are the object of as deep dedication as this. My musician friend would have given up her marriage in a moment if it had hampered her growth in her music.

Strangely, we seem to make an absolute out of commitment only in the case of marriage and children. All other commitments are recognized as being a matter of degree and subject to change. If a young man drops out of graduate school to develop a different side of himself, we do not consider him morally deficient for breaking his commitment to finish his education. We recognize that he may go back later, or that he may turn toward something different. When we try to make an absolute out of marital commitment, however, we deceive ourselves. Nearly always, in the real world, it is a matter of degree—a question of how much and how long.

Commitments change. A marriage starts off with a commitment of each spouse to the other, but in the partners' hearts and minds limits are soon put on it. "I love my husband," says a woman who has had two affairs, "but this doesn't mean I would take *anything* from him. There's a limit. He knows it and I know it." One of the things this woman would not take is indifference to her feelings and wants. Her affairs were a clear signal as to where her limits are. So was Diane's. So were Dee's. So, in their various ways, were all the other affairs we looked at.

Commitment, I think, is as real as it ever was. But it has never been total or permanently fixed. Nothing that's human is static or stays put forever. Human relationships evolve, they shift, they move together and apart. How could Diane or Eva or Dee or Suzanne know at twenty what would fulfill her life at forty? Said a woman wondering about marriage, "How can you promise never, for the rest of your life, to be attracted to another man?"

The kind of marital commitment that will probably remain valid as long as marriage survives is for the partners to care enough for each other to nurture and enrich the marital relationship while it lasts. Marriage has too long been considered a status, not an opportunity or a challenge. What marriage really means is the voluntary undertaking of a long-term learning and growing process (as one of our young couples recognized in their rewrite of the wedding vows). Marriage asks that we learn to care, to give each other encouragement and emotional support, to express affection, to help each other over the hard places, to be considerate, to be in touch with our own and each other's feelings, to allow each other room to grow and develop, to share, to communicate clearly, to trust, to negotiate differences, to fight constructively when at odds, to avoid hurting or limiting or ridiculing or smothering each other. Many—probably most—couples assume that this also requires sexual faithfulness. But some feel it does not.

FIDELITY

If the meaning of marital commitment is changing, the meaning of marital fidelity is likely to change along with it. Fidelity in general means faithfulness, and infidelity, unfaithfulness. But in marriage, infidelity has specifically meant "violation of the marriage covenant by adultery" (from my old Webster's). This puts the distinction between fidelity and infidelity squarely on a sexual basis. Is this not a very narrow view? The new meaning of commitment would seem to shift fidelity from sexual faithfulness to faithfulness in the broader sense of being devoted and caring. The broader faithfulness could include being our best self, cultivating our finer feelings, and becoming more whole persons. The older and newer concepts of fidelity are not necessarily in conflict, but for some people, and under some circumstances, they may be.

Becky spoke from the perspective of a woman tied to a mean, crippled husband. Said she: "My minister preaches about fidelity. And I know he'd say I'm a faithless woman. Reggie, my husband, would say the same if he knew what I've been doing. But I don't *feel* faithless. I feel so faithful it's ridiculous. If I were faithless, I'd have walked out on Reggie years ago. Yet I'm not ready to abandon a sick man who needs me."

Is fidelity something you owe, like a debt to a bank? The older wedding vows imply that it is. If it is owed, the fact that the debt was contracted years ago doesn't relieve you of the obligation to pay it. Or is fidelity something voluntarily given or withheld? The newer marriage concepts seem to lean in this direction. Eva, for whom fidelity has always been a basic moral imperative, has this to say: "How can you speak of marital fidelity if you don't have a relationship with your spouse? What is there left to be faithful to? I haven't had a husband for years." Eva feels faithful to her God, her children, and, of course, her lover-priest. But not to her husband who, she feels, is husband in name only. To her, fidelity is a gift, and she bestows it with grace upon the man she really loves: her adored Father Gordon.

What about the conflict between different fidelities? Father Gordon, faithful to his beloved Eva, found himself unfaithful to his priestly vows. Diane, unfaithful to her husband, Richmond, is totally faithful to her lover, Andy. And Sydney, in love with two women, wants to be faithful to both—probably an impossibility under the assumptions of our present culture.

Rustum and Della Roy have expressed the startling thought that if the sexual exclusivity of the marriage contract is not loosened, monogamy itself could suffer.[2] Society has long equated monogamy with a monopoly on sexual relations. But the Roys believe this monopoly is becoming a threat to monogamy itself and that, if religion and social custom insist on rigid adherence to it, many people are likely to turn away entirely from monogamy. As the Roys see it, monogamy should be tied, not to sex, but to "the much more basic concepts of fidelity, honesty, and openness, which are concomitants of love of the spouse, but which do not necessarily exclude deep relationships and possibly including various degrees of sexual intimacy with others." Their concern is that guidelines be provided "to help steer [people] from the dangerous to potentially creative relationships . . ."

TRUST

When old traditions are in the process of change, there is inevitable conflict. Alterations in the meaning of commitment and fidelity can tear people and marriages apart and bring excruciating emotional pain. Trying to avoid these agonizing conflicts produces secrecy, and along with secrecy comes loss of trust.

Do affairs have to be secret, with all the betrayal and distrust that this implies? The fact is they usually are. People who think themselves honest in every other way and for whom honesty is an important personal value may nevertheless feel driven to lying about extramarital affairs. In the end they don't trust; they sense a barrier between themselves and their spouse that they don't know how to overcome. They may not be sure their own track record of dependability has been so clear that their spouse will believe in them wholly. Have they always done what they promised? If they said they would be home by six o'clock, were they home at six o'clock? Were their accounts of events strictly true, never slanted? Few of us can answer yes to all these questions. So the basis of some distrust has already been laid by the time many affairs take place.

In most marriages, affairs—if they occur—are kept secret for several very potent reasons. Preserving the marriage is one, since some spouses, hearing of an affair, will simply walk out and start divorce action. Another is fear—fear of the spouse's (and other people's) reactions; fear of hurting the spouse; fear of the condemnation, disapproval, and possible threats that would follow. Some spouses, like Richmond (who wanted to murder his wife) and Rosalie (who destroyed her "perfect" marriage), react in extreme anger. I asked Andrea (quoted at the beginning of Chapter 2) whether she had considered confessing her affairs to her husband. "He'd be terribly hurt," was her answer, "and would never forget. . . . He'd be angry because he was being good while I was screwing around." She's now working on improving her marriage.

A third reason, for some individuals, is financial dependency. A woman like Becky, for example, dependent on her husband's income, may be unwilling to risk breaking out on her own, especially if she had devoted her life to homemaking and child raising and has few marketable skills.

A fourth reason may be concern for the extramarital partner, whose reputation, job security, marital status, and sometimes even life could be threatened by exposure. And there may be concern for the spouse and family, if any, of the extramarital partner. There's a "no-tattletale" ethic at work here; even children learn early not to tell on their friends.

Suzanne, who wrote the words quoted at the beginning of this chapter, paints a vivid and humorous picture of what a secret affair can be like. Recovering from surgery, she's looking back at her life.

> *I had five years of being a jack-in-the-box. When the phone rang I'd have to leap up the stairs to check extensions, then down to the basement, then back to the kitchen to guard against possible intruders. I did have a household with children. Many times it wasn't even him. . . . Other times he'd say, "Wrong number, I'm sorry." But for some strange reason it made me feel content. . . .*
>
> *Plans for our clandestine rendezvous took extreme caution. Believe me, there is no safe place. That brought me to the Groucho Marx disguise. My embarrassed lover, supposedly having an affair with a tall beauty, opened the car door, and out came a goggled character, bowlegged and limping, with her head nearly hidden under a huge babushka. The only rejection I ever felt from him was when he'd lead me to our room, fumbling with the key, anxious to hide this monstrosity. But that was part of the affair. I must never be recognized. I trembled with fear of recognition—my hands were like ice and my teeth were chattering.*
>
> *But once in the room, all this was forgotten. We were together alone. Alone not just to share our bodies but our many unsolved problems. You see, he too needed someone to love him for his many beautiful qualities.*
>
> *It was strange that I didn't feel shy. But it was his constant approval of me that melted my shyness. Never, while growing up with my parents and siblings, nor during my twenty-year marriage, had anyone approved of me so completely.*
>
> *My breasts, though small, were to him exciting and adequate. An incision on my abdomen was a thing of interest and concern. A blemish on*

my skin, he would never ignore but gently slide his fingers across it, letting me know that whatever the imperfection, it was all part of me and every part was loved. He taught me to love with no inhibitions. Everything brought us closer together. We needed no wine and roses—being together in itself was intoxicating.

But could Suzanne tell her husband? Lord, no! He never found out. Nor did her children. Now two years have passed since the ending of her affair. She's trying to work out a closer relationship with her husband. She cares enough for him to want to do this, so in this respect she is not, and has not been, totally unfaithful. But she'll never tell him of the affair. It would be a blow from which she's afraid he—and their marriage—might not recover.

As long as people don't have the inner security and strength to acknowledge that they can't meet all their spouse's wants and needs, affairs are likely to remain secret. Not because people don't want to tell, but because the risk is too great. Or the discomfort too much to bear. The way most of us have been brought up, our response to learning of a spouse's affair would range from "How disgusting!" to "You don't love me any more." Nearly all of us, in such a situation, see a rival. And we bristle like a porcupine or explode like a bomb. Moreover, we feel frightened and betrayed. Trust evaporates. The basis of our marital relationship is damaged. We see an extramarital affair as an enemy of everything our marriage means to us. And we're caught in a bind because our spouse would probably hide an affair (if he or she had one) for fear of these very reactions.

But how realistic is all this? Suppose we find out our spouse is having an affair? We say we've been betrayed and we can trust our spouse no longer. But we need to ask ourselves how much trust we had in the first place. How about the gun-waving Richmond, who wanted to kill his unfaithful wife? He had said, "I trusted her as I trusted my own right hand!" It would be more accurate to say that Richmond was taking her for granted, which is a very different thing, and that he didn't really want to know the truth. For knowing the truth about Diane meant knowing the truth about himself, and he couldn't endure that. In affair after affair, it turns out that trust is not the basic issue it appears to be at first glance. The issue is more likely to be deficient self-knowledge and a wounded ego.

Take Rosalie, who broke her "perfect" marriage in a storm of bitterness when she discovered that Frank had been "playing around" with Norene. She claimed she had trusted Frank implicitly. Had she? She had long ago been programmed by her parents never to trust men. Her claim of a "perfect" marriage was mostly a cover-up for her own misgivings. She had never trusted Frank, really; she had never trusted any man.

My observation has been that *real* trust between marital partners who are loving and close is not often betrayed. People who have been truly intimate for a number of years know a great deal about each other's character structure and value system. Would you want to betray the trust of someone you love and who loves you? Could you, in fact, deceive someone you feel very close to? From what I've seen of secret affairs, I suspect that the secrecy, if maintained long, is often part of a subtle game being played by the marital partners in which one spouse transmits an unspoken message to the other: "If you're having an affair, don't let me know about it because I couldn't stand it—I'd take revenge on you!" This must have been Richmond's attitude toward Diane's affair (which he *had* to have suspected), Jack's attitude toward Daisy's affair (she was the sexy grandmother), and David's attitude (at first) toward Eva's affair with her priest.

There are some spouses who simply don't care very much. Jimmy paid so little attention to Monica that it is obvious he was indifferent to what she did. Theirs was a marriage that should never have taken place.

A trusting and loving spouse reacts entirely differently to an affair than an untrusting, unloving one. Francine trusted Sydney. He acknowledges that his affair with Barbie was a betrayal of his wife's trust, and he feels badly about that. Yet she doesn't upbraid him. She's trying to understand. And she's trying very hard to overcome what she recognizes to be her failures as a wife. She loves Sydney still, and he loves her. The trouble is now he loves two women, one of whom he can no longer be with.

Then there's Kevin and Deborah (Chapter 4) who have the sexually open marriage. It was not always open. Before it became so, Deborah had two extramarital affairs while on holiday without her husband. Kevin's reaction was one of understanding. He said of this event, "I know how Debbie felt. I knew how she reacts to loneliness, and her being on vacation by herself was my fault. She's a free woman and I wouldn't have dreamed of trying to put a fence around her. (She wouldn't have let me anyway.) But, on the other hand, I couldn't have stood it if I had always been wondering and imagining what she was doing with whom. That would have been torture—I love her too much. She feels the same about me. Since we both recognize this and respect it, we are careful now never to hide our affairs from each other, nor to abuse each other's trust."

Telling one's spouse about an affair can, under some circumstances, be a cruel act. We pointed out earlier that some partners do it intentionally to hurt the spouse, saying in effect, "Aha, I've found someone I like better than you." Others reveal their affairs because they feel guilty and want to unload the guilt on the spouse ("I'm a louse! Kick me!"), or they imply that it is the spouse's fault. ("You drove me to it.") Then there are the cases I've mentioned where confessing an affair to a spouse may expose the extramarital partner to danger. In this instance, keeping an affair secret is a matter of personal safety. A woman in an affair said to me, "If my husband found out about my affair, I'm afraid he'd kill me and my lover, too." A paranoid spouse is especially dangerous.

There are cases where a person in an affair tries to persuade his or her spouse to have an affair. The feeling is, "If she/he has an affair too, then I needn't feel so guilty about mine." Mate swapping could be one outcome of such an agreement. Another outcome might be the sexually open marriage. Or a still different outcome—a very common one—might be the attitude that "I won't question your affairs if you are discreet about them and keep them decently under cover." In other words, mutually agreed-upon secrecy!

When affairs are secret, there is no getting around the fact that a secret affair is deception and that deception is incompatible with trust. One of the reasons the spouse of someone in an affair feels so cheated is because he or she was not informed; a piece of vital information about the marriage was withheld. This may be harder to take than the fact of the affair itself. Suppose Dee's husband had found out what his sexually lively wife had been secretly doing behind his back? Would his reaction have been outrage, like Richmond? A feeling of being unloved and rejected, like Francine? Indifference, like Jack and Jimmy? Confusion? Hostility? Unfairness? The feeling, "While I've been working my ass off for this woman, she's been playing around with other men"? The feeling, "She lives off my money, but gives her love to someone else"? Or sympathy and understanding—but with limits—like Kevin? It could be any of these. But Dee herself probably has a fairly accurate idea of what it would be, and that is why she keeps her affair secret. So does Suzanne.

OK, let's grant that Dee and Suzanne were being unfair to their husbands and that the husbands had every reason not to trust their wives. The wives obviously don't entirely trust their husbands either, or they wouldn't find it so necessary to hide their affairs. So the mistrust is mutual. How did it come about? Did the affairs cause it? Or was there lack of trust before the affairs started? And if so, why?

Trust rests on the ability of people to depend on each other, to fulfill the promises they make to each other and not to let each other down. What do you expect of your spouse when you marry? Most people take sexual fidelity for granted. But should you take it for granted any more than you take your spouse for granted? Is there nothing you need do to earn it and have the right to expect it? If you had a traditional church wedding, you made a promise to *love and cherish,* or its equivalent. If your spouse has an affair, thus violating the traditional wedding vows, you might ask yourself whether you have loved and cherished as you promised. If you haven't, weren't the vows already broken? And by you? Perhaps by both? This is a question rarely asked.

Loss of trust does not generally come about suddenly as the result of an extramarital affair. Trust has its origins in childhood—with parents who do not let the child down, who are at home when they promise to be, who give help and comfort, who tell the truth and do not spring unpleasant surprises, who do not ignore or abuse the child's feelings or punish harshly or unjustly. A child who trusts his parents will probably grow into an adult who trusts the people he loves. And even a spouse's secret affair may not destroy a trust so well grounded—for a person who trusts this deeply can also understand and forgive.

10. Coping With Your Spouse's Affair

> My first reaction to my husband's affair was a feeling of betrayal. . . . I was immobilized. . . . I was afraid that revealing the full extent of my grief and pain would repulse him. On the other hand, I thought perhaps he wanted to see this very display of emotion. He said he had hoped I would hold him and declare my need and love for him and desire for him to stay with me. But just then I couldn't. The following morning . . . when he began to caress me I dissolved into tears. . . . I felt a deep bereavement—that I had lost him. It was a physical pain that would not subside. . . . I was thrown into despair. I felt I couldn't compete with the excitement and exhilaration of a new love; that even if he stayed, he would always dream of what might have been and that I had irretrievably lost a part, if not all, of him. . . . Later we made love, but he was impotent and frustrated. . . .
> Emily

SIGNS OF POSSIBLE INFIDELITY

Suppose you suspect your spouse (or lover) to be involved with someone else. All the little signs are there: subtle changes in the relationship between you, a strange awkwardness and difficulty of communication, a feeling of evasion, a tension you can't quite put your finger on. Something is different—what is it? You feel mounting anxiety.

Your spouse doesn't seem to want to talk about it. If you mention your anxiety, you are brushed off. ("I'm just the same." Or "Sure I'm changing—isn't everybody?" Or "Stop worrying! Our marriage is OK.")

Your spouse has rather suddenly shown a new interest in personal appearance and style, perhaps taking exceptional care with clothes and grooming (if formerly careless) or perhaps becoming stylishly careless (if previously conventional and neat). He or she is making new efforts to get rid of extra pounds around the middle, maybe jogging three times a week and going on a health-food kick. Or possibly the reverse: smoking, drinking, and eating more. You may observe your spouse making or receiving telephone calls at unexpected times and talking in a low voice as if not wanting to be overheard.

Your sexual relationship has changed. It may have become more constrained, less satisfying, and less frequent. Or perhaps it's the opposite: Your spouse is more turned on than before, more exotic, wants sex oftener, wants to experiment with new positions of intercourse, and enjoys oral-genital sex that used to be a no-no. If the sex has become more exciting, you may nevertheless feel a lack of emotional intimacy; something seems to be missing. Is your spouse, while having sex with you, fantasizing about having it with someone else? And might that someone be a person he or she has actually been with? The thought disturbs you.

IF YOU'RE A WIFE

If you're a wife, you may find your husband (who had been adequate as a sex partner) suddenly having trouble with impotence and unable to sustain an erection. You seek possible explanations—extreme fatigue, preoccupation with financial or other problems, worry about his job, mental depression, physical illness, etc. None seems to apply. You sense his embarrassment and frustration. Or he may have started suddenly to act like a sex-starved, hot-blooded sexual athlete, taking you by surprise. There are other signs. He seems often moody, irritable, and withdrawn for no visible reason. He has lost (or regained) his interest in several long-cherished hobbies and activities. There are sharp shifts in his personality: He's less stingy and more generous; less conservative and more liberal; less rigid and more experimental. He's bought new underwear (bikini style), dresses a little more youthfully and with a more sportive touch. Or maybe he's wearing jeans for the first time instead of business suits and is beginning to grow a beard. Condoms seem to be missing from his secret drawer in the bedroom dresser.

He's spending more time away from you, too—on business trips, conferences, overtime work, night school, evening meetings, luncheons, entertainment of clients, parties at homes of business associates, or whatever. He has reasonable-sounding explanations for all this, but he's increasingly touchy if asked questions such as: "Where are you going tonight?" or "What time do you expect to be home?" And now he's following a new pattern of coming home after you've gone to bed and fallen asleep. It's as if he doesn't want to face you at that hour.

IF YOU'RE A HUSBAND

If you're a husband worried about your wife's fidelity, you may feel a sudden diminishing of her sexual passion, though it's easier for a woman to feign passion than for a man. (The flaccid penis can so easily give a man away.) Or perhaps your wife is concentrating on not letting you know of her sexual cooling-off and is putting on an act of being passionate that doesn't quite convince you. Or she may actually be more passionate; her affair, if she's having one, may have aroused her sexually so that she's more erotic and wants to make love frequently in new and more exciting ways. Maybe she's having multiple orgasms that she never had before. (Where did she learn that?)

You also may have observed other new things about your wife. She is beaming with a new air of self-confidence, is more socially outgoing and assertive, now reads the latest popular novels, speaks the psychological language of the younger generation, perhaps orders fancy hors d'oeuvres like clams casino and occasionally tells a risqué joke without blushing. You might have noticed also that your wife is dressing in a more modern style, using more makeup (or less makeup), and has just purchased an attractive wig. You remember feeling stunned, momentarily, when you thought you saw her put a diaphragm case in her tote bag just before leaving to visit her mother for the weekend.

Your wife also seems to spend more time away from home, shopping more (and taking longer to do it), eating out more, going to more evening meetings, visiting more with friends, etc. You may be particularly uneasy about her spending so much time with a girl friend who's known to have had several extramarital affairs. And if your wife is a career woman, she may be absent frequently on business or professional trips and related activities. Innocently, perhaps. But can you be sure?

DEALING WITH SUSPICION

By dwelling on all this, you can work yourself up into quite a state and possibly even precipitate the crisis you are afraid of. For distrust is an enemy of healthy human relationships. There could be adequate reasons for the suspicious signs you observe; your spouse may be going through a personal crisis or inner change of some kind. Shouldn't you give your partner the benefit of the doubt? Or is this a shaking up you both need to force you to deal with the unresolved problems of your marriage?

How do you handle a deepening suspicion that's in danger of corroding your relationship with your spouse? If you've been close to your spouse and accustomed to sharing your doubts and anxieties, you may openly tell your feelings: "I'm uneasy about our relationship." Or "I don't feel the closeness we once had." Such a direct expression of your feelings need not accuse or provoke. It merely says what's bothering you. It invites an honest response. Your partner may be concerned about the relationship too, and may have been wondering how to approach you about it. As long as he or she is not thrown on the defensive, the whole matter could be opened up for exploration. Your partner may even be glad to have it come out into the open. It can be hard living with a dark secret. But if your partner evades a sincere response, you'll at least know that whether there's an affair or not, your relationship needs to be revitalized.

Some people, shrinking from an open confession of their feelings, try detective tricks to catch a spouse. They check telephone bills for unfamiliar or frequently called numbers or calls to strange places. They examine credit card charges. They search (a wallet, purse, briefcase, glove compartment of the car, dresser, or clothes closet) for names, addresses, telephone numbers, private bank accounts, love letters, gift sales slips, and motel or restaurant bills. They tap telephones. They record mileage changes on the family car. They make discreet inquiries of their children, or around the neighborhood, or at the spouse's place of work. They watch for lipstick smears, hickeys on a spouse's skin, or new odors of perfume or after-shave lotion. One woman insisted on long hours of lovemaking when she suspected her husband had just made love with someone else. Another woman set a trap for her husband by saying, "I saw you coming out of a motel with so-and-so," when actually she hadn't (but her guess was correct). Some people have been known to hire a detective to trail and record their spouse's comings and goings.

But snooping on a spouse can be devastating to a marriage. And it is likely to yield very little. Suppose, for example, you noted an unexplained charge on the telephone bill or a suspicious-looking credit card purchase. There could be a perfectly innocent explanation. If you asked, "Who were you calling in Phoenix, Arizona, on the twelfth of January?" or "I notice you drove fourteen and a half miles in the car yesterday," your spouse could well retort, "So you're checking up on me, are you?" And suppose you found a lipstick smear in your husband's car (or, if you're a husband, a man's handkerchief in your wife's). What would this prove except that somebody was riding with your spouse? Even lipstick on your husband's shirt collar proves little; for all you know, his secretary may have kissed him (and missed) because he had just raised her salary.

If you find anything really damning, you will have to confront your spouse anyway. So why not confront to begin with and simply say, "I'm worried about our relationship?"

An indirect approach sometimes used is to address a seemingly casual remark to your spouse such as, "Sometimes I wonder what I'd do if you had an affair." You hope this will precipitate a discussion of "what ifs," holding the subject at arm's length without your having to reveal any personal anxieties. But your spouse might demand, "Why are you asking? Don't you trust me?" Then you could be plunged into the very dialogue you're trying to avoid.

If you're blunt and straightforward, you might simply demand to know. "Are you having an affair?" Up would go your spouse's defenses, you'd probably get an indignant denial (which may or may not be a lie), and the gap between you and your spouse could be wider than ever.

You might say nothing; simply watch and wait. This neatly postpones action. Meanwhile, you might learn a great deal. It gives you time to think and get better control of your emotions. On the other hand, some people (like Jack, Daisy's husband, who ignored the evidences of her affair), continue to watch and wait for years until they are frozen in this posture; they never do confront. But if you do this, you may never take any steps to rebuild or enrich your marital relationship. Eventually your spouse may get the impression you don't care or are afraid to face the issue. If you have a dull, boring marriage, like Charlotte's (Chapter 3), it may become even duller and more boring while your spouse turns increasingly to the extramarital partner for emotional satisfaction. Or else your marriage breaks up.

In the end, if you want your marriage to survive, you'll probably need to talk out your feelings openly with your spouse. But take care how you do it. There are ways that disrupt and ways that heal.

DISCOVERY—AND INITIAL REACTIONS

A common reaction of people, when they first begin to wonder whether their spouse is having (or has had) an affair, is to take an ostrich approach: "I can't imagine my wife in bed with someone else." "My husband is too prudish." "My spouse would be overcome by guilt." "It's just impossible." Troubled by an image they can't bear to bring into focus, ostrich people put their heads in the sand; they refuse to face the possibility of a spouse's infidelity. Children, relatives, and friends, too, often react this way. Such a posture can be maintained for long periods of time—or forever—because family members realize that once an affair is exposed or acknowledged, something may have to be done about it—and they don't want to have to do it.

If it becomes clear that your spouse is really having an affair, the knowledge is almost certain to come as a shock. Your initial reaction is vital, because it may have a lot to do with whether your marriage is wrecked or reclaimed. Faced with an unfaithful spouse, what would you do? Withdraw into cold silence? Pretend it didn't happen? Raise hell and resort to violence? Leave and start separation and divorce proceedings? Or would you remain in the marriage but punish your spouse, lay a heavy guilt trip on your spouse, never let him or her forget, demand constant explanations of your spouse's comings and goings, etc.? Would you punish or expose the "other woman" or "other man"? Would you retaliate by having an affair of your own? Or would you plead for your spouse's love and make a frantic attempt to reestablish a relationship?

All these are very human reactions, but any of them could damage or destroy your marriage.

There are other possible reactions. Would you discuss the situation and your feelings about it with your spouse? Or with a close friend or a clergyman? Would you examine honestly the state of your marriage and face up to how you might have contributed to your spouse's affair? Would you respond with sympathy, understanding, support, and reassurance? Would you get professional help? Would you try to work on the strengthening of your marriage? These are mature responses, and they are real choices if you prize your marriage.

THE DIFFERING RESPONSES OF MEN AND WOMEN

Men are often more upset by their wives' affairs than women by their husbands'. The notion that men are less emotional than women is a myth. Men merely hide their emotions more, often even from themselves.

Their emotions may pile up undetected until they explode (as in Richmond's case) or their emotional life burns out from within and dries up (as in Jack's).

One reason some men are so deeply disturbed by their wives' affairs is that they may carry deep within them surviving remnants of the ancient tradition I mentioned before—that their women *belong to them.* Many modern men are under the impression they have outgrown this attitude, but the emotional residues remain. The man's view, felt in his gut, is "She's mine!" And he'll fight to keep her for himself. Many women, on the other hand, have long had to bear up under the knowledge of their husbands' mistresses and sexual roaming. Through ages of conditioning, women seem to have become the more adaptable sex. Often they are closer to their feelings than most men, and therefore are more at home with emotions and more competent at dealing with them (though there are exceptions). It's not that a woman is less hurt by a husband's affair than a man by a wife's, but simply that the woman, in many cases, is better equipped to cope.

THE TIDES OF THE EMOTIONS

The discovery of a spouse's affair can be devastating—the emotional equivalent of having a limb amputated without anesthetic. Even if you don't love your spouse, you may discover a degree of emotional attachment you had never believed existed. Your relationship may be one of dependency rather than of love; but the agony is there just the same.

You are likely to go through a series of emotional phases:

1. First: amazement, disbelief, confusion, and/or disorientation, or else an attidue of "I knew it all along!" If the evidence is too strong to permit the ostrich approach, or if the spouse has confessed, this phase moves swiftly into . . .

2. Raging emotions: anger, fear, betrayal, anxiety, wounded pride, hatred, resentment, a sense of irreparable loss, rejection, sorrow, despair, perhaps terrible guilt, and self-abasement. Though your spouse had the affair, it may be you who feels guilty because you may consider yourself to blame. Or you may feel debased, unattractive, abandoned, or worthless because your spouse has turned away from you.

3. There may follow aching disillusionment, alienation, loneliness, and self-pity, or a smoldering desire to punish and retaliate.

4. Then, a desire (or compulsion) to learn all the facts of the affair—or, if you are of a different temperament, a wish not to know anything about it at all. If you press for the details, it may be because you want to feel the pain, or store up ammunition to clobber your spouse, or get a sexual "kick"; perhaps you hope you might gain insight into what the affair offered that the marriage did not. Perhaps you may feel several of these reactions at once.

5. After the first phases pass, an evaluation and assessment of

yourself, your spouse, your marriage, and your family. You begin slowly to recover your spirits. You may be able to think more calmly now and consider what the future may hold.

6. Then, exploring the alternatives you face: e.g., terminating your marriage, reconciling yourself to your spouse's affair, trying to build a closer and more rewarding relationship with your spouse, or having an affair of your own. You weigh the effects each of these choices would have on you, your spouse, and your children.

7. Making or postponing decisions about the future—of yourself, your marriage, and your family.

8. Finally, learning to live with what has happened or is happening; maintaining or rebuilding your damaged self-esteem and participating actively in life, with or without your spouse; and putting behind you, if you can, the experience.

Your first thought when you learn of the affair may be, "My spouse doesn't love me anymore!" You feel rejected. Someone else has taken your place. But yielding to this feeling is like surrendering in a war before the first battle is fought. You may be greatly in error in assuming that your spouse has rejected you, or that you've permanently lost out to the extramarital partner, or that your marriage is finished. None of these things may be true. They might ultimately become true if you react in panic, rage, retaliation, or hysterical clinging; but if you relate constructively with your spouse, you may be able—in time—to shift the advantage in your favor.

One thing you can do is count your assets. You're *married* to your spouse. The other person isn't. Unless your relationship has been very poor, that can be a real advantage. You have a better opportunity to assess your marriage and seek to make it more meaningful for you both. You have a chance to see and talk with your spouse every day (presumably) and may be able to tap into his or her feelings. What are your partner's (and your own) needs and wants that are not being met in the marriage? Might your spouse be longing for more responsiveness, affection, and intimacy? More sharing of interests? Better communication? More sex, or better sex? More recreation? More time with you? Have you been too preoccupied with your career or your children or your own personal interests to give your spouse much attention? Is it possible that what looks like a decline in love for you is really a decline in your spouse's love of himself or herself? Does this call for your understanding and sympathy? What can you do to enliven or enrich your marriage? What changes in priorities would you need to make?

It may be especially hard to face up to the rivalry of someone younger and perhaps more energetic, vivacious, and physically attractive than you. But physical attraction is often overrated. Infatuations are apt to be temporary. Remember that you have assets, too. Your body may not be quite so alluring, though you probably can improve it. But your personality, the fruit of years of life's experiences, may reflect a richness that could, in the long run, more than offset the temporary fascination of a luscious young body. Maybe all you need do is make full use of your assets—and wait.

Consider the possibility that your spouse's affair may not have been caused by dissatisfaction with you or your marriage. It may have arisen out of emotional patterns and needs of your spouse, or of extended separation from you (such as working in another state or another country), or may be a result of the stage of life your spouse is in. He or she may, for example, have reached a point where there is need for reassurance of continued attractiveness to someone of the opposite sex. Your own reassurance on this point may not be enough; your spouse may discount what you say and want evidence from someone else. This may be something you'll just have to live through with such forbearance and understanding as you can summon up. An affair having any of these roots may not be in any way a repudiation of you and may be fairly short-lived, but it can be painful even when you understand this.

You may feel your spouse has done a terrible thing to you. Our traditions encourage this feeling. But consider that your spouse may feel terrible about it too. Isn't it possible that he or she feels guilty, miserable, and vulnerable, and is hungry for your understanding and support? It could be. Even if there is no evidence of this, your spouse may be trying to hide such feelings or refusing to admit them. Yet a willingness on your part to listen constructively, to try to understand, and to be sensitive to your partner's feelings could act like a healing balm. Kevin's willingness to understand Deborah's early affairs drew these two together in a closer bond than they'd achieved before.

Affairs don't strike out of the blue. Nearly always, as we've pointed out, there's been a long buildup. Most of the buildup probably has been internal and therefore not easily observed: a matter of hopes and dreams and, perhaps, personal growth—or personal deterioration. If you were surprised by your spouse's affair, it could mean that you were not very close to your spouse. It could also mean that your partner is a very private person who doesn't readily reveal the events and changes taking place within. The two of you may have been slowly drifting apart without your conscious awareness. Has your relationship perhaps become dull, boring, and dispirited? Have you passively allowed this to happen? Because if you have, you unquestionably share some of the responsibility for your spouse's turning to someone else. It's no use letting yourself be consumed with self-denigration. Rather, try to put some life back into your fading relationship.

It's possible, of course, that it is too late to repair your marriage. If you or your spouse has been insensitive and unaware and allowed your marriage to deteriorate beyond the point where you both want to reclaim it, it may be time to let it go. But if you want to save your marriage, don't assume it is dead until the fact becomes evident beyond any doubt.

SAVING YOUR MARRIAGE

If your objective is to preserve your marriage, your spouse's affair might turn out to be the catalyst you both need to transform it. An affair, as we've seen, may be a growing experience for both partners. Your spouse may have been learning from the affair what a qualitative relationship is like, and what is needed to sustain it. He or she might eventually apply that knowledge to the relationship with you. Would you be open enough to accept it? Would you be willing to work on the revitalizing of your marital relationship?

It was this latter course that Emily took. (Emily is the author of the lines quoted at the beginning of this chapter.) She was at first overwhelmed by grief, a sense of loss, a feeling of hopelessness, and, of course, the emotions of rejection and anger.

"After I got a grip on myself," she wrote, "I told my husband my feelings. He acknowledged them and said he feared that his affair would always stand between us. That evening we explored the effects his leaving would have on the children and their image of him, on his financial status and life-style, his status in the community and relationship with his parents and mine. He maintained, however, that these were not the chief deterrents to his leaving, but that *I* was. . . . He said he was prepared to stay with our marriage—but our marriage must be made very different from what it had been. . . . Later we made love, but he was impotent and extremely frustrated because he wanted to make love to me very much. I could feel his pain and it distressed me.

"The following day he greeted me after work with the most expressive hug I had felt from him in a long time. After dinner we discussed again our feelings . . . and how we might alter our relationship. We explored those patterns in each of us that tended to turn the other off. We also explored how these patterns had come about. Once again we made love, and again he had difficulty maintaining an erection. I felt a deep hurt for him and for myself, wondering if this was a reflection of his feelings for me or of his guilt, and anxious about whether it would be a continuing problem. . . .

"*It's my belief that if my husband had not told me of his affair we would not have had a chance of progressing into a new and better relationship.* I wanted to build upon this experience to achieve that goal. I wanted also to continue therapy to overcome my excessive emotional dependence on my husband. I intend to replace my too-dependent self with a more autonomous self. Thus I could learn to face either a separation from my husband or the enrichment of our marriage, whichever would eventually come about."

Emily's recital sounds deceptively calm because she wrote it after her emotional turmoil had subsided. But she had maintained throughout the experience sufficient self-control not to indulge in hysterical recriminations like Rosalie's, or in frantic clinging or pleading that might have pushed her husband away. By her concern, openness, self-respect, and attempts to understand, she kept her marriage intact. How permanently, it's too early to tell. But even if he eventually decides to leave, she's a stronger person than before.

WORKING AND GROWING TOGETHER

A spouse's affair can be like an emergency alarm. Its message is, "Examine yourself, your partner, and your relationship—or take the consequences." Where and how do you begin to do this? One of the first essentials is better communication.

When we speak of communication, most of us think of communication between persons. But there's an even more basic kind of communication: that between *different parts of yourself*. Inadequate internal communication is usually at the root of defective external communication. Where internal communication generally fails is in the transmission of feelings. We don't always acknowledge our feelings to ourselves. Instead, we too often suppress, ignore, or dismiss them. As a result we issue false signals to ourselves and hence to others, and in this way our relationships with people are undermined. This is a prime cause of a deteriorating marriage or of any deteriorating relationship.

Denied feelings very often surface in an extramarital affair. Consider how your spouse came to be involved with the other person. Very likely this happened through a mixture of emotions that he or she probably only partially understood. There were doubtless dreams and longings, anxieties and misgivings, fears and wonderings, sadness and joy, excitement, infatuation, possibly guilt and shame—a vast array of feelings, some in conflict with others. Yet unless your spouse is an exceptionally aware person, it's almost certain that he or she was not clearly conscious of all these feelings, didn't sort them out or acknowledge them, didn't communicate them internally or externally or appraise where they were leading. Your spouse somehow got into the affair, and may now be wondering how it came about or how to get out of it. The inner processes that led to it may be only partially grasped.

Now you yourself are in a somewhat similar position. You're buffeted by feelings of every variety and are not sure of what they all are, where they came from, or where they are leading. Are you able to sort them out, acknowledge them, and decipher their meaning? Do you feel the sorrow as well as the anger? The compassion as well as the contempt? The love as well as the hate? If you are aware of these many feelings coursing through you and can identify and think about them, you have effective internal communication.

As a therapist working with individuals, couples, and families faced with crises, or who simply want to develop their personal and interpersonal competence, I teach a ten-step approach* to help people open up their internal and external communication so that these storms of feelings begin to make sense and can be constructively dealt with. Here are the steps as they would apply to coping with a spouse's affair. They can be readily learned and, with practice, mastered.

1. *Working with your feelings.* Feelings flicker through your consciousness sometimes like dreams or ghosts. They are there, and a moment later they aren't. Often only intense feelings like rage, fear, or passionate love seize the front of the stage and stay in consciousness for any extended length of time. But you may deceive yourself by this. Many of the intense emotions that dominate your consciousness are harsh, like hate or terror. They can eclipse gentler feelings such as mature love, sympathy, sadness, and compassion. Yet the softer feelings are within you, too, and it is these that can help you most in a crisis . . . or to grow as a person. You need to seek them out and build on them if you are to heal your relationship with your marital partner. For feelings lie at the heart of whatever you think or do.

Fortunately, if you are emotionally healthy, harsh feelings tend in time to burn themselves out unless you hamper the healing process by pouring fuel on them by raking up past injustices, dwelling on old hurts, etc. Softer feelings, because they are constructive, have much greater staying power in the long run. But you may have to seek out these feelings and give them a chance. To do this requires conscious effort. You need to ask yourself at a particular moment, "What am I feeling now?" If you feel, for example, rage, then ask, "What else am I feeling?" The answer cannot be "nothing." There is an endless river of feelings of every variety flowing in you at every moment. If you are aware *only* of the dominating emotion, your inner communication channels are partly blocked.

Not only do feelings flow ceaselessly within you, but they often include parts of coexisting opposites: joy-pain, love-hate, fear-trust, excitement-boredom, confidence-anxiety, etc. Everyone has experienced loving and hating at the same time, or felt simultaneous joy and pain. But rarely do we separate them consciously and look at them individually. Underneath your resentment you may feel, for example, a touch of sympathy for the pain your spouse may be feeling. Capture that feeling and build upon it.

Examine your feelings in your present setting. What is going on *now* in your life? What evoked your feelings? What are you doing at *this* moment? What is your spouse doing? How are you reacting to your spouse? How is your spouse reacting to you?

How I work as a therapist is described in detail in my college textbook, Open Family and Marriage: A Guide to Personal Growth *(C. V. Mosby Co., 1976), coauthored with Dana G. Finnegan. This text can be used in courses which focus on personal growth, marriage, and family enrichment. A supplementary book for the courses is* Open Family Living *(Doubleday and Co., 1976) coauthored with John U. Ayres.*

If you feel *fear,* ask yourself what brought on this fear. Is it fear of being supplanted by a rival? Is this a new fear or an old one? Have you dreaded being displaced in someone's affection at an earlier time in your life—perhaps when a younger sibling got more of your parents' attention than you did. Are you replaying the fear of loss of affection you felt then? Are you sure your present fear is justified? Is it possible you are too emotionally dependent on your spouse?

Or is it the feeling of *rejection* that hurts most? Your spouse's affair may feel to you like a slap in the face. Did you feel rejected as a child? Did you ever feel unloved by your parents, or peers, or siblings, or teachers? Did it injure your self-esteem? Is this what you are feeling now? Yet you survived all those earlier rejections. You'll survive this one, too (if, in fact, it is a rejection). And suppose your spouse's affair is not a rejection of you at all, but rather a new and exciting experience that he or she could not share with you?

There are, no doubt, feelings of *sadness* and *disappointment*—the feelings that Emily experienced so deeply. You grieve for what seems an irreparable loss. If it's not the marriage itself you feel to be lost, it is something precious in the marriage—trust, perhaps. Can the marriage ever again be the same? In time you may find that it can—not just be the same, but better. That depends on how you and your partner work things out.

Whatever your feelings are, they are yours and you must take responsibility for them. Do you blame your feelings on someone else? ("He infuriates me!" "She drives me crazy!") This is avoiding responsibility for what you feel. Nobody infuriates you or drives you crazy. By saying somebody does, you are handing over to another person the power to control your emotional life. You may react to someone's words or actions by being furious, but it's *your* reaction—the fury is all yours. You could have made other choices—you might have been amused or sympathetic or curious; there are any number of other ways of reacting. If you have a pattern of attributing your feelings to others, you cheat yourself by not learning how to deal honestly with feelings.

Becoming aware of and identifying feelings is a learnable technique. I teach it to all my patients and students because it's the basic step of internal communication through which people are enabled to gain control over their lives. Like other hazards of life, violent emotions are far less fearsome if you have learned their nature and powers. But you have to work at understanding them. With practice, you can learn to feel your feelings at the moment they come into being; you don't let them slip by unacknowledged. If you feel irritation with something your spouse has said or done, you catch the feeling as it occurs and note what evoked it. You deal with it at once; you communicate it, if appropriate. ("I'm bothered when you do such-and-such.") You don't let irritations pile up to burst forth later.

If the feeling is one of happiness or relief or affection or sadness—whatever it is, express it. Be as open as you can. Emily did this successfully: "I told my husband my feelings." Her husband was encouraged by this to confide his own feelings. There were further discussions: "After dinner we discussed again our feelings . . . and how we might alter our relationship." It was this open communication that led the way toward their attempt to put new life into a relationship that had gone partly stale. If each had kept his/her feelings bottled up, there could have been no coming together. But don't confuse expressing and communicating feelings with bursting out with them (like Richmond's "I'll kill her!") or acting them out (like the unfortunate Rosalie).

2. *Gathering information.* A festering sore in any crisis is apt to be lack of information. You have little accurate knowledge of your spouse's affair—probably only what he or she has chosen to tell you. You tend to fall back on suspicions, guesswork, and surmise. This is risky. A surmise can be entirely wrong. One of the chronic troubles in unhappy marriages is the use of surmise instead of fact—a direct result of poor communication. If you see a worried expression on your spouse's face, do you ask what's troubling him/her? Or do you silently speculate on the cause? Perhaps you guess that your spouse is worried about his job. But suppose your spouse is worried not about his job but about your drinking habits? Unless you bring out the facts by direct communication, you could annoy or worry each other indefinitely.

Extramarital affairs, because of their secrecy and the embarrassment that so often accompanies them, can produce endless wrong guesses and mistaken judgments. You may imagine your spouse to be wildly in love with the "other man" or "other woman." But that may not be true at all; the affair may have been triggered by temporary loneliness or a fleeting desire for comfort or a passing sexual urge—there could have been any number of reasons. The affair itself may have been a failure, a disappointment. Your spouse may be afraid to tell you his real feelings out of shame, embarrassment, or fear of hurting you or being hurt by you, whereas you might have preferred to know the truth regardless of the pain. Living in a welter of confusion and half-knowledge is like trying to find your way in a pea-soup fog with open manholes at your feet.

If you can't communicate verbally with your spouse, the messages between you may be restricted to body language: the stiffening of muscles, the rigid or relaxed postures, the pulling back or pushing forward of the body, the tight facial expressions, the movement of the eyes, the turning toward or turning away. These may tell more than words do, for many of the body's movements and postures are unconscious and reflect accurately the emotions within. But they do not disclose the reasons for the emotions, and guesses about those can be very wide of the mark. If you ask your spouse, "Are you having an affair?" and your spouse's body response betrays a startled chagrin, you could be mistaken in assuming that this reveals guilt. It could reflect amazement or embarrassment that you should entertain such a thought, or a fear that you might have guessed his or her fantasies. You could easily read more into body language than is there.

3. *Acquiring insight.* As communication improves, the fog gradually lifts and the realities can be discerned more clearly. Things that had made no sense begin to fall into place. You begin to understand what really happened and get a feeling as to why it happened. This is *insight.*

It was a flash of insight that led Emily to write: "It's my belief that if my husband had not told me of his affair, we would not have had a chance to progress into a new and better relationship." She saw clearly that if this jarring crisis hadn't occurred, she and her husband would inevitably have drifted further apart; she might never have understood what was happening or why, and ultimately the marriage would probably have died. This was a very mature insight, arrived at only after a painful struggle with her feelings and the beginning of more open communication between her husband and herself. True insight has an "aha!" quality that distinguishes it from surmise or guesswork. It sometimes bursts upon you like a revelation after struggle and contemplation.

4. *Negotiating.* Two people living together have to learn to negotiate, otherwise one tends to impose his will on the other. But negotiation is not only between persons. There is also internal negotiation between the different parts of yourself. You experience inner conflicts where one part of you is warring against another part. Yet when there are decisions to be made, a resolution has to be found. You need to negotiate it within yourself.

You may, for example, be faced with the question of whether to preserve your marriage or dissolve it. One part of you may insist on ending it since your spouse has proved unfaithful. ("I can never trust him/her again.") Another part of you may want to rebuild your relationship ("I can't bear the thought of breaking up!") Resolution of your internal conflict directly affects any later negotiations you may carry on with your spouse. You reflect on the possibilities and consequences of each choice. You may want to discuss these possibilities and consequences with your partner. Or better yet, explore with your spouse the inner conflict itself. ("I feel torn apart.")

Assuming you both want to continue the marriage, you have many questions to resolve together, all of which involve negotiation. What kind of marital relationship do you both want? Is it to be one of closer intimacy and more sharing of thoughts, feelings, and values? Or do you both want greater privacy and independence? Are you willing to give each other greater freedom? What understandings will you have about each other's friendships? About the children? What commitments will you make to each other? Do you mutually agree to sexual fidelity? Can you live with it if your partner is unwilling to promise this? Do you love each other enough to make allowances for each other's mistakes? Do you feel you can grow closer over the years?

The essence of negotiation is that each issue be considered fairly, with each partner willing to listen to the views of the others. It's not negotiation if you interrupt your partner, refuse to listen, issue ultimatums, pound your fist, or attempt to override or ridicule your partner's views. Nor is it negotiation if you passively give in to the other's demands. Negotiation is, by its very nature, a *process between equals*. It requires not only a willingness to take the other's preferences into consideration, but a willingness to make your own preferences clearly known; for if your partner doesn't know what you prefer, the negotiation is one-sided and biased and you may be left dissatisfied. In negotiation, neither partner may get everything he wants, but the result is not felt to be unfair by either one. Each makes allowances for the needs, values, and preferences of the other. Each is willing to let the other make a difference—to shed new light, to modify an opinion, or to change a feeling.

5. *Exploring alternatives.* There are always alternatives to any proposed course of action; negotiation calls for a willingness to consider them and try new approaches. If you allow no alternative to breaking the marriage, negotiation is at an end (or may never have begun).

You may have taken for granted (as lots of people do) that the only acceptable response to a spouse's infidelity is divorce. But that's only an assumption based on a particular value system. It may be your choice, but it's certainly not the only possible choice. Several of the spouses we met earlier made other choices. Daisy's husband, Jack, for example, ignored Daisy's affair (a poor choice because it provided no impetus for building a better relationship with Daisy). Not much interested in preserving her marriage, Henrietta responded to Harry's affair by seeking an affair of her own. Charlotte's husband reacted to her affair by calling her a slut. Emily and Francine are trying to revitalize their marriages.

You may not care for any of these choices, but the fact that they exist is important. You may choose a still different alternative. Stay as flexible as you can. If your value system limits your choices too drastically, you may wish to explore the value system itself. There could be circumstances in which you might choose to discard a value you had long held rather than break a relationship that is precious to you. This was the case with Eva and Father Gordon, whose views on the sanctity of marriage changed under the pressure of their love for each other.

6. *Making decisions.* The time for decisions has come. You've avoided power plays, yet haven't let yourself become the victim of one. You and your spouse have negotiated as equals. You're not about to make a compromise that leaves either of you dissatisfied or resentful. You've made plans that are reasonably acceptable to you both. On some points you may have agreed to disagree. That's all right, too, if each of you respects the other's position and doesn't try to impose his own view.

When your decisions are finally made, you accept responsibility for them. If you later regret a decision, you don't blame it on your spouse. ("He made me agree to this.") If you negotiated fairly, neither of you "made" the other agree to anything.

7. *Implementing your decisions.* Implementing means carrying out your decisions and accepting the accompanying risks. Every action involves

risk. So does inaction. You take a risk every time you step out of bed—or stay in bed. Doing nothing or deciding nothing is a decision in itself, and usually not a good one.

So it is with marital decisions: staying married or breaking apart, granting freedom or trying to limit it, giving or withholding love, sharing feelings or keeping them hidden, etc. Experiment. See what works and what doesn't. Some decisions may turn out to have been mistakes. If so, you may be able to alter them. Perhaps you'll need, in some cases, to renegotiate. If you stay open, there's a good chance you can modify faulty decisions—just as a pilot, finding wind driving his plane off course, makes compensating adjustments to offset his error.

8. *Building a new life-style.* Whatever your decisions, you will be entering a new way of life. If you've chosen separation or divorce, you'll be learning to live without a spouse and in a new kind of relationship with your children. If you've decided to remain in your marriage, it will not be the same relationship with your spouse that you had before. Hopefully you'll be practicing much greater openness and healthier communication. You will have to devote time and effort to this; it will not come easily. Yet the process of personal growth is also exciting and liberating. These new ways, perhaps strange or uncomfortable at first, will come to seem more natural and right as you gain experience with them. You'll find increasing satisfaction with the open approach as you enjoy the heightened warmth, intimacy, and affection it brings. You'll not want to drift back to the old ways. As you practice human relationship as an art, you build in personal and interpersonal competence and make the new approaches more and more an integral part of your life. In this way you lay the groundwork for a long-term qualitative relationship with your spouse and family. Because communication with your partner will be more effective than in the past, you'll have less reason to feel anxiety and distrust. There won't be a need to check out constantly whether your spouse still loves you or is being faithful; you'll know these things in your heart because you and your spouse are in good communication and rapport with each other.

9. *Teaching your competence to others.* As you become skilled in these new ways of interacting, you'll be increasingly able to help your spouse and other family members to develop their own competence in the arts of communication and human relationship. As you reach out to them, they are helped to reach out to you. And you and they can grasp hands and move on together. Communication, in the long run, needs to be two-way. If one partner keeps his guard up and refuses to communicate, it can become very difficult for the other to stay open for long.

10. *Living out the new approach.* Ultimately, as you become accomplished in maintaining healthy human relationships, it becomes second nature to apply your skills. They are no longer "techniques." They have simply become the way you live and interact with yourself and with people. You don't any longer need to ask yourself "What am I feeling?" You've learned to know your feelings. You don't need to tell yourself "I must

acknowledge and express my feelings." You do that naturally. You don't have to say "I must communicate." Communicating your feelings, values, expectations, thoughts, and hopes has become part of the new person you now are. This is being "born again" in a psychological sense. You're a more considerate, affectionate, understanding, and lovable person than you were. You are better able to love yourself as well as your spouse and family—and to be loved.

GUIDELINES FOR REBUILDING A DAMAGED RELATIONSHIP

There are no fixed rules. But I can suggest guidelines that may be helpful.

1. Try not to be hostile or vindictive. Anger and hostility aren't the same, though they often go together. You can freely admit you're angry and yet not be hostile. Anger is apparent enough anyway, whether you try to hide it or not. But hostile reactions—humiliating your spouse, laughing at him or her ("that's ridiculous!"), showing contempt or sarcasm or indifference to your spouse's feelings—can undermine your relationship and shut off communication entirely.

2. Don't push too hard to open up a reluctant spouse. People communicate only when they are ready and when they trust you sufficiently.

3. But, on the other hand, don't use your spouse's reluctance as an excuse to withdraw and give up attempts to communicate. Keep trying, but without prodding or nagging. You'll learn when to ease off.

4. Never assume what your spouse is feeling or thinking. Ask. Faulty assumptions can wreck your relationship.

5. Don't take your spouse for granted. That is fatal to a relationship. Let your spouse know that he or she is important to you.

6. Avoid questioning *why* ("Why did you do it?")—at least in the beginning. To answer honestly a "why" question, your spouse would need to understand many complex aspects of the extramarital experience. Such a question assumes that he or she has already come to grips with "why." But until he or she has, a quick answer to "why" is likely to be evasive, defensive, and incomplete. Better go easy in this area until you're reasonably sure your "why" approach won't be interpreted as an unspoken accusation, "you bastard!" or "you bitch!"

7. Try to get feedback from your spouse. Encourage your partner to tell you how he/she feels about you, and give respectful attention to what you hear. Don't belittle or discount the other's feelings.

8. If your spouse has trouble getting in touch with his or her feelings, try to help and encourage without seeming to probe.

9. Be as open as you can, even if you feel sometimes vulnerable. Your openness will help your spouse be more open.

10. If things get too hot or uncomfortable as you interact, back off. Sensitive areas may take time and tact to deal with. There's no hurry. Try again at a more appropriate time.

11. Beware of self-pity. It will drive your spouse away. Pick up the pieces of your life and go forward.

12. Try to keep your sense of humor. If you can laugh at yourself, you're miles ahead.

Coping with the infidelity of a spouse can (if you let it) open for you the door to coping with yourself, and through it you may increase your capacity to cope with any crisis. This can convert what seemed at first to be a disaster into a lasting asset that can serve you well all your life.

11. Coping With Your Own Affair

THE CHALLENGE: CAN YOU COPE?

Problems and anxieties haunt most couple relationships at one time or another—extramarital affairs as well as marriages. Both call for a capacity to *cope*. The dictionary defines cope: "to contend or deal successfully with." That capacity was what many of the people having extramarital affairs described in this book had lacked to a considerable degree, and that is why their suffering was so great.

If you are in an affair, you may find yourself plunged into tearing conflicts of emotions and confusions of values that exceed anything you've had to deal with before. You may feel, on the one hand, the joy of a new love with its pleasures, excitement, anticipation, and wonderment. But you may also feel anxiety, uncertainty, heartache, disappointment, shame, guilt, and fear of discovery. Your values and views about marriage may be upended. Your strict prohibitions about affairs may suddenly have vanished. From a one-to-one relationship with your spouse you are now in a triangular situation where the lives and feelings of three or even more people are involved. The opportunities for heartbreak—as well as euphoria—are increased in geometric proportion. How do you cope?

In the previous chapter, *Coping With Your Spouse's Affair,* I described a ten-step approach to opening up internal and external communication so that emotional storms can be better understood and constructively dealt with. The first of these steps, you may recall, is *working with your feelings*—becoming aware of your feelings, identifying them, considering where they came from, how appropriate they are, etc. These same steps can unlock the doors to coping with your own affair and, in fact, with any problem or crisis. They can enhance your relationships with others and remove obstacles to your personal growth. Through them you can become much more aware of who you are, how you got to be who you are, and how you think and feel about yourself.

For some people, as we've seen, an affair can be a positive and creative experience; for others, a disaster. The way you experience it depends greatly on your self-knowledge, your motivations, your understanding of the other people involved, and your capacity to deal effectively with your life. That's how following the ten steps of the system can work for you: After becoming more aware of your own feelings, you can begin to gather information, acquire insight, negotiate (with yourself, in this case), explore alternatives, implement your decisions, build a new life style based on new intrapersonal and interpersonal skills, teach your newly acquired competency to others, and finally actually *live* the new approach.

STAGES OF AN AFFAIR

Like all couple relationships with emotional depth, an extramarital affair is likely to proceed through an identifiable sequence of stages. While the order and significance of the stages will undoubtedly be different for different individuals, I've isolated at least six of the most frequently reported stages, each with its own set of coping problems. At any stage, the unfolding process may be accelerated, halted, or even reversed.

We've observed that an affair usually does not come about unless two people are ripe for it—when there is an emotional dry spot in their lives, an unsatisfied sexual desire, a concern that life is passing them by, a worry about their attractiveness to others, an uncertainty about their masculinity or femininity, a resentment against their spouse, a desire to prove something or to get even with someone. Or when there is an urge to explore new and exciting relationships, to learn about oneself and others, to try out new behavior, to break out of rigid patterns and experiment with alternative life styles. When the emotional stage is set, an accidental meeting, an inadvertent touch, an admiring glance, an unexpected opportunity to be alone with someone, an almost imperceptible body signal, a whiff of perfume, a nostalgic feeling (stirred, maybe, by a strain of music or the color of a dress)—any of these can ignite an affair.

STAGE 1—FANTASY

Affairs begin in the mind with fantasies and daydreams. Far more people imagine themselves having affairs than actually have them, just as many more people dream of getting rich than ever acquire wealth. The dreams and anticipations of an affair are part of the joy—and part of the sadness. Your coping problems begin when you discover that the reality does not match your dreams.

Dreaming of an ideal is a very human trait. A man imagines a perfect woman—beautiful, enchanting, warm, affectionate, a wonderful sex partner—who lives only in his fantasies but influences his outer life. He may think he sees her in his neighbor's wife; yet he is seeing, not the real woman, but a picture of her conjured up in his mind. A woman imagines a perfect man—strong, kind, dependable, handsome, a great lover—who lives in her fantasies but affects the way she reacts to people. She may think she sees him in a coworker or boss; but she too is not seeing the real person. Who in the actual world can compete with such dreams? A harried wife, weary after a day's work and trying to make dinner, do the laundry, and tend the baby—can she match her husband's secret golden girl? Can the husband—overweight, irritable after his day's work, and absorbed in watching TV—compete with his wife's "white knight"? The seed of an extramarital affair is planted right there in these dreams and disappointments. It may never come to bloom. But if the fantasy is nourished, it can lead to that whirlwind of passions and imaginings we call romance.

Romance carries with it an element of mystery, even a touch of the miraculous. People have been known to throw caution to the wind and to risk their lives and fortunes just to be together. Romantic involvement can produce profound alterations in a person's habitual or expected behavior, sometimes converting prudence into daring, timidity into bravery, aloofness into gregariousness, passivity into assertiveness, guardedness into spontaneity. If you have been romantically involved, no doubt you can think of other changes which have taken place in your personality.

How did you integrate the "new you" into the environment formerly occupied by the "old you?" How did your spouse respond to your apparently "uncharacteristic" behavior?

STAGE 2—CHOOSING AN EXTRAMARITAL PARTNER

Because this stage is interrelated with the previous one, it's difficult to predict which will come first. If you've been fantasizing about a romantic involvement, you may already be in the process (consciously or unconsciously) of casting about for a suitable partner. Do you know yourself well enough at this point to be sure your choice is the most appropriate one for your particular needs and desires?

Virtually all choices you make are the result of a combination of intellectual and emotional factors. In some people, the intellectual component is dominant (the cooly rational type who always "uses his head"). Others are guided primarily by emotions. ("I just had to do it; I don't know why.") But even when one factor is dominant, the other is never completely absent. Both thoughts and feelings are always at work influencing your behavior—sometimes without your conscious awareness. The most appropriate choices, therefore, are those made when both intellect and emotions are allowed equal play, neither hampering the other.

The same principles, of course, are operating when you make a decision whether to have an affair—and with whom. If you allow emotions to push all reason aside, you could find yourself caught in a destructive relationship. On the other hand, a decision made on purely intellectual grounds could be interpreted as exploitative, manipulative, and unfeeling.

By putting your heart and head together, you gain increased understanding of your own motivations and can better assess yourself in relation to the other person. As we saw in Chapter 7, there are other options to having an affair; no one *has* to have one. But just as the variables listed in Chapter 7 give some indication of why a person might choose to have an affair, they also influence the choice of partner.

In the affairs explored in this book, both emotional and intellectual factors were clearly operating as each individual selected a partner who fitted his or her needs at the time. Becky (with the mean crippled husband) picked unexciting but understanding men who would be kind to her and give her comfort. Diane, Richmond's wife, picked a man who would love her passionately with wine, poetry, and flowers. Daisy, in a very dull marriage, picked a middle-aged sexual athlete with whom she could "live it up." Sydney, the screenplay director, picked a charming and exciting woman (Barbie) who entranced him. Monica, with her sexually repressed background, picked an adventurer to teach her about life (but had to dump him later). Harry, the playboy, picked a young admirer whom he could impress as well as enjoy. Henrietta, his wife, picked a steady man with whom she felt companionable and secure. Deborah, on her two holiday trips, picked men with whom she could enjoy an exciting night or two but who would not pursue her afterward to disturb her marriage. Eva picked her idea of a perfect man, her priest, who truly loved her. Dee, bored with her marriage, picked men with whom she could have wonderful, unrestrained sex. Charlotte, with a dictatorial, punitive husband, picked a glamorous rock star, partly to spite her spouse. Dr. Jensen, the dentist of a hundred affairs, unerringly picked women who would be grateful for what he gave them, but would not make trouble for him.

Based on these and many other cases, it is possible to set down certain personality characteristics you might look for in an extramarital partner . . . and in appraising *yourself* as a partner.

Desirable qualities for an extramarital partner

A person possessing some (or all) of the following characteristics would be expected to make *positive contributions* to an affair:

• Someone reasonably well-adjusted, on good terms with himself or herself and without any serious personality or emotional problems.

• A person willing to enter an affair out of free choice—not as an escape from dealing with personal inadequacies or difficulties, not to gratify an insatiable sex drive, nor to bolster a weak ego, nor to meet his or her own all-consuming needs.

• A person able to accept fully his or her status as an extramarital partner without self-deception, inappropriate guilt or desire to displace the spouse.

• A person who is honest, sincere, in touch with inner feelings, sensitive to and considerate of others' feelings, able to give as well as to receive intimacy, and an effective communicator. It is unlikely that such a person would be unduly demanding, possessive, or exploitative.

• A person able to cope with difficulties, disappointments, and hurts without suffering excessive emotional pain or causing others to suffer.

• A person who would not allow the affair to threaten or undermine his or her own marriage and family situation or to interfere with work and other responsibilities.

• A person who can be discreet and able to keep secrets. This person, however, is also able to be open and honest about the relationship when appropriate.

• A person willing and able to make sufficient time available for the extramarital relationship.

• A person having a sense of responsibility and dependability which would prevent him or her from being reckless and impulsive.

• A person comfortable with his/her own sexuality, who finds sex pleasurable, and who functions comfortably either with the spouse or with others.

Undesirable qualities for an extramarital partner

In contrast, there are personal characteristics that could be expected to contribute to *difficulties* in an extramarital affair. If possible, try to stay clear of:

• The overeager, possessive person who wants to own you. If you're not careful, he or she *will* own you and extricating yourself could take the skill of a Houdini.

• The very suspicious, jealous, and controlling individual who wants you all to himself or herself and bristles at any possible rivals, including your spouse.

• A habitually hostile, critical, punitive, intolerant person. He or she may be sweet to you, but don't be fooled—if this is the pattern, your turn will come!

• The manipulative person who exploits others and seeks pleasure, power, and personal advantage.

• The very dependent person who leans on you and constantly calls on you to bolster his or her self-esteem. It may be flattering for a while, but you are in trouble when the relationship gets burdensome (and it probably will).

• The extremely emotional person whose ups and downs in mood can entertain but can also exhaust you. When you try to end the relationship, there may be hysterical scenes or even threats of suicide.

• The sadomasochistic person for whom a relationship is built on inflicting hurts and being hurt.

• The very immature person whose impulsive, uncontrolled behavior makes for unreliability. He or she could betray you in a moment of pique.

• The very demanding person who expects more and more from you. You will eventually reach a limit and rebel—but can you easily break it off?

Of course, these lists are by no means complete. You can probably add other characteristics—desirable and undesirable—from your own life experiences and those of people you know. I make no attempt to define the best (or worst) choices of an extramarital partner, just as I certainly would not recommend—or advise against—having an affair at all! My object is simply to assist you in charting your own direction as you evaluate the alternatives.

STAGE 3—DEVELOPING CLOSENESS

Just as the first two stages can take place concurrently, so can the next two—"Developing Closeness" and "Sexual Intercourse." Which comes first depends on the individuals involved and the circumstances. For some, sexual intercourse occurs first; deep emotional involvement and companionship may develop later—or may not. These could be people who have more inhibitions on the emotional and intellectual side than on the sexual. On the other hand, many affairs begin with a gradually growing friendship and intimacy.

You are drawn to someone. You share thoughts and feelings. You become closer, trust each other more. How far and how fast you move depends on many factors—your personality, the time you have together, the frequency of your meetings, your circumstances and, of course, how you relate to intimacy.

As emotional ties grow stronger, so also may their physical expression. Touching increases. Many of us are starved for touching. We didn't get enough as we grew up and we may not be getting enough from our spouses. An inadvertent (or advertent) touch can light a person up. It may start innocently: a hand on the shoulder, a pat on the arm or knee. A light kiss on meeting or parting. No affair, this; and it may never become an affair. But there's a process at work.

The idea of an affair may occur to you at some point and begin to grow in your mind. You may think about reasons or justifications for having an affair. You may even invite opportunities for an affair to occur. You hope. And, maybe, you're afraid.

Couple relationships tend not to be static indefinitely. The touching may not long be confined to the arm, shoulder, or cheek. There can be, of course, progressive steps. Some people jump over them and proceed quickly to genital involvement. Others do not. The unfoldment, for them, is much more gradual so that social, intellectual, and emotional intimacy can keep step with physical intimacy. The process usually calls for trust—the feeling that you are wanted for yourself and are not being used only for someone else's gratification. Each stage of progressive intimacy may require a new level of trust. One woman who has engaged in several extramarital affairs writes: "I can't relate to one-night stands. I'm not sure I ever want one because, for me, sexual passion means giving up some of my control, and that calls for *trust.* And how can I trust a total stranger? . . . I have to feel *cared for,* not just an object."

Generally, as your level of trust and intimacy increases, so does the intensity and depth of your feelings. You perceive the other person with new eyes. The possibility (or probability) of sexual intercourse carries a whole new set of emotions, both positive and negative. There may be feelings of excitement, adventure, newness, joy, and ecstasy; or there may be shyness, self-consciousness, uncertainty, guilt, reluctance to break with convention, fear of punishment, self-doubt, wondering what the other person will think, and whether your body is attractive enough, and whether you can really carry it through.

STAGE 4—SEXUAL INTERCOURSE

Now the clothes are coming off. And the relationship alters its character even more. Not only does the extramarital relationship change; the relationship with your spouse probably has changed, whether the spouse knows it or not. You have stepped out of one space into another, like Alice moving into the looking-glass world. You sense that your friendship with this person will never again be the same as before.

Once sexual intercourse has been accomplished, the relationship meets the traditionally accepted definition of a full-fledged extramarital affair. You may choose to stop after a single sexual experience; an extramarital affair doesn't have to continue beyond this point. Or you may have reached a beautiful emotional and physical peak that you'll want to experience again. You've made connection in the most intense and physically intimate of ways with someone who is special to you.

Your affair may grow more passionate and sexual. It may be hard to be away from your lover. Can you cope with your impatience and frustration at having to be separated—even for brief periods of time? Or do you begin to take greater risks, inviting the suspicion of friends, children, and coworkers? And suppose your spouse, seeing clear signs of your anxiety or excitement, guesses what is happening and confronts you? Can you field the questions without giving away the truth? Or can you answer honestly, taking full responsibility for the outcome?

STAGE 5—SETTLING IN

As the initial excitement and novelty fade somewhat, you may begin to look at your situation with more objectivity. Perhaps you look more closely at the relationship you have with your spouse. Which of the two relationships is more satisfying? Are you learning from your affair how to build and maintain a qualitative relationship? Could you make use of this new knowledge in your marriage? You may look at your marriage more critically. You may challenge yourself, "Do I want to preserve my marriage?" If you had a choice, would you marry your extramarital partner? You ponder these and other questions.

As an affair continues, its character often changes. The intensity may increase. You may, like Diane, grow emotionally closer to your lover as time goes on; or you may, like Monica and Slim, eventually begin to drift apart. Instead of being something special, the affair may begin to take its place in your day-to-day life and fit around your other activities. Of course, the same dynamics that affect any couple relationship can affect affairs.

Like marriage, an affair may remain unchanged, grow in quality, or deteriorate. Because of their nature, affairs are generally more tenuous and less stable than most marriages. Even when the emotional and sexual excitement is gone from a marriage, there are still children, home, possessions, family, financial, and legal ties which can keep a couple together indefinitely. But once the juices have stopped flowing in an affair, the relationship usually just dries up.

STAGE 6—WINDING DOWN

Coping with the termination of any close personal relationship—whatever the reason—may call for all the emotional resources a person can muster. Who has not experienced the pain of separation from beloved friends upon graduation from school or when moving from one city to another or from one job to another? Certainly the pain is even more acute when a close relationship ends through death. Affairs, like all relationships in life, are destined to end eventually. And because of the emotional needs that probably caused them to *be* in the first place, dealing with the heartaches as the affair winds down can require significant coping skills.

Of course, not all affairs will end abruptly as Charlotte's did when she found her rock singer with another woman, or as Becky's first affair, and the Frank-Norene affair did when they were discovered. More often, the flame simply burns itself out for one or both of the partners. Sometimes the experience of the affair and the self-confidence generated by it has helped a partner to grow and broaden his or her own contacts and interests, thereby making the affair itself less important than it once was. Sometimes, one or both partners decide to apply the newly-learned relationship skills to strengthening his or her own marriage. Or, an affair may end because it has begun to seem too risky and the complications too great; or, because one of the partners has become excessively possessive, perhaps insisting that the relationship be exclusive or permanent. Repeated quarrels and misunderstandings may also lead to the termination of the affair; or, perhaps one or both partners have outgrown the relationship; or one or both have become interested in somebody else; or because the interest, excitement, and magic have simply worn off.

Of course, these are only a few of the reasons why affairs end. We've noted others in this book: Suzanne stopped because of feeling guilty; Deborah kept her affairs brief by prior understanding with her extramarital partners; Renee quit her affair when she found it destructive to her ego; Monica quit when she got tired of Slim.

The ending of an affair, however, does not always mean the end of the relationship. Sydney's affair with Barbie ended when divergent careers separated them, but they are still close friends. A friendship may continue on a number of levels even after the sexual aspect has ended. Some partners find they can build even more qualitative and enduring friendships without sex. Perhaps the elements of trust, openness, and emotional intimacy generated by the sexual affair make possible a more relaxed, honest, and meaningful friendship. The affair between Eva and Father Gordon grew into a marriage following her divorce.

No matter how the affair ends (unless, of course, it ends in marriage), it is unlikely that both partners will have reached the same degree of readiness to terminate at the same time. This is, perhaps, the most painful aspect of the Winding Down Stage and the part requiring the greatest degree of emotional maturity. It can be agonizing for the partner who continues to love while the other is ready to move on. Not only is there pain over the loss, but often feelings of rejection, isolation, and abandonment. Nor is it any easier for the partner who has made the decision to end it. Too often, an extramarital partner can't bring himself or herself to be straightforward enough to say, "We've had wonderful times together, but I would like to end it." Instead he or she may retreat through increasing periods of silence and longer intervals between meetings. If the partners are in a position to see each other frequently (such as neighbors or people who work together), this emotional withdrawal may be especially difficult.

Even when a direct and honest confrontation does take place, both partners may still have hurt and painful feelings to deal with.

While each stage of an extramarital affair carries with it its own special coping problems, feelings of frustration and anxiety can follow the partners throughout their relationship, no matter how fulfilling it may be.

COPING WITH SECRECY AND DECEPTION

The need to maintain secrecy and deception is almost universal, unless yours is an open marriage like that of Kevin and Deborah. Every meeting with your extramarital partner, whether in public or in private, involves risk. If you can acknowledge the dangers, you'll be better prepared to deal with the situation. Consider those times when you encounter your extramarital partner in public such as at work, in the neighborhood, or at a social function. The fact that you are acquainted with each other may be no secret; the fact that you are lovers probably is. Can you maintain just the right degree of detachment and indifference toward each other when under other people's scrutiny? Either too much distance or too much friendliness could cause your spouses and others to take notice. Then, too, your deadpan expression—or that of your partner—could be misinterpreted by either of you as real rejection, creating anxiety and misunderstanding.

When you meet in public and it is *not* known that you are acquainted, it may take the skill of an accomplished actor to avoid sneaking glances at each other and to pretend that the two of you are strangers.

Your private meetings, of course, pose even greater risk. When you and your extramarital partner are together, you need to take special care that you aren't spotted by anyone who might recognize you; yet furtive actions like glancing around to make sure you are alone or seeking remote motels or dimly lighted corners of restaurants are apt to attract attention. Registering at a motel can create dilemmas. Should you use your real name or an assumed one? What if you are asked for identification? There could be problems if you try to falsify the license plate number and make of your car. And suppose your car is recognized by someone when it's parked where it "shouldn't" be? Traveling together in the same car presents still other problems. In addition to the risk of being spotted together, what do you do if you have car trouble or an accident? You also have to make sure that nothing belonging to your partner is dropped or left behind in your car and vice versa.

Communicating with your extramarital partner can also be hazardous unless you are able to make and receive phone calls without arousing suspicion. Sometimes a trusted friend can transmit messages. If you have to write letters to each other, a post office box might provide some degree of anonymity, but the name of a box holder can no longer legally be kept secret.

Exchanging gifts could mean trouble unless the gifts are ones that you or your extramarital partner might be likely to buy for yourselves. Personal items, accessories, and clothing might be a safer bet than expensive jewelry. And what do you do with the receipts? (It was the discovery of the receipt for the jade necklace that led Rosalie to uncover Frank's affair with Norene.)

Maintaining secrecy can, itself, be frustrating, especially if you're bursting to release your bottled-up feelings about your affair, perhaps the most exciting experience of your life, with someone other than your extramarital partner. Do you have a best friend with whom you can discuss the intense emotions and new experiences? If you are trying to cope with feelings of uncertainty and ambivalence about being in an affair, is there someone with whom you can safely talk?

A threat of disaster hangs over many affairs in the form of physical illness. I know of several situations in which men suffered heart attacks while making love to their extramarital partners. In one such case, the woman called an ambulance and got her lover to the hospital in time. However, in another instance, the woman panicked, ran out, and her extramarital partner died. No one likes to contemplate such eventualities; yet, being able to handle a crisis of this magnitude may mean the difference between life and death.

COPING WITH DISTANCE, PERIODS OF SILENCE, AND LIMITED TIME TOGETHER

One of the more unhappy situations extramarital partners face is being separated for extended periods of time. When lovers live far apart or one must travel a lot on business, the pain of being separated can be especially acute.

How you handle being apart depends a great deal on your own needs and the nature of your relationship. Some people with strong physical and/or emotional desires for constant company might take the "out-of-sight, out-of-mind" approach and bed down with the nearest available partner until the lover returns. Sometimes, this is understood and accepted by both extramarital partners, and the incidence of other sexual encounters just isn't mentioned by either. But many other extramarital partners are faithful to each other over distance and time. During periods of separation, they might channel their energies into new activities, their jobs, and their families.

One of my patients, whom I'll call Mel, described his feelings about being separated from his extramarital partner who lives in a distant city.

"It's been four months since I've seen Bea, and you asked in what ways I miss her. I miss her voice—merely to hear it on the phone sends shivers through me. I miss her accent, her smile, her vivacity, the way her eyes dance—she's entrancingly young and alive. I miss the smoothness of her skin, her funny walk (caused by a slight spinal problem), the light touch of her hands, her smell, the feel of her tongue, the softness of her breasts. I miss the way she responds to me as we make love, willingly, naturally, with nothing held back. I miss our total absorption in each other, the completeness we feel with each other. I miss her fiery temperament when she is angry with me. I miss the protectiveness I feel toward her when she is sleeping in my arms.

"But, most particularly, I miss a feeling of happiness I have when I am with her—of contentment, satisfaction, fulfillment."

I asked Mel what he would miss in his wife, Terry, if he were separated from her for a considerable time. His answer: "I know I'd miss her understanding and devotion that's been steadfast through twenty-two years of living together. (Even as I say the number '22' I can scarcely believe it has been that many!) I would miss her stability, strength, intelligence, and efficiency. It is only of late that she has responded to me very much physically, so it would be too soon to miss that. There's such an amazing contrast in styles between the two women! Perhaps it is because I have had so little real passion in my life—so few experiences where I felt strong emotions—that I miss mainly the physical and sensual aspects of Bea after having tasted them with her."

Even when lengthy separations are not a problem, one or both partners may feel frustration if they long for more time with their lovers than is available. Of course, external circumstances such as family and work responsibilities, commitment to other activities and limitations on available meeting places may be the source of this problem. On the other hand, one partner may be putting pressure on the other for more time than he or she is willing to give. Such a situation, if not faced and discussed openly, can lead to the cooling off of the affair.

The longing for more time with her extramarital partner impelled a woman to write the following:

TIME

If you want our love to grow
        see me
        touch me
        caress me
And give me Time.

Time is your most precious gift.
Through it I awaken to you . . .
        to your needs
        to your wants
To us.

We need time
        to walk
        to talk
Time to be together
        in
Contented silence
        or
Excited being.

Unless you give me time
        I will not grow
I will not be able to give you time
        or love
        or myself.

Lonely without you
Saddened by your leaving
I want more time.

Time . . . the enemy
        and best friend.
Ambivalence . . .

Short affairs are less subject to the demands for more time since they are often gone into (like Deborah's early affairs on her holidays) with an understanding that they are simply here-and-now experiences, not to be continued.

Because of the inherent impermanence of most extramarital relationships, any lack of contact, no matter how brief, can give rise to anxiety. ("Does he/she still love me?" "Has he/she found someone else?" "Does his/her spouse suspect?") Silence may not reflect a deliberate withdrawal. Partners in an affair are, in a sense, living a double life. As I've mentioned, they have obligations to their families, to employers, and to other people—and also to their own personal growth. There are conflicting demands for their time and energy. But even when this is recognized, silences are hard to bear. A woman in an affair expressed the sadness and anxiety of such a silence in these lines:

SILENCE

The silence between us grows longer with each passing day.
Cross it
Reach out to me and pull me back beside you.
Hurry—before it is too late.

Silence breeds fear in my heart.
Have I done something, said something?
Not done something, not said something?
I fear and my fear grows.

Silence makes me sad.
It belies the wish to need and be needed.
Feelings cannot grow in silence.
Silence can destroy the fragile flame you have awakened in me.

Flames need to be fed, but silence does not nourish.
I think of our moments together.
Does your silence mean I was a fool?
Did I make you into someone you are not?

You did not take me in silence.
You did not leave me in silence.
And yet silence grows between.

COPING WITH A CRISIS

For many people, coping with a crisis situation is less confusing than coping with ongoing anxieties and pressures; but others, faced by crisis, fall apart at the seams. Crises demand immediate action; you don't have time to ponder alternatives or agonize over decisions and, often, there isn't time or opportunity to change your mind. Therefore, your first course of action needs to be constructive because you may not have a chance to rectify it.

Many of the people described in this book hadn't given much thought to the emotional consequences of an extramarital relationship; yet the possibilities of a crisis occurring in an affair are very real. How you handle a crisis says a lot about the kind of person you are. Do you know enough about yourself to predict how you would react if you were caught in an affair and were confronted by a shocked and distraught spouse?

Would you run away and hide until it is safe to come back (as you might have done when a child)? Would you, instead, deny everything? Shrug off your affair and pretend it is unimportant? ("Oh, that? It's nothing to get upset about.") Make excuses? Blame your spouse for your affair? ("I did it because you never gave me any affection.") Would you blame your extramarital partner? ("He/she seduced me.") Confess and ask your spouse's forgiveness? Plead for your spouse to be reasonable? ("After all, dear, think of the spot I was in.") Promise to break off your affair immediately and never get into another? Or would you continue your affair in defiance of your spouse's protests? Would you walk out and end the marriage? Or move in with your extramarital partner (if you had the opportunity)? Would you hate yourself and expect punishment? Would you feel depressed and helpless? Angry and vindictive? Or sad and anxious?

Or, would you talk with your spouse about the affair and explore the possibility of strengthening the marriage? Would you be able to share your feelings honestly? Could you acknowledge (to yourself and/or your spouse) the positive aspects of the extramarital relationship in terms of your own needs, wants and desires and expectations?

EXPANDING YOUR CAPACITY TO COPE

My approach to the dilemmas of coping is to help an individual develop the inner strength and ability to become a more mature person so that he can deal with any crisis, now or in the future.

Let's see how the ten-step system referred to earlier would expand your capacity to cope. Through increased self-awareness, you'd gain greater understanding of how you and other people feel. With this understanding, your course of action could become clearer. You could stay closer to reality and not be sidetracked by self-deception or wishful thinking. You'd learn to be flexible in your responses; you wouldn't need to fall back on fixed, rigid positions or stereotyped reactions such as Rosalie's. You'd be honest with yourself and thus be honest with the other people in your life. You would become strong enough to take responsbility for your feelings and actions, as Eva and Father Gordon did, and not blame them on somebody else. You'd balance your several responsibilities: those to your spouse, to your extramarital partner, to your children, to your extramarital partner's spouse and children, and to yourself. You won't slip and slide into situations; you'll know more about where you are going and why you are going there.

When you have moved in this direction (the direction of personal growth), your approach to extramarital affairs may undergo a change. You'll recognize the difference between what you *want* and what you *need.* You do not "need" an affair in the same sense that you need food or shelter. But you may desire one for reasons you think are valid. You may long for a qualitative human relationship that you feel you're not getting in your marriage. You may want practice in developing such a relationship, and you may face obstacles to doing so in your marriage. You may want more love in your life, more affection, more sex, more excitement, more enjoyment. You may want a new experience with a new person. You may want to enjoy a new body or to be challenged by a new mind. But you'll recognize all these as wants, not needs; and if you decide to pursue them, you'll take responsibility for the consequences.

If you decide to have an affair, you probably won't go into one for destructive reasons such as retaliation for your spouse's affair, or to make your spouse jealous, or for conquest, or to gain power over someone. As I mentioned earlier, affairs entered into for such reasons are likely to be dangerous and damaging. Your notion of an ideal partner in an ideal affair could be quite different from someone else's. For example, you might want an intense emotional involvement because that is what you are not getting in your marriage. But your extramarital partner may want to *avoid* a deep emotional involvement because of the threat to his/her marriage and other complications. That difference in goals could set the two of you at cross-purposes. However, if you have developed skills in communication, you may be able to reach an understanding. One of my male patients put it this way: "Know what you're looking for in the other person and share it with her. Also, help her share what she is looking for. This way you'll both know where you stand."

If you're honest with yourself, you'll face up to the risks you are taking and not deceive yourself into believing there isn't any risk. There's *always* a risk. Not merely risk to you but to other people as well. You are never completely secure, no matter how private you think your meetings are. As Suzanne put it, "Believe me, there is no absolutely safe place!" You might manage to keep an affair secret for years if your spouse is not particularly observant, but your chances of doing so may decrease as time goes on. Even the risks of pregnancy and venereal disease are not entirely absent, for the best contraceptive devices can fail. And you have to consider the risk to your own peace of mind and stability. What will the emotional conflicts and moral struggles do to *you*? How will the way you see and feel about yourself be affected? Can you handle all this?

Few people, of course, are able to look so rationally and coolly at an affair they are about to enter. But being in touch with who you really are will always be helpful, for it strengthens the rational segment of your total personality. You will act with more regard for potential consequences, and not be propelled into an affair by unknown motivations.

CHANGING YOUR PERSPECTIVES

The recurrent theme throughout this and the previous chapters has been that self-knowledge is the key to coping. Getting to know who you are, how you got to be that way, and what you want to become will assist you to gain a clearer picture of your alternatives. We've seen repeatedly the way in which personal needs, wants, and characteristics have determined individual courses of action—that the same set of circumstances may not elicit the same set of responses from different people. And that even the same person will not necessarily act in the same way all the time. The more you know about yourself, the more control you will gain over all situations in your life.

Personal growth is the outcome of having moved out of rigid patterns of thinking, feeling, and acting. You can develop alternatives and make choices based on a variety of changing factors—both within yourself and in relation to outside circumstances.

Learning about yourself can be an exciting and stimulating process. You did not spring from a seed full-grown like Botticelli's *Birth of Venus*. Just as you can trace a complicated mathematical formula back to the basics of elementary arithmetic so, too, can you trace a complicated human being back to the elemental units of social learning and conditioning.

Where did your attitudes toward religion, education, raising children come from? Why did you choose the career that you did? What influenced your choice of marital partner? Are you passive—or competitive? Comfortable in a crowd—or a loner? What are your values concerning politics, money, sex, marriage, extramarital affairs? All of the ways you think, feel, and behave; all of your attitudes, values, and expectations; your rules, beliefs, and ideas of right and wrong constitute the foundation and framework of your day-to-day living. How did you get them?

Innumerable directives, instructions, attitudes, values, emotional responses, and nonverbal signals (such as refusal to talk about certain matters, like sex) have been impressed upon you over the years by parents, siblings, teachers, acquaintances, religious leaders, employers, etc. Some you have incorporated into your personality unaltered. Others were either modified or rejected altogether. Some of these inputs have been helpful. Some have not. Some are out-of-date and some are still relevant.

I call these Prescriptions for Living,[1] or PFLs (I pronounce them "piffles"). They are one-liners that influence what you think, how you feel, and how you act. Many are simple like, "Look both ways before you cross the street." "Thou shalt not kill." "Be polite to your elders." "Don't trust strangers." "Sex before marriage is wrong." "Do unto others as you would have them do unto you."

Prescriptions for Living make up the conscious and unconscious codes by which you live. They take a variety of forms. Some are directions you give yourself. ("I mustn't show my feelings.") Some are orders you give yourself and others. ("Obey the rules.") Some are permissions you allow yourself. ("It's okay to express and share my feelings.") Some are expectations. ("A husband ought to support his wife and children.") Some are value statements. ("I believe in marital fidelity.") Some are statements about yourself. ("I'm comfortable in intimate situations.") Some are statements of what you want or enjoy. ("I like meeting people.")

So deeply embedded are many of your PFLs that you are scarcely aware they are there; you do not ordinarily examine them. Nevertheless, they influence you at every moment, affecting what you say, how you say it, what you do and feel, your gestures, your facial expressions, your tones of voice, the choices and decisions you make, and much else.

The trouble with many PFLs is that they may continue to operate inappropriately when you (or the times) have outgrown them and the conditions requiring them have changed. Because many basic ones were acquired in childhood, they may retain a naive and childlike quality that doesn't keep pace with the needs of the maturing adult. Old PFLs that are no longer appropriate can restrict your life or even endanger it, hurt your relationships with people, hamper your personal growth, and undermine your capacity to cope.

The ways you characteristically think and feel about yourself—your self-concept—generally reflect the messages you incorporated when growing up. Do you like yourself? Are you happy with the life you have carved out for yourself? Do you feel in control of your destiny, able to take responsibility for your mistakes and to move on from there? Or, are you like many of us whose experiences in childhood have led us to feel inadequate, fearful of making mistakes, unable to cope with problems or new situations? Do you, somewhere in the deep recesses of your mind, still hear the voices of parents, teachers, siblings, and peers saying things like:

> *You always muddle things.*
> *You never do anything right.*
> *Modesty is a virtue.*
> *You'll never amount to anything.*
> *You're stupid.*
> *You always look a mess.*
> *Nice girls don't do that.*
> *Big boys don't cry.*
> *Why can't you be like . . . . ?*

These things may not have been said on purpose to hurt you. But they could have left wounds. Children tend to believe what they are repeatedly told about themselves. Unless you later repudiated these disparaging messages, you may still be limping along believing negative things about yourself that simply aren't true. And even worse, you may have been taught that it's conceited to think well of yourself.

You can, however, learn to identify these built-in put-downs and recognize them as enemies of your well-being. You can deny their authority to continue undermining your self-concept. You can believe and say to yourself,

> *I'm competent and attractive.*
> *I'm lovable and worthwhile.*
> *I'm a unique person.*
> *I'm a developing, growing person.*
> *Life offers me endless possibilities.*
> *I enjoy new experiences.*
> *No one makes me feel what I feel.*
> *I'm responsible for myself and my feelings.*
> *I am comfortable showing my feelings.*
> *It's okay to believe in myself.*

Growth enhancing PFLs flow out of statements like these and

others beginning with *I like, I want, I enjoy, I'm willing to, I can, I prefer, I feel.* Self-affirmation, however, is not to be mistaken for self-indulgence. Positive feelings for oneself must be integrated with positive feelings for others. If carried to an extreme, the permissive PFLs can lead to a hedonistic, self-centered life-style that can be as destructive as the too rigid, self-condemning style.

The same principles apply to the Prescriptions for Living regulating how people characteristically behave toward each other. PFLs, in fact, give stability, consistency, and structure to life and provide a kind of "social glue" that holds people together through shared attitudes, beliefs, values, and expectations. In spite of their advantages, however, PFLs can be excessively restrictive and limiting when expressed in terms like *ought, oughtn't, should, shouldn't, must, mustn't, do, don't, can, can't, always,* and *never.* While some may be valid expressions of desirable moral conduct, others may be part of a closed and inflexible life-style characterized by fixed opinions, inflexible rules, tightly defined strictures of right versus wrong, good versus bad, black versus white. These suggest a kind of rigidity that can block honest communication, negotiation, and problem solving.

PFLS ABOUT SEX, MARRIAGE, AND EXTRAMARITAL AFFAIRS

One of the reasons an extramarital affair shakes up people so profoundly is that the rules, expectations, and values they previously held about sex and marriage (such as, "Sex outside of marriage is wrong") are suddenly torn loose from their moorings. As a woman with a strict church upbringing put it, "All of a sudden everything you learned morally goes astray." You may be doing something specifically forbidden by your religious beliefs (like Eva and Father Gordon). You may be unfaithful to a spouse who believes you to be faithful. These strains on your inner integrity can be agonizing; yet they also can offer a rare opportunity for personal growth, as Emily and her husband found.

The immediate problem posed by an extramarital affair is that you almost certainly have not been trained to handle a sudden, radical shake-up of your Prescriptions for Living. Practically no one has learned in childhood (or later) the degree of openness and flexibility required to meet this kind of challenge. You have been briefed about life—taught a lot of things your parents and teachers believed to be true (and perhaps were true under the conditions they knew). But now you suddenly need a debriefing to prepare you to meet new conditions.

Note how Rosalie's PFLs totally unfitted her for dealing with the crisis produced by discovery of her husband's extramarital affair. As I described earlier, her PFLs were formed under the conditions of the Nazi regime during World War II. Some of them were "Never trust men," "Men are beasts," and "Infidelity in marriage is unforgivable." Her PFLs put Rosalie in a psychological straitjacket that left her no emotional maneuvering room. As a result, she broke up the marriage that until then she had boasted was "perfect," drove out a sensitive and—in many ways—considerate husband whom she really loved, hurt the lives of her children, and shut herself in emotional and social isolation. A tragedy!

PFLs can victimize people in other ways besides making them rigid. We met Dr. Jensen who claims to have had about a hundred extramarital affairs, not because he loves women deeply but because his life has been an unending search for a love he couldn't find. Some of his PFLs like "Take advantage of every opportunity to learn" had helped him become a competent oral surgeon; but he also had PFLs like "Keep your feelings hidden" and "Don't get emotionally involved" that handicapped him in forming intimate relationships.

The concept of extramarital affairs rather quickly exposes the PFLs people have about sex and marriage. I described PFLs as the elemental units of social learning and conditioning. The primary source of such learning is the family. Because the PFLs concerning sex and marriage were indoctrinated by the very institution they were designed to uphold, these values tend to be stronger than most others. A child growing up within a family experiences daily his parents' attitudes about marriage and sex. Some of these may be discussed openly; more usually, the child learns by observation. He sees the interaction between his parents; he overhears their conversations about outside activities and friendships (although maybe not in great detail); he may experience an atmosphere of warmth or one of hostility. If the family is a deeply religious one, he has been exposed to the values held by his particular religion regarding sex and marriage.

A person growing up in a family holding traditional Western values might be likely to hold the following PFLs concerning sex, marriage and extramarital affairs.

> *Love, honor, and* obey.
> *I can't love two people at the same time.*
> *My mate will satisfy all my needs.*
> *My spouse belongs to me.*
> *Till death do us part.*
> *If I'm married, I can't have intimate friends of the opposite sex.*
> *If I can't make my marriage work, I'm a failure.*
> *Thou shalt not commit adultery.*
> *People who cheat on their spouses are bad.*
> *Adultery has to lead to divorce.*

Holding some or all of these PFLs does not, of course, guarantee that a person will not engage in extramarital affairs. They will, however, be likely to exert a strong influence on the way each spouse reacts to the situation. The one in the affair will probably have to deal with feelings of guilt and ambivalence. The other spouse will probably react with feelings of hurt, rejection, and anger if the affair becomes known.

The greatest conflicts arise when one spouse is locked into the traditional PFLs concerning sex, marriage, and extramarital affairs and the other is oriented toward personal freedom. People oriented to freedom may seek broadened human experience. They may enjoy getting acquainted with new people and forming new relationships. There is undeniably some potential for extramarital affairs in this orientation. And their PFLs having to do with sex and other matters may be quite different from the traditional ones. These people may be more relaxed about exploring new options. They may not condemn others whose choices are different from theirs, but neither do they try to be different for its own sake. They may engage in extramarital affairs, but they don't *have* to. Ideally, they would be comfortable with their spouses exercising the same options, although this may not always be the case (if negative PFLs concerning jealousy and possession are still operating!)

If you and your spouse are to reach any kind of understanding, it must begin with the identification and examination of the Prescriptions for Living that each of you holds. Then you can apply the ten-step process of the Interactional Therapeutic System to build in new styles of thinking, feeling, and acting—both as individuals and in your relationships with your spouse, extramarital partner, and others.

Hunting down your PFLs can be a fascinating and rewarding exercise. Where did your PFLs, whatever they are, come from? Are they ones that strengthen your ability to deal with the realities of life? Or do they tie you in knots? Do you want to keep all of them? Or can you let some go and modify others? What are the outgrown ones costing you and other members of your family? Is it a price you really want to pay? The choice is yours. But, before you make any decision, try on the following PFLs for size. They offer specific ways of looking at your relationships with other people and suggest alternatives for your future.

> *I love people and I learn much from them.*
> *I enjoy intimacy.*
> *New people and new experiences can be very exciting.*
> *Every new experience enriches my life.*
> *When my life is enriched, my marriage is enriched.*
> *No one owns me, nor do I own anyone else.*
> *I prize my friendships with others.*
> *Sex with a new person might be one of those new*
> *   experiences—but it doesn't* have *to be.*

We've seen in the last two chapters that the skills required to cope with extramarital affairs—either your spouse's or your own—are the same that you need to cope with almost any life situation. Through learning them, applying them, and practicing them in your day-to-day activities, you can gain a greater degree of emotional maturity, self-confidence, and control over your life than you ever had before. You are the sum total of your life experiences. You can use your past, in the light of your present, to enhance your future.

12. *Marriage and Affairs: No Turning Back*

I have tried to lift extramarital affairs out of the realm of the dark and forbidden and present them as very human events having a vital bearing on people's lives. Contrary to convention they may be—and perhaps they strike a lethal blow at the tottering, half-sick invalid that some people feel modern marriage has become. The basic message that comes to me from the majority of people in affairs is a cry for something better, a search for a greater intimacy with another human being . . . a hesitant journey on a thorn-strewn route to personal fulfillment.

Based upon the experiences of hundreds of people, many of whose stories are presented in this book, the reality is that extramarital affairs bring both *joys* and *disappointments* . . . and can be constructive or destructive in outcome. As with any human relationship, there is no such thing as an affair that is *totally* positive or *totally* negative . . . there are components of both. The truth is that an affair does not occur in a protected vacuum. It is never an isolated event, separate from people's marriages or from their total lives. Lives continue, circumstances change. Joys of an affair may give way to sadness; disappointments become delights. Needs and wants which birthed an affair may be denied, altered, or fully achieved.

But no matter what the experiences and outcomes, there are useful insights to be gained strongly affecting the institution of marriage and the individuals within it.

Marriage, which has undergone far-reaching changes in the past generation alone, seems destined to continue in this process . . . perhaps, at even a greater pace. I am referring not to changes in the external form of marriage, but to ways people perceive it and live it. We have touched on many of these changes; now let's sum them up and try to get a feel for where marriage is headed.

Both the divorce rate and the proliferation of extramarital affairs show that marriage is less and less of a *binding commitment.* Two words have expressed the traditional meaning of marriage: *unite* and *wedlock.* We all know what *lock* means; it suggests a prison cell. The term *unite* implies that a married couple has ceased to be two individuals; the pair has merged to become "one flesh." In actuality, it is the wife who "merges" most. She gives up much of her individuality and even her name. The husband keeps his separate personhood *and* his name. Significantly, the word *marriage* is derived from the Latin *maritus,* which means *husband.* One of the many signs of change today is the increasing number of women who, although married, insist on keeping their original names.

What many modern couples want and expect when they marry is

not a binding, mandated commitment but a close *personal relationship.* Like their parents, they want to make a life together. They want a home. They want to feel they can depend on each other, help each other, be a friend and companion to each other, work together to build a future. Each wants to know the other will be there when he or she comes home. But they don't want to be locked in to each other so that options for other close relationships are forever closed.

The two concepts of marriage—as a binding commitment and as a close relationship—are in some respects incompatible. Relationships between people hardly ever remain static over a long period of time; they either grow stronger or they wither and sometimes make way for new relationships. For as people change and grow, their needs, values, ideas, feelings, and expectations change. But the concept of a binding commitment, cementing two people together for life, must, in order to preserve itself, resist and restrict change. Change is threatening to such a relationship because as marital partners are permitted outside opportunities for personal growth, they face the possibility of either growing together or growing apart. The influences of a rapidly changing society exert enormous pressure on partners locked into a binding commitment, and it is increasingly difficult for such a relationship to survive.

The *status* of being married was once supremely important for a woman, less so for a man. Not any more. Being single or divorced no longer draws the disapproval or pity it once did, and being an "old maid" no longer terrifies. While marriage still gives a woman a certain degree of prestige in the eyes of the world, it is a derived position. Now more and more women are demanding status of their own—to be acknowledged as people in their own right. If a woman marries, she expects to continue to grow, not to be submerged, certainly not to lose her identity. Her grandmother never thought of marriage in this way.

Marriage has been *male dominated* from the earliest recorded times. Apparent exceptions, such as the legends of female-dominated societies before the rise of Greece and Rome, are lost in the mists of antiquity. Male supremacy has been the most consistent feature of cultures that differed in almost every other respect; this has been embedded in legal systems, religious doctrines, and social systems everywhere. The move toward equality in marriage has faced huge obstacles because of this; but change has definitely begun and will continue—probably at an even faster pace than before.

We have looked at the emergence of women, their growing capacity for economic independence, and, through contraception, their freedom from unwanted childbearing. We saw these developments having a revolutionary impact on marriage. The concept of sexual equality is penetrating cultural and even religious areas where only a few years ago it was unheard of.

Change, by its very nature, is not always smooth. Sometimes the pendulum swings too far in the opposite direction before it strikes a new balance. The rise in women's expectations is likely to precipitate further disharmony in marriage, at least for a time. Many men feel threatened by the growing independence of women; many women, meeting male resistance, feel frustrated and enraged. Yet, I believe that men and women are beginning to understand each other better and future marriages will probably be far more stable and more satisfying as a result. Furthermore I am convinced men are discovering that freeing the woman frees them, too, and both will ultimately benefit.

The very thing that has attempted to keep marriage intact in the past may lead to its undoing today. I'm referring to the concept of marriage as a *closed unit*—a walled-in estate, private, and inviolable. Traditional wedding vows have expressed this in terms like "forsaking all others." Such "turned inwardness" or "closedness" of marriage discourages and makes suspect outside relationships of any depth except on a couple-to-couple basis. My experience as a therapist helping people to improve their marriages convinces me that the barriers to outside relationships which this concept imposes are doing more than anything else to kill traditional marriage. It is the locked-in concept of the marriages they have known that causes many young people to want to pass up marriage altogether.

I believe that if marriage doesn't open up and accept the risks that go with openness, many people (including some already married) will abandon it. The ideal of openness is beginning to gain ground. Openness does not, in itself, mean unrestrained sexuality. Openness means that internal and external barriers to relationships are, at least, relaxed. The human being is preponderantly a social creature, not made to live in isolation. Outside activities and meaningful relationships are essential to emotional health. In years past, it was unthinkable for a married woman to participate without her husband in activities outside the home. Today, it's not unusual for either marital partner to take part alone in sports clubs, adult education courses, dance clubs, music clubs, theater groups, choral groups, art associations, political organizations, etc. These offer opportunities for anyone to broaden and enrich his or her interpersonal life, which is an important component of openness.

In an open relationship, the partners stop building walls around themselves and each other. They give each other freedom by actively encouraging each other's personal growth and broadened contacts with people. They mutually share their feelings and thoughts, they care about each other, they communicate freely and openly, they do not impose their will on each other, and they become sensitive to one another's needs and feelings. Openness becomes a way of looking at life and of living it.

As openness is experienced, outside relationships become less of a threat to the marriage. Each partner can find friends with whom to pursue the interests and activities that the spouse does not strongly share. Such relationships can become intimate—not necessarily sexual—although that possibility is there.

In the past, of course, relationships of married people with individuals of opposite gender have been feared, even forbidden. There is the classic story of the husband who, learning that his wife had lunch downtown with a man she had known since school days, exploded, "A married woman can't have male friends!" Thus, in one blow, he ruled out half the human race as acceptable friends of his wife. Does he put the same restrictions on himself when he regularly lunches with female business associates?

In reality, freedom to have friendships—of both sexes—can strengthen and enrich a marriage. They offer each marital partner the opportunity to grow as a person by experiencing and sharing a variety of new perceptions and insights which can often be enhanced by the input of a different gender. (Understanding the views held by a member of the opposite sex can help one to understand the spouse better, too.) Living with such a mate is often more exciting than living with one whose horizons are limited by rigid convention.

Even when both partners in a marriage subscribe to the principle of openness, usually they agree to place their own relationship ahead of any others. They treat each other as responsible adults capable of deciding for themselves how far outside relationships should be permitted to go. They care for each other and trust each other. All ideas of ownership are abandoned. Fidelity is understood as continued loyalty to the basic commitment to protect and secure the primary relationship of the marriage. It is not just a promise to have sex only with one's spouse. Thus the meaning of adultery is altered.

That such a marriage can exist seems preposterous to many people for it requires shifts of basic Prescriptions for Living that have been embedded and virtually unquestioned for millennia. But we have entered an age when rapid shifts in basic attitudes are, in fact, taking place. One has only to look at the de-tabooing of premarital sex and the relative acceptance of unmarried people of the opposite sex living together. The softening or lifting of prohibitions on married people having close relationships with people of the opposite sex—including extramarital sex—is catching up.

As the barriers to friendships with the opposite sex come down, many of us find ourselves sadly lacking in the skills needed to develop such friendships. When we were children, we experienced relationships with peers of both sexes on a variety of levels. As adults, the relationships we form with members of the opposite sex tend to fall into only two narrow categories: the casual, superficial encounters with people we never get to know really well, such as business associates, bridge or tennis partners, people we meet briefly at cocktail parties, etc.; and "dating" relationships where lovemaking and sexual intercourse are the focus.

The type of relationship that few of us are able to enjoy comfortably with people of the opposite sex are affectionate, intimate friendships *not* specifically centered on sex—friendships in which we can care and be cared about, share thoughts and feelings, be open and close to each other, yet not feel obliged to have sexual relations. Ironically, that *obligation* to have sexual relations probably developed out of society's taboo against *friendships* with members of the opposite sex! Many men and women simply never learned how to relate to each other as adults without the sexual component. For example, if a man says to a woman (whether or not either of them is married), "How about dropping over to my place this evening?" it is generally assumed by both that he means much more than showing her his rare book collection or playing his favorite record albums. He means to go to bed with her. Both know it; and if she accepts his invitation, it is further assumed that she is agreeing to a sexual experience. But why shouldn't these two be able to enjoy a friendship without intrusion of the sexual element? Why can't she just enjoy his books, his records, or his conversation if she doesn't want to be sexually involved? Why should she feel that if she turns down sex she will offend him? And why should he be offended? Why should the two of them be caught in this bind?

Even though a sexual relationship may develop from an intimate friendship, it doesn't *have* to. When sex comes in too fast, it can circumvent the steps which a deep friendship needs in order to evolve. The relationship may never return to those more deliberate steps of getting acquainted, sharing thoughts and feelings, and finding common ground on which to build intimacy. The man and the woman can both lose out.

As marriage moves in the direction of openness and offers the opportunity for men and women to interact more comfortably on all levels, there may be less pressure on them to engage in extramarital affairs. Many will find that the option of forming intimate friendships provides them with the qualitative relationships they might otherwise have sought through an affair—but without the pressure to have sex. The resulting nonsexual friendships can still be warm and affectionate, meeting many intellectual and emotional needs of the friends, unencumbered by the sexual component. Such friendships will tend to be less threatening to a marital partner, especially if both spouses continue to uphold their agreement to place their relationship ahead of all others. Under these circumstances, there is less need to maintain secrecy and deception, thereby eliminating the anxiety, frustration, guilt, and jealousy that invariably accompany clandestine maneuvers.

This new concept of openness reaffirms the equality of males and females, a condition which is not possible under a closed system.

Even if the intimate friendship should become sexual, I see no inherent reason why it would weaken a strong marital relationship. On the contrary, it could strengthen it further because the decision to enter an extramarital affair would probably reflect some of the more positive and constructive reasons which have been cited throughout this book. These people would have more self-knowledge, would be more realistic, and, better able to cope.

The freedom for husbands and wives to develop more qualitative intimate friendships gives them another advantage—ready-made potential external supports in time of crisis. Such a crisis might even be the disintegration of the marriage. With outside close friends of either or both sexes to bolster them, what could otherwise be a catastrophic event might now be less damaging and painful for both marital partners.

As I look toward the future, I envision not only marriage—but society in general—becoming less depersonalized and more open and democratic. Even though elements of reactionary conservatism will always be at war with change, our society can never completely return to the old beliefs and assumptions. Human awareness has changed too much and the social order has been altered too profoundly. The institution of marriage will continue to reshape itself into new styles. Although conventional marriage will serve the needs of many, new forms of couple relationships will also emerge, providing many options from which to choose. Some variants of marriage are already being tried "without benefit of clergy" such as threesome marriages (two women and a man or two men and a woman), two-couple marriages, group marriages, homosexual marriages, etc. Perhaps some of these will become legally recognized. In themselves, they may reduce the desire for extramarital affairs.

These changing concepts of marriage offer no comfort to those concerned about high divorce rates. The ideals of open relationships, personal growth, and equality are not focused on marital permanence for they accept the inevitability (and desirability) of change. A marital relationship that grows and deepens over a lifetime is a wonderful thing to behold. But it requires that two people either grow in the same direction at about the same rate, or that the partners accept and are comfortable with different rates of personal growth.

Options for change are definitely available for those in conventional marriages. New Prescriptions for Living can be adopted by both partners in a marriage to make their relationship more compatible with the external changes in society. Some of these might be:

1. Our commitment in marriage is to nurture our relationship and encourage each other's development and personal growth.

2. We believe in being open toward each other and not hiding matters that affect our relationship.

3. We agree to put our own relationship first, ahead of any relationship we form with others.

4. But, we don't own each other and don't put restrictions on each other's outside relationships.

5. If either of us loves somene else, this does not mean we have ceased to love each other.

6. An affair would not necessarily destroy our marriage. Close intimate relationships with others, if not allowed to displace the marital relationship, could enhance our marriage.

7. We can manage and deal constructively with feelings of jealousy, rivalry, and anger that might arise.

As marriage becomes more qualitative in the future so, I believe, will extramarital affairs. Already there seems to be a significant reduction in superficial one-night stands, and greater emphasis on more meaningful and longer-term extramarital involvements. As more creative marriages are pursued this will, in turn, encourage the pursuit of more creative friendships and affairs. The concurrent experiences of marriage, intimate friendships, and affairs, whenever they occur, will be blended more constructively and will permit a healthy cross-pollination resulting in positive contributions to each.

As extramarital affairs move out of the shadow of marriages and we really understand and respect them as important dynamic human encounters, I believe that people will become increasingly aware of their own multiple motivations for desiring, for having, and for ending affairs. Future extramarital partners will be less subject to unconscious forces propelling them into unhealthy and destructive relationships. Because of the expanded options available, the motivation for affairs will be more identified with the *desire* for richer human experiences instead of *need*. Due to their greater self-knowledge, people involved in affairs will assume an increased responsibility for themselves as well as become more considerate of others. The need to blame anyone, including one's self, for having an affair will, consequently, recede.

As for the prevalence of actual extramarital affairs in the future . . . well, it's a guessing game. In Chapter 1 we looked at a variety of studies and the limited research findings on affairs from Kinsey's respondents in 1953 to *Cosmopolitan's* "Cosmo Girls" in 1980. My "guesstimates" for the end of this decade would far exceed Paul Gebhard's current ratio of sixty percent men and thirty-five to forty percent women engaging in affairs. By the year 1990, I predict that those figures will increase to seventy-five percent men and sixty-five percent women. This, I believe, will be the result of the expanded opportunities for interpersonal relationships outside of marriage—for both men and women, the softening of harsh and punitive attitudes toward people in affairs, the expansion of intimate friendships, the increase in the maturity of marital partners, and the strengthening of marriage itself.

The best expression for me of where we have been, where we are, and where we are going can be summed up in the following lines:

GROWING

When we were young, we were told
What to think,
How to act,
And not to feel.

Then time passed and we were told
You owe it to yourself
To please yourself,

To be yourself,
To be.

But if you are you
And I am I
Is that all there is?

With you, I become more than me.
I grow, you grow, we grow.
I can be me,
You can be you;
Together we can be us.

We are growing, sharing, caring . . .
Showing others it's good to feel.
And they're freer . . .
*   to be . . .*

Reference Sources

Introduction
1. Amitai Etzioni, quoted in article, "The New Morality," *Time*, November 21, 1977, p. 117.
2. Tony Lake and Ann Hills, *Affairs: The Anatomy of Extramarital Relationships* (London: Open Books, 1979), p. 6.
3. Ibid., p. 9.

1. Extramarital Affairs—Past and Present
1. William Graham Cole, "Religious Attitudes Toward Extramarital Intercourse," ed. Gerhard Neubeck, *Extramarital Relations* (Englewood Cliffs, N.J.: Prentice-Hall Spectrum, 1969), p. 55.
2. George P. Murdock, *Social Structure* (New York: Macmillan, 1949).
3. Committee on Marriage and the Home of the Federal Council of the Churches of Christ in America and the Committee on Christian Family Life of the National Council of Church Women, *A Christian View of Marriage*, 1940, p. 14.
4. Bishop John A. T. Robinson, *Honest to God* (Philadelphia: Westminster Press, 1963), pp. 110–112, 118.
5. Rustum and Della Roy, *Honest Sex* (New York: New American Library, 1968), p. 121.
6. Kenneth and Betty Woodward, "Why Young People Are Turning Away from Casual Sex," *McCall's*, April 1974, p. 127.
7. Robert Athanasiou, Phillip Shaver, and Carol Tavris, "Sex," *Psychology Today*, April 1970, pp. 39–52.
8. Gerhard Neubeck, "The Dimensions of the 'Extra' in Extramarital Relations," ed. Gerhard Neubeck, *Extramarital Relations* (Englewood Cliffs, N.J.: Prentice-Hall Spectrum, 1969), p. 20.
9. *Statistical Abstract of the United States, 1979* (Washington, D.C.: United States Department of Commerce, Bureau of the Census, 1979), p. 46, Chart 60.
10. Special Report, "Saving The Family," *Newsweek*, May 15, 1978, p. 67.
11. *Current Population Reports*, Series P-20, No. 349, "Marital Status and Living Arrangements: March 1979" (Washington, D.C.: United States Department of Commerce, Bureau of the Census), p. 26, table 4.
12. Quoted by James J. Lynch, *U. S. News and World Report*, June 30, 1980, p. 47.
13. Paul C. Glick and Arthur J. Norton, "Marrying, Divorcing and Living Together in the U.S. Today," *Population Bulletin*, No. 5, Vol. 32 (Washington, D.C.: Population Reference Bureau, Inc., 1977).
14. *Statistical Abstract of the United States*, 1979 edition, p. 81, table 117.
15. *U. S. News and World Report*, June 30, 1980, p. 47.
16. *Newsweek*, September 22, 1975, p. 48.
17. Report from the Population Reference Bureau, prepared by Thomas J.

Espenshade of the Urban Institute; Associated Press release, October 7, 1980.

18. *Current Population Reports,* Series P-20, No. 352, "Household and Family Characteristics: March 1979" (Washington, D.C.: United States Department of Commerce, Bureau of the Census), p. 7, table 1.

19. *Statistical Abstract of the United States,* 1979 edition, p. 82, table 120.

20. Lionel Tiger, "Omnigamy: The New Kinship System," *Psychology Today,* July 1978, p. 14.

21. Information based on U.S. Census data, *Time,* November 27, 1977, p. 111.

22. Morton Hunt, *Sexual Behavior in the 1970's* (New York: Dell, 1974), p. 263.

23. Shere Hite, *The Hite Report* (New York: Dell, 1976), p. 73.

24. *Newsweek,* August 1, 1977, p. 47.

25. *Statistical Abstract of the United States,* 1979 edition, p. 396, Chart 650 and p. 400, Chart 660.

26. Gail Sheehy, *Passages* (New York: E. P. Dutton, 1976), pp. 378–379.

27. James Ramey, *Intimate Friendships* (Englewood Cliffs, N. J.: Prentice-Hall Spectrum, 1976), p. 6.

28. Sheehy, op. cit., p. 379.

29. Alfred C. Kinsey, Wardell B. Pomeroy, and Clyde E. Martin, *Sexual Behavior in the Human Male* (Philadelphia: W. B. Saunders, 1948); and Alfred C. Kinsey, et al, *Sexual Behavior in the Human Female* (Philadelphia: W. B. Saunders, 1953).

30. Yoon Hough Kim, "The Kinsey Findings," ed. Gerhard Neubeck, *Extramarital Relations* (Englewood Cliffs, N. J.: Prentice-Hall Spectrum, 1969), p. 66.

31. Morton Hunt, *The Affair* (New York: New American Library Signet, 1969), p. 26.

32. Anthony Pietropinto and Jacqueline Simenauer, *Beyond the Male Myth* (New York: Times Books, 1977), pp. 278–279 and 282.

33. Robert J. Levin, "Premarital and Extramarital Sex," *Redbook,* Vol. 145, October 1975, p. 42.

34. Robert R. Bell, *The Sex Survey of Australian Women* (Melbourne, Australia: Sun Books, 1974).

35. Morton Hunt, *Sexual Behavior in the 1970's,* op. cit., p. 263.

36. Quoted Larry and Joan Constantine, Plenary Session, Future Families of the World Conference, April 1975, University of Maryland, Ramey, op. cit., p. 145.

37. Linda Wolfe, "The Sexual Profile of That Cosmopolitan Girl," *Cosmopolitan,* September 1980, pp. 254–257 and 263–265.

2. Myths About Affairs

1. Richard Farson, "Why Good Marriages Fail," *McCall's,* October 1971, pp. 110, 170.

2. John F. Cuber, "Adultery: Reality versus Stereotype," ed. Gerhard Neubeck, *Extramarital Relations* (Englewood Cliffs, N. J.: Prentice-Hall Spectrum, 1969), pp. 190–196.

3. Shere Hite, *The Hite Report* (New York: Dell, 1976), pp. 164–165.
4. William H. Masters and Virginia E. Johnson, *Human Sexual Response* (Boston: Little Brown, 1966).
5. James Ramey, *Intimate Friendships* (Englewood Cliffs, N. J.: Prentice-Hall Spectrum, 1976), p. 21.
6. John F. Cuber and Peggy R. Harroff, *The Significant Americans* (New York: Appleton-Century Crofts, 1965).
7. Alfred C. Kinsey, et al. *Sexual Behavior in the Human Female* (Philadelphia: W. B. Saunders, 1953), p. 434.
8. Ray L. Birdwhistell, quoted in interview by Gail Sheehy, "Can Couples Survive?" *New York* Magazine, February 19, 1973, p. 33.
9. William Graham Cole, "Religious Attitudes Toward Extramarital Intercourse," Neubeck, op. cit. pp. 59–61.
10. Tony Lake and Ann Hills, *Affairs: The Anatomy of Extramarital Relationships* (London: Open Books, 1979), p. 173.
11. John F. Cuber, Neubeck, op. cit., p. 191.
12. "The New Morality," *Time*, November 21, 1977, p. 112.

4. Itch for Excitement
1. Tony Lake and Ann Hills, *Affairs: The Anatomy of Extramarital Relationships* (London: Open Books, 1979), p. 96.

5. Fulfillment
1. Ray L. Birdwhistell, quoted in interview by Gail Sheehy, "Can Couples Survive?" *New York* Magazine, February 19, 1973, p. 33.
2. Gerhard Neubeck, "The Dimensions of the 'Extra' in Extramarital Relations," ed. Gerhard Neubeck, *Extramarital Relations* (Englewood Cliffs, N. J.: Prentice-Hall Spectrum, 1969), p. 21.
3. John F. Cuber, "Adultery: Reality versus Stereotype," Neubeck, op. cit., p. 194.

7. Why, Oh Why?
1. William J. Lederer, "Videotaping Your Marriage to Save It," *New York* Magazine, February 19, 1973, p. 39.

8. No Two Alike
1. Bernard Slade, *Same Time Next Year* (New York: Dell, 1978).
2. John F. Cuber, "Adultery: Reality versus Stereotype," ed. Gerhard Neubeck, *Extramarital Relations* (Englewood Cliffs, N.J.: Prentice-Hall Spectrum, 1969), p. 192.
3. Tony Lake and Ann Hills, *Affairs: The Anatomy of Extramarital Relationships* (London: Open Books, 1979), p. 170.
4. "The New Morality," *Time,* November 21, 1977, p. 112.
5. Leon Salzman, "How Does An Affair Affect A Marriage?" *Sexual Behavior,* September 1972, p. 51.
6. Ronald M. Mazur, "The Double Standard," *Sexual Behavior,* November 1972, p. 47.

9. Commitment, Fidelity, and Trust
1. Jerome Weidman, *Your Daughter Iris* (Garden City, New York: Doubleday, 1955), p. 282.
2. Rustum and Della Roy, "Is Monogamy Outdated?" *The Humanist,* March/April 1970, p. 24.

11. Coping With Your Own Affair
1. Thomas C. McGinnis and Dana G. Finnegan, *Open Family and Marriage: A Guide to Personal Growth* (St. Louis, Missouri: C. V. Mosby, 1976), pp. 78–93.

Bibliography

Bartusis, Mary Ann. *Every Other Man.* New York: E. P. Dutton (Thomas Congdon Books), 1978.

Berger, Evelyn Miller. *Triangle: The Betrayed Wife.* Chicago: Nelson-Hall, 1971.

Boylan, B. R. *Infidelity.* Englewood Cliffs, N. J.: Prentice-Hall, 1971.

Cuber, J. F. "The Mistress in American Society." *Medical Aspects of Human Sexuality,* September 1969, p. 81.

Denfield, D. and Gordon, M. "The Sociology of Mate-Swapping: Or the Family that Swings Together Clings Together." *Journal of Sex Research,* 6(2) (1970), pp. 85–100.

Edwards, John N. "Extramarital Involvement: Fact and Theory." *Journal of Sex Research,* August 1973, pp. 210–224.

Ellis, Albert. *The Civilized Couple's Guide to Extramarital Adventure.* New York: Peter H. Wyden, 1972.

English, O. Spurgeon. "Positive Values of the Affairs." In *The New Sexuality.* Otto, H., ed. Palo Alto, California: Science and Behavior Books, 1971, pp. 173–192.

Etzioni, Amita. "The Next Crisis—The End of the Family?" *Human Behavior,* August 1974, pp. 10–11.

Farson, Richard. "Why Good Marriages Fail." *McCall's,* October 1971, pp. 110–170.

Hawthorne, Nathaniel. *The Scarlet Letter. In The Portable Hawthorne.* Ed. by Malcolm Cowley, New York: The Viking Press, 1971.

Hunt, Morton. *Sexual Behavior in the 1970's.* Chicago: Dell, 1974.

Hunt, Morton. *The Affair.* New York: Signet, 1969.

Johnson, Ralph E. "Attitudes Toward Extramarital Relationships." *Medical Aspects of Human Sexuality,* 6(4) (April) 1972, pp. 168–191.

Lake, Tony and Hills, Ann. *Affairs: The Anatomy of Extramarital Relationships.* London: Open Books, 1979.

Lawrence, R. J. "Toward a More Flexible Monogamy." In R. T. and A. K. Francoeur eds. *The Future of Sexual Relations.* Englewood Cliffs, N. J.: Prentice-Hall, 1974, pp. 66–74.

Levin, Robert. "Premarital and Extramarital Sex." *Redbook,* October 1975, pp. 38–44 and 90–94.

McGinnis, Thomas C. and Ayres, John U. *Open Family Living: A New Approach for Enriching Your Life Together.* Garden City, New York: Doubleday, 1976.

McGinnis, Thomas C. and Finnegan, Dana G. *Open Family and Marriage: A Guide To Personal Growth.* St. Louis, Missouri: C. V. Mosby, 1976.

"Mrs. X," *The Adultery Game.* New York: Pyramid Books, 1973.

Neubeck, Gerhard, ed. *Extramarital Relations.* Englewood Cliffs, N. J.: Prentice-Hall Spectrum, 1969.

Otto, Herbert A. "Has Monogamy Failed?" *Saturday Review,* April 25, 1970.

Pietropinto, Anthony and Simenauer, Jacqueline. *Beyond the Male Myth.* New York: Times Books, 1977.

Ramey, James. *Intimate Friendships.* Englewood Cliffs, N.J.: Prentice-Hall, 1976.

Rimmer, Robert. *Thursday, My Love.* New York: New American Library, 1972.

Roy, Rustrum and Roy, Della. "Is Monogamy Outdated?" *The Humanist,* 30(2) (1970), pp. 19–26.

Sager, Clifford and Hunt, Bernice. *Intimate Partners: Hidden Patterns in Love Relationships.* New York: McGraw-Hill. 1979.

Salzman, Leon. "Psychiatric and Clinical Aspects of Infidelity." In Masserman J. H., ed. *The Psychodynamics of Work and Marriage.* New York: Grune and Stratton, 1970.

Saul, Leon J. *Fidelity and Infidelity.* Philadelphia: J. B. Lippincott Co., 1967.

Sheehy, Gail. "Can Couples Survive?" *New York* Magazine, February 19, 1973.

Skolnick, Arlene. *The Intimate Environment.* Boston: Little Brown, 1973.

Smith, J. R. and Smith, L. S., eds. *Beyond Monogamy: Recent Studies of Sexual Alternatives in Marriage.* Baltimore: Johns Hopkins University Press, 1974.

Smith, L. G. and Smith, J. R. "Co-Marital Sex: Incorporation of Extra-Marital Sex Into the Marriage Relationship." In Zubin, J. and Money, J., eds. *Contemporary Sexual Behavior: Critical Issues in the 1970's.* Baltimore: Johns Hopkins University Press, 1973, pp. 391–408.

Whitehurst, Robert N. "Alternative Life Styles: Are They a Threat to Conventional Family Life?" *Humanist,* May/June 1975, pp. 23–26.

Wolfe, Linda. *Playing Around.* New York: The New American Library, 1976.

Index